THE LIBRARY
NATIONAL FOUNDATION FOR
EDUCATIONAL RESEARCH
IN ENGLAND & WALES
THE MERE, UPTON PARK
SLOUGH, BERKS. SL1 2DQ

DATE: 28-10-97

CLASS: JBD-TW   DAV

ACCN. NO: 29382

AUTHOR: DAVIES, I

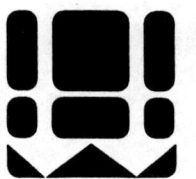 **Produced for the Politics Association**

*Studio 16, 1-Mex Business Park,
Hamilton Road, Manchester M13 0PD*

Developing European Citizens

Edited by

Ian Davies and Andreas Sobisch

Foreword by Sir Edward Heath

Sheffield Hallam University Press
Learning Centre
City Campus
Pond Street
Sheffield S1 1WB

First published 1997

Designed and typeset by Design Studio, Learning Centre, Sheffield Hallam University

Printed by Print Unit, Sheffield Hallam University

All rights reserved. No part of this publication may be reproduced, stores in a retrieval system, or transmitted in any form or by any means, electronic, mechanical, photocopying, recording, or otherwise, without prior written permission of the publishers.

©1997   ISBN 0 086339 6739

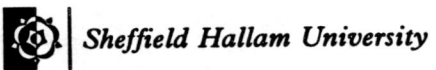

ACKNOWLEDGEMENTS

It is almost axiomatic that book projects, even edited volumes, turn out to be more difficult and labour intensive than originally anticipated. And so it is with this one. It all started with a chance encounter between the editors at the 1994 conference of the International Society for the Study of European Ideas (ISSEI) in Graz, Austria. Preliminary discussions about the need for more interdisciplinary cooperation in the area of political education quickly led to the idea for an edited volume that would seek to bridge the gap between educational studies and political science and combine lessons from both into a book that would be of use to practitioners, policy makers, and academics alike.

However, planning and doing are not the same thing, and it took another year to formulate a useful framework and convince a sufficient number of prospective contributors of the merits of this particular project. We were very fortunate that the Politics Association, and its editor, Duncan Watts, indicated very early their interest in publishing the fruits of this venture. This made it possible for us to line up a strong team of contributors, and we very much hope that readers will profit from the variety of perspectives presented in this volume.

In many ways this book - whatever its merits - is a tribute to the modern, and now indispensable, conveniences of fax machines and electronic mail. Without them this project would have been difficult to carry out, and with them there is tremendous potential for cooperation among scholars and practitioners in all fields and from all corners of the globe. If European or even world citizenship ever becomes a practical reality, these future citizens may look back at this time period as a major turning point in achieving that goal - for, as Karl Deutsch pointed out long ago, communities are bounded by barriers to communication. It follows that when these barriers are eroding communities must be expanding. Modern communication thus has the potential to bind together people of diverse backgrounds and ideologies.

Many individuals helped in the process of putting together this volume. We would like to mention especially Professor Ken Fogelman of the Centre for Citizenship Studies in Education, University of Leicester, for his help in suggesting the work from Boothville Middle School; the Europees Platform, Alkmaar, Netherlands, which organised a working visit for Ian Davies and assisted with the development of ideas about education for citizenship; the many government agencies and individuals who supplied Ian with information and suggestions. Likewise, the support from colleagues (academic and administrative) in the Department of Educational Studies, University of York, proved invaluable. On the other side of the Atlantic, Professor John Czerapowicz of John Carroll University contributed his expertise on the finer points of international law, and Dr. Nick Baumgartner, Dean of Arts and Sciences at John Carroll, provided generous financial support for travel and the purchase of data. Professor Alberta Sbragia, of the University of Pittsburgh, commented on an early draft of the conceptual framework. Sir Edward Heath has been kind enough to reschedule his other commitments and write a Foreword. Finally, we wish to thank the Politics Association and its editor, Duncan Watts, for the support we received throughout the writing process.

Last but not least we wish to thank our families who put up with the inevitable neglect that goes along with this type of endeavour.

Needless to say, any errors, omissions, and misjudgments are solely our responsibility.

Ian Davies, York, UK
Andreas Sobisch, Cleveland, Ohio, USA

This book is dedicated to
Lynn, Matthew, Hannah and Rachael Davies
and to
Laurie, Dara, Melanie and Alexandra Sobisch

FOREWORD
Sir Edward Heath

The Maastricht Treaty represented an important stage in the process of creating 'an ever closer union'. All member state nationals are now citizens of the European Union, with rights and duties. What does this mean for the average person in practice? The right to vote and stand as a candidate at municipal elections or for the European Parliament; the right to move and reside freely within the territory of every member state (subject to the limitations in the Treaty); and the right of protection by the diplomatic authorities of any other member state. European citizens can also now petition the European Parliament and utilise the European Ombudsman. I hope that these rights will grow still further in the near future.

There sadly remains much ignorance in this country of the many opportunities and rights that our membership of the EU brings. This is why the Citizens First Project is so important. This scheme aims to give all European citizens an idea of the rights and obligations for a national of a Member State wishing to live, work or study in another EU country. Since November 1996 more than 450,000 people across the European Union have used this facility.

One new article which received little attention during the arduous ratification of the Maastricht Treaty was Education. The Maastricht Treaty encourages educational co-operation between member states with particular emphasis on language learning, youth exchanges and the mutual recognition of academic qualifications. Schemes such as Socrates, Erasmus and Comenius have created huge opportunities for many students, encouraged teacher mobility and improved the links between European schools. For many students this will be their first experience of living and working abroad, using the skills learnt in this country. I am sure that they themselves recognise how intellectually and socially rewarding this training can be.

I will never forget my own first experiences in Europe hitch-hiking through Germany and Poland as a young man. I was to return there later as a commissioned officer in 1945 and 1946. I learned then that if the peoples of Europe can work together, beyond narrow national interests, that prosperity and peace could replace the bloody history of the old Western Europe. I am sure that these youth exchanges and increased educational co-operation have a similar positive effect - and one of the reasons why support for membership of the EU amongst those British citizens under the age of 35 is twice as high as amongst those over that age.

I am sure that this book will play an important role in promoting a better understanding of European Citizenship and the role of education in its development. The cultural and linguistic differences between the member states of the European Union should not obscure the scope for collective action in these fields. Unity in diversity has the potential to lead to many opportunities for the ordinary citizen as well as improving tolerance and understanding across the Union. This was always a fundamental political goal behind the original European Community - the Treaty of Rome referred to an ever closer union of peoples, not states. European Citizenship is another logical step towards this admirable objective.

CONTENTS

Acknowledgements		i
Foreword		v
Glossary		1
Contributors		3
Introduction	Developing European Citizens *Ian Davies & Andreas Sobisch*	7
SECTION 1. THE MEANING OF CITIZENSHIP		19
Chapter 1	The Reality of Multiple Citizenship *Derek Heater*	21
SECTION 2. THE CONTEXT OF EUROPEAN CITIZENSHIP: INSTITUTIONS AND POLICIES		49
Chapter 2	Developing European Institutions: Governing European Integration *Roger Scully*	51
Chapter 3	The European Union and European Citizenship *Andreas Sobisch*	73
Chapter 4	Education for European Citizenship: Review of Relevant Documentation *Ian Davies*	97
SECTION 3. EUROPEAN CITIZENSHIP: EMPIRICAL APPROACH		121
Chapter 5	Interest In, Knowledge About, and Support For the European Union *Andreas Sobisch*	123

| Chapter 6 | The Social Basis of European Citizenship
Andreas Sobisch & Stefan Immerfall | 141 |

SECTION 4. EUROPEAN CITIZENSHIP: 175
PRACTICAL APPROACHES

Chapter 7	Educational Projects for Developing European Citizens *Ian Davies*	177
Chapter 8	Foreign Language Learning and Citizenship: Issues for Lifelong Learning *Hugh Starkey*	187
Chapter 9	European Citizenship and Education for Democracy and Human Rights *Don Rowe & Jan Newton*	209
Chapter 10	Towards the Europe School: Educating European Citizens Through Whole School Development *Gordon H. Bell*	223
Chapter 11	The European Monetary Union: A Cross-Curricular Teaching Project *Peter Krapf*	253
Chapter 12	Philomel: a Project for European Unity *Ernesto Macaro*	277
Chapter 13	Boothville Middle School European Citizenship Initiatives *Mary Clark*	289
Conclusion	Some Final Thoughts *Andreas Sobisch & Ian Davies*	309
Index		315
Appendix		321

Glossary

BBC	British Broadcasting Corporation
CAP	Common Agricultural Policy
CDCC	Council for Cultural Cooperation
CFSP	Common Foreign and Security Policy
Commission	Commission of the European Community
COREPER	Committee of Permanent Representatives at the EU
Council	Council of Ministers of the EC
CSCE	Conference on Security and Cooperation in Europe
DG	Directorate General of the European Commission
EC	European Community (or Communities)
ECHR	European Convention on Human Rights
ECJ	European Court of Justice
ECOSOC	Economic and Social Committee
ECSC	European Coal and Steel Community
ECU	European Currency Unit
EDC	European Defence Community
EEC	European Economic Community
EMS	European Monetary System
EMU	European Monetary Union

EP	European Parliament
EPC	European Political Cooperation
EU	European Union
EURATOM	European Atomic Energy Community
ES	Europa-Schule (Europe Schools)
GDP	Gross Domestic Product
GDR	German Democratic Republic
HRE	Human Rights Education
ICPR	International Covenant on Civil and Political Rights
ICJ	International Court of Justice
IGC	Intergovernmental Conference
JHA	Justice and Home Affairs
MEP	Member of the European Parliament
NATO	North Atlantic Treaty Organisation
OECD	Organisation for Economic Cooperation and Development
PSE	Personal and Social Education
QMV	Qualified Majority Voting
SEA	Single European Act
Social Charter	Community Charter of Fundamental Social Rights for Workers
TEU	Treaty on European Union
UK	United Kingdom
UNESCO	United Nations Educational, Scientific and Cultural Organisation
VAT	Value Added Tax
WEU	West European Union

CONTRIBUTORS

Gordon H. Bell is Professor of Education and Principal of Bretton Hall, a college of the University of Leeds specialising in the arts and education. He has directed a number of research and development projects on the European dimension in education and worked extensively in a training and consultancy role in member states of the EU since 1976.

Mary Clark trained as a teacher at Furzedown College of Education, South London, specialising in Drama and has been teaching since 1971. She has held various posts in schools, joining Boothville Middle School in 1981. She now teaches History, Geography, English and French throughout the school and is responsible for developing Industrial and Economic Awareness.

Ian Davies is a Lecturer in Educational Studies at the University of York. His previous experience includes ten years as a teacher in comprehensive schools. He currently supervises undergraduate and graduate students in the areas of history education and education for social and political understanding. He has undertaken work relating to education for citizenship in various European countries. He has numerous publications in journals such as the *Journal of Further and Higher Education, Social Science Teacher,* and *Educational Review*

Derek Heater was the Founder-Chairman of the Politics Association. His many publications include *Citizenship: The Civic Ideal in World History, Politics and Education,* and *World Citizenship and Government: Cosmopolitan Ideas in the History Of Western Thought.*

Stefan Immerfall is Akademischer Rat and Lecturer in Sociology at the University of Passau, Germany. Among his recent publications are two books dealing with the comparative study of European societies as well as editorship of a special issue of *Historical Social Research*.

Peter Krapf was born in Oxford in 1952 and spent his first ten years in England before moving to Germany. Educated at the University of Tübingen, he teaches Politics, History and English at the Schubart-Gymnasium in Ulm. He has specialised in teaching Politics and Economics, and he has participated in teacher training and curricular work.

Ernesto Macaro is a Lecturer in Modern Foreign Languages Education at the University of Reading. His current interests include the European dimension in education and European citizenship. He is a member of the Collaborative Research in Modern Languages Education group (CRMLE). Recent publications include *Pupils' Perceptions of Europe* (Cassell 1997).

Jan Newton is chief executive of The Citizenship Foundation, a London based educational NGO promoting education for democratic citizenship nationally and internationally. Her particular interests are education for democracy and political literacy. She has written for teachers as well as developing classroom materials for use with pupils. With Don Rowe she co-edited the successful primary school materials, *You, Me, Us!*

Don Rowe is director of curriculum resources at The Citizenship Foundation, London (see above). Since 1984 he has directed a number of curriculum development projects in law-related and moral education and published a range of student materials and academic papers on these subjects. Current interests include the nature of democracy in schools and the emergence of public discourse in the primary school.

Roger Scully is Lecturer in European Politics at Brunel University, having recently completed graduate study in political science at the Ohio State University, Columbus, Ohio, USA. His research interests include British and European Union Politics, and political institutions. He is the author or co-author of articles in the *British Journal of Political Science, European Journal of Political Research, Legislative Studies Quarterly,* and *the Journal of Legislative Studies,* and co-author (with Andreas Sobisch) of a forthcoming book chapter on the British political parties.

Andreas Sobisch is Assistant Professor of Political Science at John Carroll University, Cleveland, Ohio, USA, where he teaches European Politics. He was born in Hamburg, Germany, and moved to the United States at the age of 20. He received his PhD at Emory University in Atlanta, Georgia. His research interests include European integration, political parties, and right-wing extremism. He is author or co-author of a number articles and book chapters, published in both the United States and Europe.

Hugh Starkey is Senior Lecturer and Assistant Director of the Centre for Modern Languages at the Open University. From 1991 to 1996 he was Coordinator for European Affairs at Westminster College, Oxford, from where he managed an ERASMUS curriculum development project on education for European citizenship. He has been a consultant to the Council of Europe for human rights education and to the European Commission for citizenship education. He is the author, with Audrey Osler, of *Teacher Education and Human Rights* (Fulton, 1996).

INTRODUCTION
Ian Davies and Andreas Sobisch

Among the most significant political debates in recent years are those relating to European unification. This book focuses on two important issues in these debates: European citizenship and the role of education in its development. The general aim of the book is to provide practitioners (educational policy makers, teachers, students and others) with a better understanding of the meaning and implications of the concept of education for European citizenship as well as discussing practical strategies for citizenship education.

The writers are specialists in the fields of either education or political science. All the contributors have considerable experience as academic experts and/or as practitioners. The book aims to provide a volume of authoritative but tentative reflections on the meaning of education for European citizenship. It attempts to do this through the careful analysis of historical developments, educational policy and up to date empirical data, as well as successful practical experience.

Jean Monnet once said: 'If I had to do it again, I would start with education'[1]. This book recognises the critical importance of education and allows the reader to judge the importance of particular projects within the context of insights from political science. There is already a large (and growing) literature on the separate aspects or dimensions of European unification. There has not been, however, an attempt to view these vital issues in a more integrated way. The consequence of this unidimensional approach has been the development of only an incomplete understanding. At best, loose (or at worst incoherent) characterisations of citizens and citizenship are used by educationalists and others who may be tempted to use key terms as slogans rather than helpful and meaningful constructs. It has been possible for much writing to be undertaken without any knowledge of the polity, politics and policies associated with Europe. Often that writing also has neglected the consideration of practical ways forward in such a way as to make further thinking and action more difficult. When language begins to lack meaning or is otherwise debased the dangers are clear[2].

The reality and importance of Europe (even if we may disagree about the Europe which does or should exist) are obvious. Political scientists and educators (and, indeed, all citizens) cannot afford to ignore it.

This significance can easily be demonstrated: historically, as the centre of many of the major events of the 20th century; economically, as a wealthy area with the total gross domestic product of the seventeen established democracies of OECD Europe being 31% greater than the United States and more than double that of Japan; politically, as an increasingly important actor on the world stage with the majority of democracies in the world being European[3]. The level of involvement in education is high (in the EU) with 10 million attending pre schools, 59 million in schools, and 11 million students studying for degrees and other qualifications at over 5000 universities and higher education institutes[4]. Increasing attention is being paid to the fact that the idea of European citizenship has, explicitly since at least the Maastricht Treaty, become a reality. This can be seen through the actions of the institutions of the European Union, individual states and specific schools and other organisations as they seek to develop an appropriate form of education.

Throughout the book we intend to develop discussion about political and educational issues. The title of the book has been carefully chosen: 'Developing European Citizens' is a deliberately ambiguous phrase. The political context is clearly important in work relating to education for European citizenship. When one speaks of 'developing countries' it is usually implied that those nations are moving (or, more normally, being moved) towards a particular political goal. This dimension is analysed here through a consideration of how the Union has emerged, how it currently exists, and what citizenship in it exactly means. But 'developing' also suggests that there is some sort of pedagogical project in which opportunities for promoting citizenship education are explored. The notion of education for citizenship is crucially important and yet significantly unclear in very many respects. The term 'education for citizenship' is the one employed in this book and is the most commonly used phrase for education about contemporary society across Europe and yet it is itself controversial. Does it suggest that other formulations such as civic education and political education are now neglected? There is no simple solution which is proposed but rather a range of issues and case studies are presented so as to illuminate an incomplete array of options for educational work.

Some of the key debates on the political and educational issues which affect the development of education for European citizens are referred to in a little more detail below.

i) Citizenship

There are issues fundamental to any conception of citizenship. This area is itself divided into three debates. Firstly, is it about a polity? Here we see debates which focus on the nature of education for or about a particular polity. There are obviously many controversies about which aspects of the polity need to be taught. Secondly, to what extent is citizenship about economic or social or political or moral conceptions? Some have argued that European citizenship will never come into being due to the conflicts between the traditions seen in these debates, for others it is possible for some sort of dialectic to be developed and perhaps even for human rights to be seen as universalised citizenship[5]. Thirdly, what are the purposes associated with citizenship? A few not mutually exclusive options could include academic thinking, action, dispositions relating to issues of allegiance or positive feelings towards the society that is being studied.

In recent years debates over citizenship have become even more complex with new interpretations associated with the development of postmodernist thinking. This allows for a stronger emphasis on, first, the roots of citizenship seen through the prism of individual or communal identity, and second, on the extent to which those debates are perceived to be capable of resolution through the methods of the so called Enlightenment project (i.e. rational discourse within a framework which holds fast to the value of the modernist goals of improvement)[6].

ii) Europe

What sort of Europe is being considered, how far are we towards any particular goal, and what actions need now to be taken? The language of certainty is often employed for political purposes. For some, we have no choice but to accept the existence of a unified (if not necessarily uniform) Europe:

> The train left the station long ago and even though the ride may be bumpy, the destination unclear, the design of the engine uncertain and the relationship among the engineer, the guard and the passengers still evolving, it is too late for anyone to leave the train without risking severe injury[7].

There are others, however, who would dispute such a contention.

> Ultimately, however, there was no option but to stake out a radically different position from the direction in which most of the Community seemed intent on going, to raise the flag of national sovereignty, free trade and free enterprise - and fight. Isolated I might be in the European Community - but taking

the wider perspective, the federalists were the real isolationists, clinging grimly to a half-Europe when Europe as a whole was being liberated; toying with protectionism when truly global markets were emerging; obsessed with schemes of centralisation when the greatest attempt at centralisation - the Soviet Union - was on the point of collapse. If there was ever an idea whose time had come and gone it was that of the artificial mega-state[8].

It may be more sensible to attempt to avoid such simple prescriptions. Rather than stark choices between, for example, widening and deepening, it is possible that the European Union may do both at the same time. Similarly, the debate over flexibility, usually seen as a mutually exclusive choice between, on the one hand, a multispeed Europe with all countries having the same destination but reaching it at different times; and, on the other, the variable geometry of a Europe which allows for different destinations for different countries may be an unhelpful way to understand the issues[9].

The nature of 'Europe' itself and any form of citizenship within 'Europe' is far from clear. This book discusses three commonly formulated frameworks: education for European citizenship as characterised by the European Union; education for citizenship in the various countries of Europe which means taking account of the ways in which national programmes have been designed and about the extent of the fit that is claimed between that and the broader European picture; and also, those notions of education for European citizenship which are formed by transnational European groups with the best known and most prestigious of these groups being the Council of Europe.

The first formulation which puts the emphasis on the European Union is given sustained attention. The latter two formulations are given less attention but are nevertheless important for a number of reasons. The principle of subsidiarity in the European Union means that consideration must be given to the actions of states within Europe (even if that Europe is already a part of the Union).

Other countries are currently making efforts to join the Union and so the debates on citizenship and education should not be restricted to factors and aspects which can exist only within a particular constitutional framework. Indeed those debates would be very artificially limited if such a restriction were enforced. It is also important to make clear that this book is not concerned to promote simplistic commitment to one form of citizenship including that of the European Union. The nature of European citizenship as given in the Maastricht Treaty is not considered by many commentators to be perfect and a critical dimension needs to be included which takes account of the possibility of ensuring a professional educational approach rather than merely inculcating particular allegiances.

iii) Education

There are enormously difficult issues which relate to the development and implementation of education for citizenship. Much of the implementation debate relates very strongly to the other dimensions mentioned above. It is not possible (in anything more than a superficial manner) for teachers to ignore the nature of Europe or of citizenship when teaching any students. Those who claim not to take account of such issues are either unaware of all aspects of their professional work, which may be recognised by others even if not by themselves, or they are being disingenuous. Teachers are European citizens, or, at least, operate in a world where Europe is already much more than a geographical entity.

And yet the challenge of educating about Europe is very difficult indeed. At the very time when citizenship has become a reality in at least a legal sense, there are a number of fundamental issues about the notion of Europe and its relationship with individual states and citizens that must be considered by those who wish to educate for citizenship. The meaning of Europe is unclear:

European politics are often complex and ambiguous, European affairs are usually far removed from everyday lives and most people believe they have no control over European decision making[10].

This sorry state of affairs was recognised in 1996 by John Bruton at the beginning of the Irish Presidency of the EU when he declared that 'most people haven't a clue what Europe is trying to achieve'[11]. The strength of national identity, the xenophobia of much of the output of the media, the lack of determination to give official recognition to Europe in nationally determined curricula all mean that there are many fundamental obstacles for educators to overcome. But even if those factors were not present there would still remain many difficult issues. Should there be a framework which relates fundamentally more to cognitive than affective matters; should it be assumed that active citizens need to be given the opportunity to take action during a period of compulsory education or would the nature of any action be regarded as potentially undemocratic and so best avoided; should the focal point of education for European citizenship be seen as relating to language learning, to economic, social or political understanding through established academic or integrated issue based study; should the experience of student exchanges be seen as essential or a merely a luxury for young Europeans taking the contemporary version of the grand tour? Whatever decisions are taken a teacher will seek to make the work interesting for students and will again find challenges to overcome. 'Colourful personalities, dramatic events and clash of policies have been in short supply in the evolution of the Community'[12]. It is entirely possible for teachers to be so concerned to find material that will motivate pupils and students but which leads only to a situation in which the original purpose of the work has been defeated.

The Structure of the Book

There are four main sections. The first section takes the form of a single chapter by Derek Heater who explores the meaning of citizenship. He does so by concentrating on the concept and practice of multiple citizenship, historical and current, taking account of the relationships between European citizenship and national citizenship and to the complexities of such aspects as subsidiarity and multiculturalism.

Section 2 is made up of three separate chapters by Roger Scully, Andreas Sobisch and Ian Davies. Roger Scully undertakes a survey of the institutions and processes of the European Union. Andreas Sobisch places the concept of citizenship into the context of the new Europe. He does so through an examination of the key elements of citizenship as currently practised or envisaged. Ian Davies gives an overview of recent educational policy and initiatives across Europe which provide opportunities for the further development of European citizenship.

The third section deals with what could be described as empirical approaches. A chapter by Andreas Sobisch and then a chapter by Andreas Sobisch and Stefan Immerfall from the political science perspective raise issues about the extent to which European citizenship is already felt and practised and so provides a reference point for understanding the need for a coherent educational policy. The first of these two chapters examines the state of interest in and knowledge of community affairs as well as the development of a European political identity among the publics of the fifteen member states of the Union. The second considers the extent to which it is possible to identify a common set of distinct European social values such as democracy, human rights and social justice which are significant in the development of a genuine European identity.

The final part of the book is devoted to educational considerations and focuses on examples of practical projects with teachers and learners. Ian Davies places the six case studies in context by raising a series of questions for readers to consider. An attempt has been made to ensure a range of examples which allow for some consideration of a number of different aspects of the debate. Age of students, areas of curriculum and some attempt to cover a number of different geographical areas within Europe are three of the main criteria which have been employed when selecting case studies. This means that in the relatively short space available a number of very different projects affecting very different communities are presented.

However, there is, of course, much that has been omitted. There is no real consideration of some curriculum areas which may have significant potential for developing European citizens. Ian Davies has written about the possible impact of History and the importance of values education elsewhere[13], but neither have been included in this collection. An explicit and sustained consideration of other approaches, such as for example, that emanating from an intercultural education base is not included. Work with the very young has been omitted. The majority of authors are from the UK and there is no voice from a member of a country currently applying to join the EU. Very important is the omission of an example of the issues involved in the teaching and learning of European Politics. Whereas the educational projects included in this book all relate directly and unproblematically to politics and citizenship there is no real discussion of issues arising from the type of work undertaken by many post 16 school, college and university students who are following courses which examine the institutions, issues and concepts which are central to the EU. This omission, in light of recent innovative approaches to the study of academic Politics may be particularly significant (e.g. see the materials available from the Case Study Project, Department of Politics, University of York). However, any attempt to include every perspective would inevitably fail.

The work that is covered here, though, is extensive. Gordon Bell of Bretton Hall, College of the University of Leeds, reviews the various projects he has been associated with in recent years and places them in the context of the Europaschulen Project in Hesse, Germany. Mary Clark of Boothville Middle School in Northampton writes of three projects: one on leisure and tourism with a French 'flavour'; the second focused on the concept of freedom by a project on 'Boothville's Berlin Wall'; and the final project on 'The Waterloo Experience' centring around a journey to Paris with help from artists and industrialists. Peter Krapf of Schubart-Gymnasium, Ulm discusses two projects in Germany which relate to political education with particular attention to the European Union and to unemployment and European Monetary Union with materials written in German, French and English and highlighting issues in various countries. Ernesto Macaro of Reading University describes school based projects which provide a link between identity, citizenship and the teaching of languages of the European Union. Don Rowe and Jan Newton from the Citizenship Foundation, London focus on ways in which they have introduced primary and secondary school students to the European Convention on Human Rights. Using cases which have come before the European Court they provide a framework which will enable teachers in any of the member states to introduce students to the workings of the European Convention and show how these are enforced through the European Court of Human Rights, suggesting ways in which teachers might look at how these issues are encountered in the experience of ordinary citizens. Hugh Starkey of the Open University reflects on the experiences of that University in its first distance courses for foreign languages. He identifies specific citizenship issues that are raised and compares the perspectives of the course designers with that of the adult learners. The chapter explores the extent to which the course writers set out to stimulate thinking about citizenship issues and the reactions of the learners to this course content.

This book will not clear away all the major difficulties and challenges. To claim to do so would be ridiculous. The debates concerning Europe are too many and too complex for easy solutions to be offered. None of the authors in this volume are offering to engage in a vacuous fortune telling exercise. Nevertheless those authors are attempting to face squarely some of the important issues in a coherent manner and to consider constructively and professionally the shortcomings of current thinking and positive strategies for education for European citizenship.

Endnotes

1. Sultana, R. G. (1994): Conceptualising Teachers' Work in a Uniting Europe. *Compare,* vol. 24 no. 2, pp. 171 - 182. Quotation from page 175.

2. Orwell, G. (1947): Politics and the English Language. Reprinted in Orwell, G. (1984): *The Penguin Essays of George Orwell* (Harmondsworth: Penguin).

3. Rose, R. (1996): *What is Europe?* (New York: Harper Collins).

4. European Commission (1995): SOCRATES vademecum. (Brussels: European Commission). Information given on page 11 of the document.

5. Referred to by Elizabeth Meehan during a paper given at the Politics Association 1996 annual conference held at the University of York. See also Meehan, E. (1993): *Citizenship and the European Community.* (London: Sage). An interesting discussion of human rights as universalised citizenship is given in Bauböck, R. (1994): *Transnational Citizenship: membership and rights in international migration.* (Aldershot: Edward Elgar).

6. Coulby, D. and Jones, C. (1995): *Postmodernity and European Education Systems.* (Stoke on Trent: Trentham Books).

7. McCormick, J (1996): *The European Union: politics and policies.* (Colorado: Westview Press). Quotation from page 300.

8. Thatcher, M. (1993): *The Downing Street Years*. (London: Harper Collins).

9. Brittan, L.: speech made to the 1996 Politics Association annual conference at the University of York.

10. Vis, J. C. P. M. (1995): Knowledge of European Integration: statistics on the Dutch public's knowledge of the European Community. pp. 194 - 208 in *Political Education Towards A European Democracy*. Papers of a European Conference held at Maastricht, 8 - 11 October 1995. Bundeszentrale für Politische Bildung and Instituut voor Publiek en Politiek. Quotation from page 206.

11. Helm, S. (1996): Bruton Sets Out Irish Strategy for Leading EU. *The Independent*, 1 July 1996.

12. Heater, D. (undated) *Education for European Citizenship*. (European Association of Teachers).

13. Davies, I. (1996): Education for European Citizenship and the Teaching and Learning of History. In Osler, A. Rathenow, H.-F., and Starkey, H. (eds.): *Teaching for Citizenship in the New Europe*. Stoke on Trent, Trentham Books. pp. 149 - 160. The point that some form of limiting is essential is made implicitly by two recent publications in which limitations either by countries covered or by areas of study discussed is clear, i.e. Friebel, W. (1996): *Education for European Citizenship: theoretical and practical approaches*. (Freiburg: Réseau d'Institutions de Formation, RIF1); and *Evaluation and Research in Education*, vol. 10, no. 2 and 3, special issue *Education for European Citizenship*, edited by Bryam.M.

SECTION 1
THE MEANING OF EUROPEAN CITIZENSHIP

THE REALITY OF MULTIPLE CITIZENSHIP
CHAPTER 1
Derek Heater

Introduction

The Sicilian St. Paul was a citizen of Tarsus and Rome; the Englishman Thomas Paine was made a citizen of France and liked to think of himself as a citizen of the world; born of UK nationals in the UK, I am a British citizen and also, by virtue of the Maastricht Treaty, a citizen of the European Union. Contrast these examples with the singular, bilateral mutual relationship of individual and state which is usually accepted as the norm of citizenship, shorn up in modern times by the doctrine of state sovereignty. Yet the implied reluctance of this traditional format to recognise the validity of the idea and practice of a more complicated multiple citizenship denies the evidence of history, constricts theoretical investigation of the concept and inhibits its practical evolution.

The status of European citizenship is an obvious example of the extension of the basic notion of citizenship. But what is the significance and potential of this? It is easy to think of the emergence of the status purely in European Union terms. True, Article 8 of the Maastricht Treaty, which defines the status in international law, was a direct outcome of the call of the 1984 Fontainebleau meeting of the European Council for a 'People's Europe'. This, in turn, was a recognition of the need to counterbalance the Europe of the technocrats. On the other hand, the traditional concept of simple state citizenship was already showing many different signs of inadequacy. It is therefore instructive to place the idea of European citizenship in the broader context of the many different styles of multiple citizenship that have existed throughout history.

A survey of the several devices that have been used to render citizenship a more elastic concept and status and thus to allow the individual more than one civic identity reveals a basic four-fold typology. These forms of citizenship, held in conjunction with the fundamental state citizenship, may be tabulated in outline as shown in Fig. 1.

Figure 1

legally defined	dual -	citizenship of two states held simultaneously
	layered -	in federal constitutions; few multinational communities
mainly attitude; limited legal definition	below state level -	municipal, local allegiance/sense of identity
	above state level -	world citizenship

Thus two of these variations have been given legal, constitutional definition in the states or communities where they have operated; the other two often rely on citizenly attitudes and behaviour for their functioning, though in some cases there has also been a certain legal recognition of the status.

If we traverse the two-and-a-half millennia of the history of citizenship, we may identify five periods in that great span of time when the urge to break free from the constraints of 'singular' citizenship manifested itself most clearly. These are: the Roman Empire; the Renaissance; the Atlantic region c. 1775-1810; Britain and its Empire c. 1832-1939; and the world, especially western Europe, from c. 1945. The aim of this chapter is to analyse each of these eras and to conclude with some observations and questions drawn from this evidence. We shall concentrate on the last three of these periods as being most relevant to our own age.

Roman Empire and Renaissance

During the era of the Roman Empire both the practice of dual citizenship and the concept of world citizenship were developed[1]. The introduction of the right to dual citizenship was gradual and pragmatic, the result of resistance to and pressures for its concession. As Rome steadily extended her sway, the problem had to be faced that the status of Roman citizenship was both a coveted title and a means of cementing the loyalty of the conquered peoples to Rome, while, at the same time, the feeling of local identity remained with the inhabitants of these, often far-flung, lands. During the century c. 50 BC-50 AD the legal position that it was incompatible to hold both Roman and local citizenship was increasingly flouted in practice. By c. 50 AD it was quite common for men of some substance to claim both metropolitan and local municipal rights, usually in order to engage in local public affairs while enjoying the privileged protection of Rome[2].

The matter of dual citizenship in the Roman Empire was a technical, legal issue; the matter of believing oneself to be a citizen of the universe, a cosmopolite, was a question of philosophy and conscience. The latter was embedded in the Stoic doctrine of an overarching universal moral law. Originally expounded by Greeks, the ideas enjoyed a revival in Rome c. 200 BC-200 AD. But how can one live simultaneously by the dictates of one's state law and universal natural law? How can one be both a citizen of one's *polis* and of the *cosmopolis?* By the evidence of the philosopher-politician Seneca and the philosopher-Emperor Marcus Aurelius, there would appear to be two options[3]. According to Seneca, one's role as a world citizen is not citizenship in any clear political meaning of the word: it is a private contemplation of virtue, or, at best, a virtuous behaviour so long as it does not conflict with the current needs of the state or government. Alternatively, according to Marcus Aurelius, one must struggle to raise civic standards by the light of natural law and be willing to die in the attempt. The political implication of the Stoic duality of state and world citizenship is the choice of performing the latter role eremetically or heroically.

The transmission of classical thinking into Renaissance thinking led a few men to revive the concept of the *cosmopolis*. Most notable of these were the Dutchman Justus Lipsius and his French friend Montaigne. In his influential work, *Of Constancy*, Lipsius attempted to counter-balance what he believed to be the excesses of patriotism by the ideas of cosmopolitanism. Montaigne repeated Plutarch's report that Socrates claimed to be a citizen of the world, thus recruiting his distinguished name to the concept[4]. The problem of combining state and world citizenship was not, however, a vital issue. Despite the significant theoretical works of Machiavelli and Bodin, state citizenship was an exceedingly circumscribed right in practice; and few were touched by the revival of cosmopolitan theory.

Atlantic Region c. 1775-1810

We may therefore pass swiftly to the third of our periods. This was the truly pivotal era in the evolution of the modern concept of citizenship, including its potential for the development of multiple citizenship. It so happened that the endowment of the individual with the rights of citizenship by the replacement of royal by popular sovereignty coincided with the defeat of Enlightenment cosmopolitanism by the new ideology of nationalism. Yet although this convergence of two strands of thought led to the modern identification of citizenship with nationality, practical worries about the centralisation of the new sovereign power favoured the protection of multiple citizenship through the extension of the formerly rare device of federalism.

The mini-classical Renaissance of the Enlightenment brought in its train a revived interest in the idea of the *cosmopolis,* though the proud bearers of the title of 'citizen of the world' - the likes of Franklin, Paine, Diderot, Schiller - generally speaking used the term in a cultural rather than a specifically political sense. Political usage tended to run along the lines of Lipsius's distaste for uncritical and excessive patriotism. Even so, Locke provided an interesting commentary on the topic:

> By the law of nature, [he wrote] common to them all, [a man] and all the rest of mankind are one community. . . . and were it not for the corruption and viciousness of degenerate men, there would be no need of any other, no necessity that man should associate into lesser combinations[5].

Furthermore, international law was edging in the direction of recognising a quasi-world citizenship. Notice particularly the opinion of Vattel, in 1758:

> Since the universal society of the human race is an institution of nature itself, that is, a necessary result of man's nature, all men of whatever condition are bound to advance its interests and to fulfil its duties . . . . When . . . men unite in civil society and form a separate State or Nation. . . . their duties towards the rest of the human race remain unchanged, but with this difference, that . . . it devolves thence forth upon that body, the State . . . to fulfil these duties of humanity towards outsiders in all matters in which individuals are no longer at liberty to act . . . .[6]

With the exciting events of the American and French Revolutions, however, some men's thoughts did run to the vision of a world led to political unity by one or other of these new republics. A somewhat eccentric blueprint was drafted by the somewhat eccentric French Revolutionary, Anacharsis Cloots. This was entitled *Constitutional Foundations for the Republic of Mankind.* And he made provision for the democratic participation of all citizens throughout the world by means of a structure of *départements* modelled on the French system.

By the 1780s and the 1790s the terms 'citizen' and 'democracy' were indeed taking on their modern meanings, especially in America and France. In France, of course, the titles *citoyen* and *citoyenne* were worn with pride. Moreover, to demonstrate that the democratic ideas of the Revolution could be of universal benefit, the Legislative Assembly conferred French citizenship on a number of foreign sympathisers, thus creating a form of dual citizenship for those of radical persuasion. These included Bentham, Kosciuszko and Washington. What is more, two of these 'dual' citizens were nominated for election to the new assembly, the Convention. These were the Englishmen Joseph Priestley and Thomas Paine, and the latter was elected.

However, these cosmopolitan gestures were made by Revolutionary politicians who participated in the shaping of the modern ideology of nationalism by means of such doctrines as the sovereignty of the people defined as the nation and that of natural frontiers for the nation. If the ideas of the *cosmopolis,* nationalism and citizenship were all present in the political discourse of the French Revolution, the question naturally arises whether there was any attempt to meld them all into a coherent theory of multiple citizenship.

The Stoic concept of a universal natural law was certainly an unquestioned assumption of many of the revolutionaries who had received a classical education. Also, this natural law was believed to accord to all human beings certain inalienable rights. For example the preamble to the 1789 *Declaration of Rights of Man and the Citizen* makes it clear that the Constituent Assembly was drafting the rights of man clauses not just for Frenchmen but for universal application. However, it was after the collapse of the monarchy in 1792 that, during the debates on a new, republican, constitution the task of combining the concepts of natural and world citizenship was commended, albeit without practical outcome.

The most convinced exponent of this form of multiple citizenship was Robespierre. Moreover, he approached the matter from a background of deep thinking about the nature of citizenship in the straightforward, national sense. His reading of Rousseau, his participation in the constitutional debates in the Constituent Assembly and his journalism helped him to develop and marshal his thought in this context[7]. However, when discussions took place on a new Declaration of Rights and a new Constitution, he advocated in addition a cosmopolitan approach in two key speeches at the Jacobin Club in April 1793[8]. He urged the appending of four extra articles to the Declaration of Rights which already existed in draft. He accused the drafting committee of having 'utterly forgotten to recall the duties of fraternity which should unite all men and all nations'. The first of his extra articles reflects this concern:

> Men of all countries are brothers, and the different peoples must help one another according to their ability, as though they were citizens of one and the same State.

This is pure Stoic cosmopolitanism, reminiscent of Plutarch's comment that 'we should consider all men to be one community and one polity'[9].

Even so, Robespierre was anything but averse to voicing highly nationalistic comments. As a leading member of the Committee of Public Safety he used every propaganda device to unite the nation against the threats of civil and international war - to engage indeed in a nationalistic total war. Were his expressions of cosmopolitan brotherhood therefore hypocritical? Were they words embroidered into an ethical cloak to conceal a French missionary imperialism rather than an honest vision of true universal citizenly fraternity? In all probability Robespierre was sincere. His vision of a cosmopolis presupposed the overthrow of all regimes he genuinely believed to be tyrannical and the embracing of revolutionary principles, as divulged by the vanguard French republic, by all the freed nations of the world.

But in struggling to sustain cosmopolitanism, Robespierre was doomed to failure. The powerful waves of nationalism were rapidly swamping the ideal, not just in France, but in Germany too.

Before outlining the main relevant strand in German thinking, it is of interest to mention an echo of Robespierre's thought in the Mainz Republic, which briefly existed in imitation of the French in 1792-93. Here citizenship was defined in partisan, rather than national terms. In the words of Franz Dumont, 'As the basic struggle was being waged against the tyrants of all countries. . . . patriotism and cosmopolitanism became two sides of the same coin'[10].

The real struggle in Germany on this issue, however, took place in the minds of philosophers, particularly Prussian intellectuals. The cosmopolitan and nationalist ideas were reconciled by arguing that the Germans, by dint of the purity of their language and culture, had a pan-human destiny. Fichte, with the added faith in the power of Pestalozzian education, may be taken as the exemplar of this chain of reasoning. In his *Addresses to the German Nation* delivered in Berlin in 1807-8, he fused cosmopolitanism, nationalism and citizenship in his concept of 'the genuine German art of the state':

> the [German] state, in the persons of its adult citizens, is the continued education of the human race. . . . Henceforth [the German education for citizenship] . . . will be characterised by a spirit that is not narrow and exclusive, but universal and cosmopolitan[11].

Nevertheless, no more than Robespierre was Fichte able to ensure the reconciliation of the old cosmopolitanism with the new nationalism. Before the Napoleonic Wars had been brought to a close, the likes of Arndt and Jahn were expounding a brutish nationalism embraced by active, especially militarily active, citizens enthused by their identity with the chosen *Volk*.

While the cosmopolitan form of multiple citizenship was losing out to the single identification of citizenship with nationality, another form of multiple citizenship was taking hold. This was federalism.

The Americans, of course, had to face up to the question of 'layered' citizenship when they moved from being thirteen separate colonies, via confederation, to federal union. Three aspects of this process are of particular interest.

The first relates to a difficulty that arose in the 1777 *Articles of Confederation*. The so-called 'comity clause' gave to the inhabitant (sic) of a state the privileges of citizenship of any other. So, hypothetically, a non-citizen inhabitant could acquire citizenship merely by moving to another state: an anomaly tidied up in the Constitution, but illustrative of the need for careful drafting when defining multiple citizenship in law.

A more serious case of careless drafting, secondly, was the discrepancy between the preamble to and Article 7 of the Constitution. The former starts with the well-known words, 'We, the people of the United States'. The latter required that the Constitution be ratified by separate state Conventions. Was the Constitution, then, the product of the will of the singular American people or of the several peoples of the constituent states? Where lay ultimate sovereignty? Which had primacy - state or federal citizenship? It took a most bloody civil conflict to resolve the issue. Alexander Stephens, who had been the Confederate Vice-President, wrote after the Civil War:

> the *Causa causans* of [the war] . . . was the assumption on the part of the Federal authorities, that the people of the several States were . . . citizens of the United States and owed allegiance to the Federal Government . . . . the war . . . grew out of different and opposed views as to the nature of the Government of the United States[12].

This, of course, is the crucial issue in any system of multi-layered citizenship.

Nor is it only a legal-constitutional matter. It concerns also the relative effectiveness of citizenly identity with and participation in the various civic levels. This is our third aspect to the device of layered citizenship. Madison, for example, expected that state citizenship would have a greater reality for the people than the federal. He wrote that,

> the first and most natural attachment of the people will be to the governments of their respective States. Into the administration of these a greater number of individuals will expect to rise ... With the affairs of these, the people will be more familiarly and minutely conversant. And with the members of these will a greater proportion of the people have the ties of personal acquaintance and friendship, and of family and party attachments; on the side of these, therefore, the popular bias may well be expected most strongly to incline[13].

Civic competence, too, was thought to be more effectively nurtured at local than national level. Writing admittedly half-a-century later and admittedly basing his conclusions on the evidence of only five states, Tocqueville nevertheless recorded shrewd observations concerning the importance of the local levels of political activity. Indeed, he is well known for going so far as to suggest that the health of the Union's democracy was dependent on the vigour of citizenly activity not just at state level, but also the municipal. Referring to the New England citizen's attachment to his township, Tocqueville explains that it is in this small-scale context that he

> learns to rule society; he gets to know those formalities without which freedom can advance only through revolutions, and becoming imbued with their spirit, develops a taste for order, understands the harmony of power, and in the end accumulates clear, practical ideas about the nature of his duties and the extent of his rights[14].

Meanwhile, at the next layer,

> The central government of each state, being close to the governed, is continually informed of the needs that arise;

every year new plans are put forward . . . and published in the press, exciting universal interest and eagerness among the citizens[15].

In this portrait of American democracy, therefore, we have a pyramidal form of citizenship, operating at three distinct layers.

Britain and its Empire c. 1832-1939

Municipal citizenship was also a feature of our fourth period, namely, the experience of multiple citizenship in Britain c. 1832-1939. Paradoxically for a country that eschewed the term 'citizen' in its political and legal vocabulary, Britain during this era developed, or attempted to develop, strong senses of citizenship at both infra-state and supra-state levels in parallel with the extension of the rights of political and social citizenship at the national level.

The burgeoning of industrial cities and the reform of local government led in Victorian times to an extraordinary flowering of a truly realistic municipal citizenship. This took the form of an extension of the franchise, devotion to the creation of civic facilities and the growth of a sense of municipal identity and pride. Leeds and Birmingham were conspicuous examples of these trends.

John Stuart Mill famously commended the local political arena as a more effective level than the national for citizenly participation and education in his *Considerations on Representative Government*, which was published in 1861[16].

Eight years later the Municipal Franchise Act not only generally extended the suffrage but also enfranchised some women. As a consequence, the municipal electorates in Birmingham and Leeds rose to nearly a fifth of the population[17].

In the words of Asa Briggs,

> The provincial cities nurtured the sense of loyalty through rivalry with each other and solidarity against the metropolis. They used their status as regional capitals to challenge the

claims of the national capital, both culturally and politically . . . . People felt that they belonged to particular cities, and each with its own identity[18].

The archetypical and most imposing symbol of this civic pride was Leeds Town Hall, the building of which was started in 1853. However, it was the Birmingham ideal of the municipal or civic gospel a generation later, that was the apogee of Victorian civic consciousness. This was the brainchild of the Baptist Minister, George Dawson, while its most rapid period of implementation occurred during the mayoralty of the indefatigable Joseph Chamberlain. With a politico-religious zeal which he modelled on Mazzini, Dawson preached a kind of republican civic virtue for the municipal level of citizenship.

He declared that

> a town is a solemn organism through which should flow, and in which should be shaped all the highest, loftiest and truest ends of man's moral nature[19].

Chamberlain, who was mayor from 1873 to 1876, laid the foundations for Birmingham's proud claim to be the best-governed city in the world.

Two decades later Chamberlain took the post of Colonial Secretary in Lord Rosebery's administration with the express purpose of stimulating the development of the Empire. And as the Empire expanded, the need arose to define the relationship of the inhabitants of its various territories to the mother-country. Rosebery himself was a leading light in the Imperial Federation League, but this body was too nervous to contemplate political union, confined itself to trade and defence matters and foundered in 1893, nine years after its creation. Much more significant for our purposes was the search, especially from 1914 to 1939, for a formula for a supra-state Imperial citizenship.

By the beginning of the twentieth century the question of the degree of independence to be enjoyed by the Dominions (Australia, Canada, New Zealand and South Africa) and the nature of their ties to the mother-country were needing to be rethought. There was an imprecise feeling that all these countries were one community with a common nationality. There was also a confused mass of conventions and Dominion laws. All inhabitants were reckoned to be British subjects, but definitions of citizenship and nationality varied among the members of the Commonwealth[20]. Should not some legal codification and standardisation be attempted? As the years passed a number of leading figures felt that this should be attempted if for no other reason than to rein back the secessionist mood in some Dominions. The British Nationality and Status of Aliens Act of 1914 made a very tentative start. Belief in the fact of common citizenship, even if not a clear-cut legal right, was succinctly expressed in a private letter written in 1921 to the South African statesman Jan Smuts by Leo Amery (who was later to become Colonial and Dominions Secretary). He wrote that 'these independent political units are composed equally of British subjects and have thus a common and interchangeable citizenship'. He continued: 'Nothing could be more typical of this community of citizenship than the fact that you, while a South African Minister, were actually for a time also a member of the British War Cabinet . . . .'[21]

The 1931 Statute of Westminster was the great defining constitutional document of the Commonwealth; and in the drafting meetings a serious attempt was made by some delegates to tackle the issue of citizenship. It broke on the intransigence of the Irish. The agreed paragraphs were woolly, and the Home Office legal adviser on nationality considered that the common status of Commonwealth citizen had received a fatal blow. Even so, as late as 1937, the great authority on the Commonwealth, Keith (later Sir Keith) Hancock, could write,

> There is no doubt . . . that the duty of maintaining the largest possible measure of effective common or mutual citizenship

is one of the principal non-fundamental conventions of the Commonwealth[22].

Before moving on, two footnotes, as it were, are in order. One is that, of course, the granting of independence to the Indian sub-continent and the greater mobility of peoples after our period c. 1832-1939 led to yet more, equally unsatisfactory, attempts to give legal definition to the concept of Commonwealth or British citizenship.[23] The second supplementary point concerns Ireland. If the meaning of Commonwealth citizenship during this period was tenuous, the meaning of Irish citizenship was bizarre[24]. The 1922 treaty conceding Irish independence referred to the 'common citizenship of Ireland and Great Britain'. The subsequent Irish constitution promised a legal definition of Irish citizenship - but nothing happened until 1935. In the meantime, Irish citizenship and the relationship between Irish and British citizenship were in utter confusion. The Irish Nationality and Citizenship Act of 1935 abolished the common citizenship formula, though, as a Dominion, the Irish Free State, as we have seen, participated in the vague concept of Commonwealth citizenship. However, in 1948 Ireland became a republic and in the following year left the Commonwealth Yet an anomaly remained, because the 1948 British Nationality Act gave Irish citizens the privileges of British citizenship. Accordingly, today an Irish citizen resident in Britain has three legal sets of citizenship rights (such as voting) - Irish, British and EU.

Europe and the World Since c. 1945

In typical fashion, the British approach to citizenship was a muddle. For, much more commonly during the nineteenth and twentieth centuries, citizenship was identified solely with nationality. Indeed, as Reinhard Bendix has shown, citizenship was part of the process of nation-building[25]. In a negative sense, Blacks in the USA, Jews in Nazi Germany, all but a handful of the Gallicised in the French colonies, for example, were denied full citizenship status because they were not ethnically 'true'. Similarly, the Asian inhabitants of

Uganda who opted for Ugandan citizenship were discriminated against when Amin came to power. The idea that citizenship is synonymous with 'nationality', whatever that term might be taken to mean, remains a widely held assumption. Even so, since c. 1945 our fifth and final era, the nature of citizenship has again become increasingly uncertain and fluid, so that the concept of multiple citizenship has enjoyed ever greater relevance and reality.

Dual and layered forms still exist, of course. International law refers to the first of these as dual or double nationality. And the condition has been sufficiently common and caused sufficient controversy to have generated a number of legal guidelines and judgements from the Hague Convention of 1930 onwards[26]. Also, federal forms of government now exist on every continent. All geographically large countries, with the sole exception of China, are federations. However, of greater interest are three particularly recent trends. These are: world citizenship, multiculturalism and the European Union.

First, then, let us examine the meaning and force of world citizenship as an objective or ideal held in conjunction with actual state citizenship as expressed during the past half-century. The vivid horrors of the Second World War and the foreseen horrors of a nuclear third global conflict concentrated minds on the urgent need for human beings to be, and be conscious of being, citizens of the world[27]. Individuals keen on such an enterprise in the USA and France took the lead. In 1947 the American Garry Davis created a World Citizens' Registry and invited individuals to adhere to the World Citizens' Pact. The Frenchman Robert Sarrazac founded, in 1945 and 1950 respectively, the *Front Humain des Citoyens du Monde* and the 'mundialisation' movement, which committed whole villages and towns to declaring themselves 'world territories'. Similar movements, again based in the USA and France, were inaugurated in the 1970s. Hundreds of thousands of individuals in scores of countries associated themselves with such schemes, heartening for the organisers, but scarcely a critical mass. In the 1980s and 1990s the term 'world citizenship' came increasingly into use, but in very vague and unspecified, or indeed different ways.

This has raised the question of what meanings can be attached to the term in the late twentieth century. It is helpful to display four main meanings on a spectrum from vague to precise in diagrammatic form[28]. (See Fig. 2)

Figure 2

vague			precise
member of the human race	responsible for condition of the planet	individual subject to moral law	promotion of world government

Each of these four categories requires a little elucidation. The vaguest is the sense which an individual has of being a member of the human race and even having a loyalty to it unconfined by nationality, race or creed. It describes a relationship between persons either as individuals or, more often, as members of interest-groups and organisations such as professions or businesses. Ease of communication in recent decades - by both physical and electronic means - has enhanced this sense of global community to such an extent that one now readily speaks in terms of there being a global civil society[29]. In the earlier days of the United Nations its staff, committed to the impartial pursuit of world peace and justice irrespective of their individual nationalities, were considered world citizens *par excellence*.

The second meaning of the term describes the world citizen's attitude towards the planet as an ecological system. This is less vague than our first category because the holding of an attitude often leads to taking action such as donations to pressure-groups and charitable bodies or, even and more dramatically, the practical pursuit of a conservationist aim as in the activities of Greenpeace. This consciousness of - and indeed conscience about - 'green' issues has been growing rapidly since the 1970s. It is probably true to say that the current use of the term 'world citizen' in popular and journalistic parlance has this meaning attached to it more often than any other.

The third interpretation of the term 'world citizen' requires rather fuller explanation, for it contains within itself four distinct sub-meanings: this is the relationship of the individual to forms and codes of law above and beyond his or her municipal (i.e. national) law. T. H. Marshall famously analysed the nature of citizenship into its civil, political and social components[30]. Civil citizenship concerns the rights and duties of citizens in relation to law. By analogy, therefore, world citizenship must have a legal dimension. Most basic is the ancient notion of natural law, which still persists as a belief in a moral yardstick of a just mode of living for the whole of mankind. It is a belief that underlies the global environmentalist movement, especially when perceived planetary interests conflict with national policies.

The second kind of law which helps define world citizenship is international law. Although overwhelmingly designed to codify relations between states, certain principles, particularly since 1945, have been defined to offer the individual a legal identity and legal rights of a universal as distinct from a national kind. The various human rights documents and institutions, both universal and regional, provide supra-national frameworks for an embryonic civil world citizenship. In particular, the Optional Protocol to the International Covenant on Civil and Political Rights and the European Convention on Human Rights allow for individuals to by-pass and indeed complain against their own governments[31].

Thirdly, there have been tentative attempts to require individuals to conform to international criminal law beyond the constraints of their own nations. Trials of war criminals took place in Nuremberg and Tokyo after the Second World War and, at the time of writing, a tribunal is working at The Hague to prepare the prosecution of those guilty of atrocities in Bosnia and Rwanda. The key principle enshrining the idea of the individual's supra-national obligations is contained in this sentence from the Charter of the Nuremberg Military Tribunal: 'He who violates the laws of war cannot obtain immunity while acting in pursuance of the authority of the State'[32].

Nevertheless, the quasi-world citizenship features of international law are fragmentary and haphazard in the extreme. Campaigners for a more developed world citizenship have urged the creation of a fourth kind of law relating to this conceived status, namely, an efficacious system of world law. They distinguish this form of international law by insistence on a fully worked out code and courts with real power.

However, by analogy with municipal law, world law could only be credible if it were backed by a world police force. This, in turn, implies some world, probably federal, central executive authority. World citizens would owe some allegiance to such an authority, and thus we arrive at world citizenship in its fourth and most concrete shape. The idea of a world government, as venerable as Dante's *De Monarchia*, was revived, in democratic form, during the First World War. Enthusiasm was renewed after the Second. In this context, world citizenship has been conceived either in the sense of a future status, when a world government has been installed, or as the current status of those who sedulously promote it. In the latter sense, we have already seen how the likes of Davis and Sarrazac reacted in the post-war years. More recently, and with a greater sense of practicality, Professor David Held and others of a like mind have argued for cosmopolitan democracy. This means greater opportunities for popular participation in a pyramidal structure. In this scenario national parliaments would be complemented by regional and global assemblies, all popularly elected. If such a layered system of democratic politics was spread across the world, together with enforceable law, the effect would be, in Held's words,

> a binding framework for the political business of states, societies and regions. . . . People would come, thus, to enjoy multiple citizenships - political membership in the diverse political communities which significantly affect them[33].

Thus, in essence, are the varying recent interpretations of world citizenship. The second major feature of the post-war world tending to multiple citizenship is multiculturalism. The Athenian citizen was a man whose parents were Athenian, who spoke Greek and who worshipped the same gods as his fellow-citizens. How different are conditions in most states today. Virtually every state is a cultural medley, resulting from a number of causes that have been particularly evident during the past half-century. National consciousness in multinational states has become increasingly acute, witness, for example, the discontents of the Tamils in Sri Lanka and the violent fragmentation of Yugoslavia. In addition, there have been migrations of peoples on an unprecedented scale. These have been due to the collapse of colonial empires, the improvements in transport systems, the economic lure of the richer countries and the creation of many millions of refugees, often by civil wars. We may take as representative examples, Muslims in Britain, Hispanics in the USA and Hutu and Tutsi refugees in all the countries neighbouring Rwanda and Burundi[34].

These events are germane to the subject of multiple citizenship because, collectively, they have muddied and undermined the notion of singular citizenship in four ways. First, the question of civic identity may well have to be addressed in a state with cultural minorities. This problem itself has two facets. One is the question of loyalty. This was encapsulated in Britain by Lord Tebbit's 'cricket test': when the English team is playing a team from the West Indies or the Indian sub-continent, which team would be supported by British citizens whose families came from these former territories of the Empire? The other facet is the practical, usually language, difficulty of performing civic functions in the absence of basic competence. To provide an example of this issue: can monoglot Spanish-speakers be real American citizens?

The second problem derives from the first. Should the state give special rights to cultural minorities - to allow them to retain their cultural distinctiveness while enabling them to be (or become) truly citizens of the state? For instance, should Sikhs in Britain be exempt from the law requiring motor-cyclists to wear crash-helmets? Should Spanish become an official second language in the USA?

The third problem is that, in practice, social and economic rights of citizenship are often available to aliens. And if aliens are resident for a long time, the question arises whether the rights of political citizenship also should be extended to them. The issue is particularly pertinent to the position of the *Gastarbeiter* in Germany.

Fourthly, the distinction between citizens as people with rights and aliens as people without rights has been eroded by the development of codes of human rights. This is especially evident in Europe because of the effectiveness (albeit cumbersome) of the Council of Europe's Commission and Court of Human Rights.

As a consequence of these confusions, it is becoming increasingly necessary to refer to citizenship as a much more complex concept than hitherto, leading to the invention of new terminology. Iris Young has coined the term 'differentiated citizenship' to describe the need for group-specific civic rights[36]. Piers Gardner makes a distinction between 'nationality citizenship', defined by each state's municipal law, and 'new citizenship', derived from the rights accorded by other means, such as the European Convention on Human Rights[37].

The matter of multiple citizenship is of particular significance for understanding the nature of the status of citizenship in the component states of the European Union[38]. As this topic is dealt with in Chapter 3 of the present work, a few general observations will suffice here. These may be clustered into three points.

First, the creation of the European Community provided for the mobility of persons, as well as goods, services and capital, a principle reiterated and strengthened by the Single European Act[39]. A corollary to this objective was provision for the enjoyment of social security for individuals from one state working in another[40]. Together with the 'Social Chapter' of the Maastricht Treaty[41], considerable potential exists for the exercise of the rights of social and economic citizenship across the European Union, irrespective of the individual's nationality.

Secondly, the rights of civil citizenship exist in the sense that the Union's European Court of Justice and the Council of Europe's Commission and Court of Human Rights have the capacity to protect the interests of the individual citizen irrespective of nationality. Moreover, individuals have the right to present their cases.

Thirdly, the Maastricht Treaty provides for a measure of political citizenship, including the rights to vote and stand as a candidate in municipal and European parliamentary elections in the individual's state of residence, regardless of nationality[43]. Furthermore, the treaty commits member states to the principles of democracy and subsidiarity[44]. Application of the second of these principles in the light of the first could be interpreted to mean the exercise of civic rights at four levels of decision-making, namely, local, regional, state and Union.

By establishing the very concept of citizenship of the Union, Article 8 of the Maastricht Treaty unequivocally confirms the principle of multiple citizenship for the citizens of fifteen states (and potentially more if the project for 'widening' membership of the Union still further is put into practice). However, the use of the words 'potential', 'principle' and 'capacity' and the conditional mood in the above paragraphs has been deliberate: the reality of multiple citizenship still awaits full exploitation by the citizens and institutions of the European Union.

Conclusion

It will be evident from the foregoing matter that 'multiple citizenship' is anything but a precise term; rather, 'multiple' is a portmanteau word used to describe a wide variety of styles of citizenship, which, over the centuries, have placed the original meaning of that status under considerable strain. The new term is brought into play in order to rescue the concept of citizenship from being overwhelmed by three kinds of problems: the problem of definition, the problem of moral behaviour, and the problem of incompatibilities.

Despite the complications of the laws governing citizenship in the Roman Empire, the basic principles were simple: the status defined the civil and political relationships between the state and the individual, regardless of ethnic origin, and with the possibility of dual citizenship; while the concept of world citizenship was used by the Stoics as merely an ethical benchmark. However, by our own age, any attempted definition must strive to encompass an extraordinary complexity. Analysts now refer to five 'generations' of citizenship - civil, political, social, economic and environmental. The attempt to retain the modern legal identification of citizenship with nationality is breaking down before codifications of competing supra-national notions such as human rights and European citizenship. And, to cap it all, the ancient metaphysical idea of world citizenship is now, in an age of increasing global interdependence, assuming some tangible forms.

These complications would have no import beyond stretching the ingenuity of political scientists and lawyers to make sense of the confusion were it not for the moral problem. For if the individual has more than one civic identity, difficulties arise when the individual is faced with competing, even conflicting, demands on his/her allegiance. Legal clarification of the several spheres of rights and duties can help. But only so far. In the event of a clash of loyalties, the priority is left to the individual citizen's interpretation and conscience. How much simpler was the role of the citizen in the civic republican tradition of patriotic political and military allegiance to the state[45].

Confusion is worse confounded when we realise that certain features of citizenship in the contemporary world seem to raise serious questions about compatibility. To take up the allusion at the end of the last paragraph, is the experiment with a NATO multinational corps in Europe incompatible with the civic republican equation of military service with state citizenship? Or does the persistence of national military service in many states suggest that at least in this respect the classical style of citizenship is resisting the encroachment of multiple citizenship? And is the classical ideal of patriotism as a basic feature of citizenship compatible with multiple citizenship[46]? One may also question whether civil and political citizenship have any reality without the citizen experiencing a sense of identity with, as well as having duties to and receiving rights from, the polity which provides the status. The citizens of the member-states of the European Union may indeed be also citizens of the Union by virtue of the Maastricht Treaty, but how many *feel* that that European status is compatible with their national status? Conversely, individuals who feel that they are world citizens may well find that this sense of cosmopolitan identity is hardly compatible with even the most generous reading of international law on the subject.[47] Moreover, insofar as global environmental issues underpin contemporary cosmopolitanism, this global civic consciousness could well be incompatible with national economic citizenship rights when the citizen's living standards are sustained by planetary unsustainable development[48].

We may therefore conclude with the following observations. Simple, 'singular' state citizenship is an idea which cannot contain the complexities of what citizenship involves in reality. The concept can only be rescued and retain its validity if the notion of multiple citizenship is fully grasped. Yet, if that concept is undermined by the incompatibilities it contains, what is left of the very notion citizenship at all? Yet it *does* exist.

Endnotes

1. Both had been initiated by the Greeks, but rather tentatively. For dual citizenship, see the relevant pages of Sherwin-White, A. N., (1973): *The Roman Citizenship* (Oxford: Clarendon). For world citizenship, see Heater, D. (1996): *World Citizenship and Government*. (Basingstoke: Macmillan). Chapter 1.

2. For the principle of incompatibility, see Cicero (1958): 'Pro Balbo' (trans. Gardner, R.), in *The Speeches* (London: Heinemann). For a famous example of the use of dual citizenship, see the case of St. Paul in *Acts*, 21.39.

3. See Seneca (1959): (trans. Basore J. W.), 'On Leisure' in *Moral Essays* (London: Heinemann); and Antoninus, (1961): *The Communings with Himself* (trans. Haines, C. R.), (London: Heinemann) (usually referred to as his *Meditations*).

4. See Lipsius, J. (1939): *Two Bookes of Constancie* (trans. J. Stradling), (New Brunswick, NJ, Rutgers University Press) and Montaigne (1958): (Harmondsworth: Penguin). 'On the education of children' (trans. Cohen, J. M.), in *Essays*.

5. Locke, J. *Second Treatise on Civil Government*, ch. IX para. 128.

6. *Le Droit des Gens*, quoted in Green, L. C. (1967), Is World Citizenship a Legal Practicality? *The Canadian Yearbook of International Law*, vol. 25, p. 163.

7. See the two essays on Robespierre's ideas in Cobban, A. (1968). *Aspects of the French Revolution*. (London: Cape).

8. The texts, from which the following quotations have been taken and translated (pp. 463 and 469) are printed in M. Bouloiseau et al. (1952): *Oeuvres de Maximilien Robespierre*, t.ix (Paris: Presses Universitaires de France).

9. Plutarch (1957): (trans. F. C. Babbitt), *Moralia*, pp. 329-334. vol. IV (London: Heinemann).

10. Dann, O. and Dinwiddy, J. (eds.) (1988): *Nationalism in the Age of the French Revolution* (London: Hambledon), p. 163.

11. Fichte, J. G. (1968): Seventh Address. P.99 in Kelly, G. A. (ed.), *Addresses to the German Nation* (New York: Harper and Row). For a thorough discussion of the German intellectual scene, see Meinecke, F. (1970): (trans. R. B. Kimber), *Cosmopolitanism and the National State* (Princeton, NJ: Princeton University Press).

12. Quoted in Forsyth, M. (1981): *Unions of States* (Leicester: Leicester University Press) P.70.

13. *The Federalist*, no. 46.

14. De Tocqueville, A. (1968): *Democracy in America* (ed. J. P. Mayer and M. Lerner) (London: Collins), p. 85. His views were confirmed by his reading of *The Federalist*, which he much admired.

15. Tocqueville, *Democracy in America*, p. 199.

16. Chap. 15.

17. See Hennock, E. P. (1973): *Fit and Proper Persons* (London: Arnold), P. 12. This figure compares with a national average for central government elections after the Second Reform Act of 1867 of under a tenth.

18. Briggs, A. (1968): *Victorian Cities* (Harmondsworth: Penguin,) P. 85.

19. Quoted, Hennock, *Fit and Proper Persons*, p. 75.

20. This word came into vogue during the First World War. The 1914 Imperial Act declared that everyone born in the Empire was a British subject.

21. Quoted in Hall, H. D. (1971): *Commonwealth: A History of the British Commonwealth of Nations*. (London: Van Nostrand Reinhold), pp. 376-77.

22. Hancock, W K and Latham, R. T. E. (1937): *Survey of British Commonwealth Affairs: Volume 1 Problems of Nationality. 1918-1936* (London: Oxford University Press), p.584.

23. British Nationality Acts of 1948 and 1981 and Commonwealth Immigrants Acts of 1962, 1968 and 1971. For a succinct description of this legislation, see Walvin, J. (1984): *Passage to Britain* (Harmondsworth: Penguin), pp. 118-23, 217. For details of the 1981 act explained simply, see Wilson, M. (1983): *Immigration and Race* (Harmondsworth: Penguin), pp. 1-9.

24. For details, see Hancock and Latham, *Survey of British Commonwealth Affairs*, pp. 378-9.

25. Bendix, R. (1964): *Nation-Building and Citizenship* (Berkeley and Los Angeles, CA: University of California Press).

26. See Brownlie, I. (1990): *Principles of Public International Law* (Oxford: Clarendon Press), pp. 399-402.

27. For details, see Heater, D. *World Citizenship and Government*, chap. 6.

28. See Heater, D. (1995): Education for World Citizenship in *Citizenship* col 4. For an alternative classification, see Falk, R. (1994): The Making of Global Citizenship in B. van Steenbergen (ed.) *The Condition of Citizenship*. (London: Sage).

29. See, e.g., Walzer, M. (1995): *Toward a Global Civil Society*. (Providence, RI: Berghahn).

30. Marshall, T. H. (1950): *Citizenship and Social Class* (Cambridge: Cambridge University Press).

31. In practice the International Covenant is ineffective; and the European Convention covers only citizens of the member-states of the Council of Europe which allow individual applications to the Commission and Court.

32. Quoted in Brownlie, *Principles of Public International Law*, p. 562.

33. Held, D. (1995): *Democracy and the Global Order* (Cambridge: Polity). P. 233.

34. Kymlicka, W. (1995): *Multicultural Citizenship* (Oxford, Clarendon), makes the useful distinction between 'national minorities' in multinational states and 'ethnic groups' in 'polyethnic' states. Of an increasing literature on the topic, the following brief essays can also be commended: Habermas, J. Citizenship and National Identity, in van Steenbergen (ed.), *The Condition of Citizenship;* Gardner, J. P. (1990): What Lawyers Mean by Citizenship, Commission on Citizenship, *Encouraging Citizenship* (London: HMSO) Parekh, B. (1991): British Citizenship and Cultural Citizenship, in Andrews, G. (ed.), *Citizenship* (London: Lawrence and Wishart).

35. Cited, Kymlicka, *Multicultural Citizenship*, p.26.

35. Cited, Kymlicka, *Multicultural Citizenship*, pp. 198-90.

37. Gardner, 'What Lawyers Mean by Citizenship'.

38. Of the wealth of material, two very useful recent publications should be noted: Rosas, A. and Antola, E. (eds.) (1995): *A Citizens' Europe* (London: Sage); and Gardner, J. P. (ed.), (1995): *Hallmarks of Citizenship* (London: British Institute of International and Comparative Law).

39. Treaty of Rome, Art. 8a and Single European Act, Art. 13.

40. Treaty of Rome, Art. 51.

41. Protocol on Social Policy to the Treaty on European Union, signed by all members except the United Kingdom.

42. Personal access to the Council of Europe institutions is dependent on the individual's state having agreed to the principle of individual petition.
43. Art. 8b.
44. Arts. F1 and C.
45. But, see Habermas, J., Citizenship and National Identity.
46. See Aron, R. (1974): Is Multinational Citizenship Possible?, *Social Research*, vol 41.
47. See Green, Is World Citizenship a Legal Practicality?
48. See Steward, F., Citizens of Planet Earth.

SECTION 2
THE CONTEXT OF EUROPEAN CITIZENSHIP: INSTITUTIONS AND POLICIES

DEVELOPING EUROPEAN INSTITUTIONS: GOVERNING EUROPEAN INTEGRATION

CHAPTER 2

Roger M. Scully

The development of European citizenship is impossible to divorce from the broader process of European integration. The intermittent, frequently faltering, but nonetheless persistent advances in the economic and political unification of much of the continent since the war reached their most recent high-water mark in the Maastricht Treaty on European Union (hereafter, TEU or simply Maastricht). The citizenship provisions of that Treaty must, therefore, be recognised as but one - albeit highly significant - element of a much deeper phenomenon.

In that light, this chapter presents an overview of European integration, so that readers may understand the citizenship issue within its appropriate context. The first section reviews the key historical events in the development of what is now the European Union. Following that, a description of the main governing institutions that have been created at the European level will be given. The aim of the latter section is to provide a 'guide to the maze' that, to the uninitiated, European politics often seems to be.

The overall message which readers should take from this chapter is that the EU has not become what we would recognise as a country say, a 'United States of Europe'. But nor do European countries remain entirely independent of each other. Rather, they have joined in a Union that links them quite closely, and reflects an uneasy, and often confusing, compromise between the two incompatible ideals of a federal Europe and one of independent, sovereign states.

European Integration: A Troubled Evolution

The Historical Legacy: The idea of European unity is by no means new. Some, indeed, trace it back as far as the Roman Empire, when most of Europe (and much of the rest of the world) was politically united. The history of Europe since Rome, however, has more typically been one of division and periodic conflict, with idealists of European unity for the most part dismissed as impractical dreamers. A far stronger force in the 18th and 19th centuries was that of nationalism. Following the example of the French revolutionaries, people increasingly came to argue that the boundaries of countries should be set by the divisions between nations (defined as a people sharing some sense of ethnic or linguistic identity), rather than the past conquests of Princes, Kings and Emperors. Prompted by this ideal, the 19th century witnessed the uniting of most Germanic peoples in a German Empire, and Italians in a newly established Italy.

Nationalism, however, also appeared to lead, inevitably, to national rivalry. World Wars I and II seemed to testify to the devastating consequences which aggressive, assertive nationalism could produce. Proposals for greater European unity were floated in the 1920s and 30s - for example, by the French Foreign Minister Aristide Briand, and the peripatetic Austrian Nobleman Count Richard Coudenhove-Kalergi - but without success. As Zurcher comments, 'The union of Europe continued to be a concept that appealed to scholars, philosophers and occasional politicians, as it had for centuries, but the masses of the people and the organs of popular opinion remained largely uninfluenced and uninformed'[1]. During the early 1940s, however, as plans began to be made for the post-war world, many Europeans seized on the notion of a more united continent as offering a better future. Yet it was quite one thing to think in general terms about such a unity, and another entirely to actually make these ideas a working reality. Who would be included in a 'united Europe', and on what principles of government would it be constructed? To what extent would European unity mean giving up often long-cherished, or hard fought-for, national independence and identity? Could unity really prevent future conflict (given the history of numerous civil wars)? These were questions which would have to be confronted. Furthermore, it was not necessarily apparent how European unity might help Europeans deal with the most pressing problems after the war ceased: re-building a devastated continent, feeding people, and sustaining basic standards of life.

Initial Moves: Not surprisingly, the first steps taken were hesitant ones. In 1949 the *Council of Europe* was established. This organisation originally comprised ten of the non-Communist democracies of Europe, and it subsequently expanded its membership to include all European democracies. But the role of the Council of Europe in the integration process has been marginal. The primary reason is that some of the original members (in particular Britain and the Scandinavians) were unwilling to allow it to develop into a prospective European government, or to give up any of their national independence to it. Thus, while it was, and has remained, a valuable discussion forum and done particularly useful work in the field of human rights, it has done little to build links across national borders or to develop a European level of governance. Similarly, cooperation between European countries in the administration of *Marshall Aid* was limited and did not prompt the more widespread cooperation that the American donors had hoped it might[2].

The first major advance in European unity was the establishment of the *European Coal and Steel Community (ECSC)* by the 1951 Treaty of Paris. The ECSC was set up amongst only six countries - West

Germany, France, Italy, and the 'Benelux' states: Belgium, the Netherlands, and Luxembourg - where pro-unity feeling among the peoples and governments was strongest. The idea of the ECSC was developed by a French civil servant, Jean Monnet, and the French Foreign Minister Robert Schuman - partly as a means to develop European unity, but also to try to assuage the fears of many French people about the burgeoning German economic recovery. Lingering French fears of the Germans (understandable given that France had been invaded three times in the previous seventy years by Germany) were lessened somewhat by the placing of both countries' coal and steel industries - the basic materials of a war machine - under a common European authority, along with those of the other members. In the longer term, however, Monnet and others hoped that the handing over of some powers to a European organisation would develop the practice of cooperation, and that this could then be extended to other areas of life.

Shortly thereafter a much more ambtious proposal was put forward. The Pleven Plan aimed to develop a *European Defence Community (EDC)*. The idea was the response of Monnet and French Prime Minister Rene Pleven to growing pressure from France's allies, America and Britain, to allow the West Germans to contribute to Western European defence. The continuing Cold War, and the outbreak of hostilities in Korea, threatened to overstretch the resources of the western allies. Yet while acknowledging the logic of the case that the Germans should help in the defence effort, France was loathe to see the re-establishment of an independent German army. The EDC was an attempt to 'square the circle' by having German-manned units as part of a united European force, under the political control of a joint council of national defence ministers. The EDC would have been a huge advance for European unity - national defence, after all, is one of the most fundamental tasks of a government - but it never came into being. While a treaty was signed by the six ECSC members, it failed to be ratified and thus never entered into effect. The notion simply aroused too much opposition - particularly (and somewhat ironically, given who originally proposed the idea) in France, where concerns about national honour and French independence persuaded the National Assembly to reject the EDC. West Germany eventually was re-armed, but as a member of the US-led NATO organisation.

With the failure of EDC, proponents of integration returned to more cautious proposals. In 1957, two Treaties of Rome were signed by the six ECSC members. One was to create a *European Economic Community*, which aimed at completely free-trade among the six, some common policies such as on agriculture, and common tariff (import tax) levels on goods from outside the EEC. Bringing the economies of Europe closer together would increase social and economic interaction, and might, in time, help generate support for greater political unity. The other treaty created *Euratom*, which aimed to promote common research in the peaceful use of atomic energy. (The 1950s, it should be remembered, was long before the Three-Mile-Island and Chernobyl disasters, and a time when nuclear power was widely considered to be the most promising source of clean, cheap energy for the future). Collectively, the three communities later came to be known as the *European Community* or simply the *EC*.

Development of the EC: The EC's early years were successful in many respects. Trade between its members expanded considerably, contributing to a sustained economic boom for all. The agricultural policy led to a Europe almost self-sufficient in food - a stark contrast to the shortages of the immediate post-war years. Most importantly, the six became accustomed to cooperation, and conflict amongst them was rendered virtually unthinkable. The most vivid symbol of this was a French-German Treaty of Friendship, signed in 1963.

The main limits on the EC's early achievements were those imposed by the French President, Charles de Gaulle. De Gaulle opposed the Community ever becoming a federal union. He also - to the consternation of the other members - steadfastly refused to permit

British membership of the EC. Seeing the early success, Britain had applied to join, but was vetoed by de Gaulle in 1963 (and again in 1967). De Gaulle saw the UK as too closely allied to the USA, while his vision was of a French-led 'Europe des Patries' - a third force of allied but independent countries. Expanding the membership of the EC had to wait until after de Gaulle left office in 1969. The EC increased in size from six to nine countries in 1973, when Britain joined, along with Ireland and Denmark. Greece became a member in 1981, and Spain and Portugal brought the membership to twelve in 1986, all three becoming eligible for membership only after the downfall of military governments in the 1970s[3].

By the 1980s, the EC was an established part of European life. Yet it was also a disappointment to many people. While it had facilitated increases in trade, and institutionalised cooperation between its members, it was clearly a long way from a close federal union. National governments insisted on retaining a veto over many EC policies, while the most well-known of those policies, the Common Agricultural Policy, was becoming a fiasco, with vast over-production of food leading to European 'food mountains' and the destruction of surpluses, all at considerable public expense. It took the leadership of Jacques Delors, President of the European Commission from 1985, supported by national leaders like Chancellor Helmut Kohl of Germany and President Francois Mitterrand of France, to 're-launch' the integration process. The 1986 Single European Act (SEA) was a major achievement. It eliminated the national government veto over many EC policies and gave greater powers to the European Parliament. Its centerpiece, however, was the completion of the common economic market within the EC countries, by sweeping away hundreds of 'technical' barriers to trade (such as extensive customs checks, and the use of health and safety laws to render illegal in one place goods produced in other EC countries), and also granting complete freedom of movement for capital, services and labour. But in addition, the SEA was important as a first step in Delors' wider programme of advancing the economic and political unity of Europe. He used the success of the SEA to generate a favourable momentum for his efforts, which were to reach their culmination at Maastricht[4].

The European Union: The Maastricht Treaty, agreed in December 1991 and formally signed early the following year, created the *European Union (EU)*. The EU incorporated the EC, as well as formalising government-government cooperation on foreign policy issues and cross-border anti-crime efforts into two separate 'pillars' of the Union, the Common Foreign and Security Policy (CFSP) and Justice and Home Affairs (JHA). This rather confusing arrangement means that institutions like the Commission (discussed below), remain European *Community* institutions, while being 'associated' with cooperation between national governments in the two non-EC areas. In practice, the term 'EU' has tended to replace 'EC' in popular usage, even though the EC still exists as part of the broader EU.

Of more substantive importance, Maastricht included provisions for greater powers to be given to the European Parliament; set out 1999 as the latest date by which countries (except Britain and Denmark, which gained 'opt-outs' allowing them to decide later) should begin replacing their national currencies with a single European currency if their economies were ready; and established European citizenship. A separate 'protocol' on minimum standards of social protection for workers was also agreed at Maastricht between all of the countries except the UK. Although nearly coming unstuck in referendums in Denmark and France, which revealed much public confusion and even some hostility[5], Maastricht was another distinct advance in the integration process. Whilst that process has often been troubled and uncertain, the fifteen EU member countries (Austria, Sweden and Finland became the newest members in January 1995) are now economically and politically unified to a degree unimaginable forty years ago[6]. And although the 1997 Amsterdam Treaty contained but minor additional advances, it just as clearly gave little joy to those 'Euro-skeptics' in some EU countries who would like to see the reversal of integration.

The European Union Today

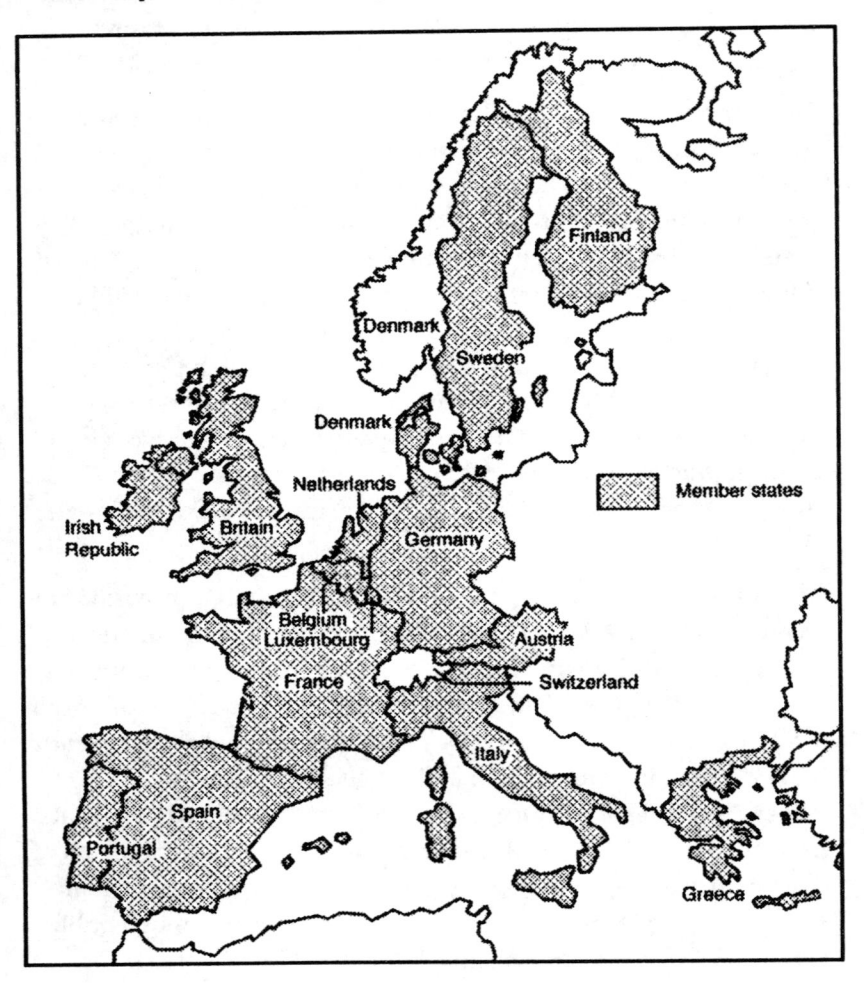

Governing European Integration: The Institutions

Like the development of integration as a whole, the institutional structure of the EC bears witness to compromises between the desire of some to establish strong European-level structures of governance, and the belief of others that power should remain essentially in national hands. The result is a rather untidy structure in which the influence of national governments remains strong, but is far from the whole story.

The Council of Ministers and European Council - 'Institutionalised Inter-Governmentalism': The Council of Ministers and European Council are the institutions through which the governments of the EC member countries retain substantial influence, if not quite complete control, over European affairs. The Council of Ministers was established with the formation of the ECSC, and after the Rome treaties came to operate over the entire range of EC activities. At any one time, the Council has fifteen members - one minister from each member government⁷. Who that minister is, however, varies according to the subject under discussion and its perceived importance. On fairly significant matters of more general policy, countries will usually be represented by their senior foreign or European affairs ministers. More run-of-the-mill matters may mean deputy or junior ministers attending, while meetings devoted to more specialist areas will usually mean that the minister in charge of that policy portfolio will represent his or her country. Thus, many of the meetings during 1996 devoted to sorting out the 'mad cows' crisis were attended by the British agricultural minister, the appropriately named Mr Hogg, and the other fourteen national farming ministers.

The Council of Ministers is effectively the main chamber of the EC's legislature. All major European laws, and the Community budget, must receive approval from the Council. Prior to the SEA, countries were granted a veto over virtually all policies, meaning that unanimous consent was required for nearly every significant decision. As can be imagined, this tended to make the EC policy process extremely slow and encouraged difficult decisions to be avoided. In recent years, however, an increasing number of decisions have been subject to what is known as 'qualified majority voting' (QMV). Under QMV, countries receive a vote allocation which is somewhat weighted to account for their size.

Table 1: Qualified Majority Voting in the Council Of Ministers

Country	Votes in Council	Population (1995 approx, Million)	Votes per Million population
Germany	10	80.2	0.12
Italy	10	57.8	0.17
UK	10	57.6	0.17
France	10	57.2	0.17
Spain	8	39.1	0.20
Netherlands	5	15.1	0.33
Greece	5	10.3	0.49
Belgium	5	10.0	0.50
Portugal	5	9.8	0.51
Sweden	4	8.7	0.46
Austria	4	7.9	0.51
Denmark	3	5.1	0.59
Finland	3	5.1	0.59
Ireland	3	3.5	0.86
Luxembourg	2	0.4	5.00

Total Votes in Council = 87
Qualified Majority = 62 (Blocking Minority = 26)

As Table 1 shows, the largest four countries receive ten votes each, while Luxembourg, the smallest, receives two votes. Nonetheless, Germany is much more than five times as big as Luxembourg, so the smaller countries generally get relatively more 'voting power' per head of population. On the other hand, three of the largest countries grouping together can form a 'blocking minority', while up to eight of the smallest would be needed to do the same. Proposals by some of the larger countries to re-weight the votes, giving themselves greater power, were predictably resisted by the smaller states in the Amsterdam negotiations. In areas of law where QMV is used, proposals received by the Council from the Commission and/or Parliament can be approved as they are by a qualified majority, but unanimity in the Council is generally required for them to be altered[8].

About 100 meetings of the Council are held every year, usually in Brussels, the semi-official capital of the EU. The meetings are chaired by the minister of the country holding the *Presidency of the Council*. This rotates between all of the member countries, with each taking a six-month term. The Council presidency gives a country some ability to shape the direction of the policy agenda being pursued, although six months is generally too short a period in which to have a decisive influence. A presidency is likely to be most effective not only when a country has considerable diplomatic skills, but when it is following a similar agenda to its immediate predecessor(s). There can thus be a cumulative effort. The obverse, however, is that successive presidencies with divergent aims and priorities, or ones that are simply incompetent, can hamper the EU as a whole. While cumbersome, the rotating presidency system seems unlikely to be eliminated as many national governments are reluctant to adopt the only obvious alternative of allowing the Commission to chair meetings, which would give the Commission greater control over the policy agenda.

The *European Council* is the name given to the now-regular summit meetings of the EU heads of government. Until the 1970s, this form of meeting was rather rare, although bi-lateral summit meetings were more common. Since 1974, however, meetings of all the heads of government have occurred two or three times a year, and have been termed the European Council. The idea of regular summit meetings was developed out of a widespread perception of the need to give the EC greater direction and leadership. The meetings generally deal with broad policy issues, particular crises, and plotting the future direction of the integration process. They provide, in short, a place where the 'buck stops' - where problems cannot be pushed any higher, and where major decisions must be taken. Thus, the Maastricht Treaty is known after the European Council held at the Dutch town in December 1991, where the final shape of the treaty was hammered out between the national leaders.

The summits are hosted by the country currently occupying the Presidency of the Council of Ministers, and will generally be located at some country estate or chateau, where the national leaders can meet in a degree of comfort as well as privacy and security. They generally take place over a long weekend, with the leaders assembling on Friday evening, and then continuing until Sunday night. Formal sessions, which include all the national leaders and their foreign ministers, along with the Commission President and Vice-President, are interspersed with dinners and informal coffee and breakfast meetings where two or three of the leaders may meet alone. These latter, more intimate and private encounters are where much of the deal-making apparently takes place. Even in the formal sessions, however, great onus is placed on the skills of the national leaders, who must be both well-prepared and persuasive if they are to achieve their aims. John Major, for example, while an unimpressive speechmaker, was apparently highly effective in the European Council forum, where his command of detail and personal charm were far more salien qualities. The meetings do, moreover, allow for national leaders to interact fairly regularly and to get to know each other. Often this can help to build or solidify ties - Chancellor Kohl and President Mitterrand developed what became a close working relationship partly through European Council meetings[9].

Taken together then, the Council of Ministers and European Council epitomise the 'inter-governmental' approach to cooperation, by which national governments negotiate with each other, rather than handing powers over to a European body above the national level. However, with their regular meetings and highly formalised rules, they also represent a highly institutionalised form of inter-governmentalism and show how deeply embedded the practice of cooperation has become in western European politics[10].

The European Commission: The forerunner of today's European Commission was the *High Authority* of the ECSC. This body was intended by Monnet and Schuman to be the driving force of integration - overseeing existing policy, developing new proposals, and having some degree of executive discretion to take decisions within general parameters set down by the Council of Ministers. When the EEC and Euratom were set up, they were each given a Commission of their own to fulfil a role similar to the High Authority, but under somewhat tighter control from the Council of Ministers. Eventually, in 1965, the three bodies were merged into one European Commission, thus ending a rather silly and wasteful duplication of structures.

The Commission is headed by twenty Commissioners, who are nominated by the national governments[11]. Commissioners are usually people who have previously had a fairly prominent role at the national level, either as politicians or senior administrators. The current British Commissioners, for example, are Sir Leon Brittan, who was formerly Home Secretary and Minister for Trade and Industry, and Neil Kinnock, previously Leader of the Opposition. One of the twenty is designated President of the Commission, an appointment which can sometimes be the subject of contention between national governments. Once nominated, the President, consulting with his nineteen colleagues and with the national governments, will determine the allocation of policy responsibilities between the Commissioners[12]. Each Commissioner will have the responsibility of overseeing existing policies within his area, as well as developing new proposals. Proposals, however, must be approved by the full Commission before they can become official Commission policy; in the Commission meeting they are subject to a majority vote, in which the President, like all his colleagues, can be outvoted.

Although charged with the oversight and execution of EC policies and laws, the Commission is unable to fulfill this role by itself. Contrary to the media image of the vast 'Brussels bureaucracy', the Commission is actually a rather small and slimly resourced organisation, given the scale of its responsibilities[13]. Thus, it has to depend on national bureaucracies to help execute much policy. Nonetheless, the Commission is far from powerless and irrelevant. It does have some ability to take decisions in narrow, generally technical, areas of policy. It also has the sole right to introduce draft legislation, and while the Council and Parliament can often require that the Commission bring forward proposals in particular areas, they cannot determine the content of those proposals. Under QMV rules (see above), this can give the Commission a degree of influence.

More generally, some Commission leaders, most notably Jacques Delors (President from 1985 to 1994), have shown how the Commission can shape the direction of the integration process. Most Commissioners favour European unity, but effective ones like Delors are those who act as 'policy entrepreneurs' - using their knowledge of national governments' concerns and EC activities to shape proposals that win the widest coalition of support, and manage both to address the policy priorities of governments and advance integration. There is little the Commission can force national governments to do. Rather like the domestic powers of theUS President, the Commission is at its most effective when it exercises the 'power of persuasion': in other words, when it can get national governments to *choose* to move in the direction the Commission desires[14].

The European Parliament (EP): The European Parliament is the only EC institution whose membership is directly elected by the people. This was not always the case. The EP began life as the *Common Assembly* of the ECSC, with its membership originally consisting of national parliamentarians from the six member countries, who would be nominated to serve in the Assembly for several years. The Assembly not only lacked any direct mandate of its own but also was originally virtually powerless, possessing only the right to be consulted on policy and the rather extreme sanction of removing the entire High Authority from office for the equivalent of 'high crimes and misdemeanours'. Thus, it was more a discussion forum - or a 'multi-lingual talking shop' as some were inclined to dismiss it - than a genuine parliament or legislature. When the Rome treaties were signed, the Assembly's remit was extended to cover the EC as a whole, but it remained almost powerless.

Since the 1950s, however, the European Parliament (which it began to call itself in 1962), has slowly developed a more important role in European politics. In the 1970s, it was granted greater powers over the EC budget. It also gained the right of delay over legislation when the Court of Justice, in the famous **Isoglucose** judgement, insisted that legislation could not be passed by the Council before the EP had formally presented its opinion. (This allowed the EP to delay by simply not giving its opinion for some time). Moreover, after many years of argument, the first EP elections were finally held in 1979. Elections had long been resisted by those who feared that a democratic mandate would allow EP members to press for greater powers. These fears have indeed proven to be well-founded. The Parliament has consistently and vigorously lobbied for an enhanced role, notably in its 1984 Draft Treaty on European Union, where it demanded more powers as part of a deepening of integration. These demands were somewhat met by the SEA, which gave the EP greater ability to amend some legislation, and a veto which could only be overturned by a unanimous Council of

Ministers. The TEU was a further step forward, with the Parliament now having full 'co-decision' power on some matters, meaning that it could delay, amend, or issue a veto which could not be overridden. Maastricht also gave the EP approval power over each new Commission after it was nominated: votes were held on the nominee for the new Commission President, Jacques Santer, and his fellow Commissioners in 1994 and 1995.

While the EP did not yet have full co-decision powers on a majority of EC laws, its ability to shape legislation was now considerable. Indeed, in practice, in recent years it has probably influenced a greater proportion of laws than the national legislatures of many of the EU members. Further, whilst the 626 members serving in the EP came from across the political spectrum (from neo-fascists through to Communists, although a clear majority belonged to one of the moderate groups within the chamber - the Socialists, Christian Democrats or Liberals), most were committed both to deepening European integration and to giving the EP a more substantial role within that united Europe. National governments continued to be lobbied in this direction, and the campaign achieved considerable success at Amsterdam. Indeed, given that the Parliament's role is currently understood by only a tiny fraction of the public, in future years the attention of EP members may well turn away from the issue of gaining more powers, and towards that of making greater efforts to connect with the citizenry of Europe. In this latter area, despite its democratic mandate, parliament still has a long way to go[15].

The Court of Justice: The Court of Justice is the supreme court for European law. The Court is not to be confused with the European Court of Human Rights - which is entirely separate from the EC, and rather more famous[16]. But, by using the founding treaties of the EC and subsequent amendments as its core constitutional texts, the Court of Justice has developed a role whose significance is increasingly recognised.

The Court has fifteen members, usually high-ranking former judges or legal scholars in their own countries. These members are nominated for six-year, renewable terms by agreement between the national governments, with one of their number serving as President. The Court, supported by a lower *Court of First Instance*, sits in Luxembourg, and issues decisions which address whether EC laws are consistent with the treaties, or whether EC laws are being upheld in all the member states. Unlike some constitutional courts (for example, the US Supreme Court), Court of Justice opinions are issued alone without any dissenting views being aired, even if there has been disagreement among the fifteen justices.

A number of Court opinions have made their mark on the path of European integration. The 1963 **Van Gend en Loos** decision established the principle of the 'direct effect' of European law; i.e. that it was binding on individuals and institutions, in addition to national governments. The 1979 **Cassis de Dijon** case first articulated the principle of the 'mutual recognition' of health and safety standards between EC countries that was to form an important part of the single market strategy used in the SEA. The 1980 **Isoglucose** case (discussed above) shaped the balance of power between the EC institutions. More recently, the **Bosman** ruling has brought about substantial changes in the football transfer market and, of greater significance perhaps, attracted wider public attention to the Court, as well as indicating how far European law now impacts on people's daily lives. While, by its nature, it has a low political profile, the Court is a highly important actor. Calls in recent years by British 'Euro-sceptics' for the Court's powers to be trimmed are merely one illustration of the increasing recognition of this fact[17]. Such calls, however, were ignored in the Amsterdam treaty.

Other Institutions: Three other bodies deserve at least a mention. COREPER is the French acronym for the *Council of Permanent Representatives*. This body comprises the Ambassadors to the EU (designated 'Permanent Representatives') of each of the members countries. All fifteen, or their deputies, meet on a regular basis and cooperate with the Commission to ensure that business can be as well-organised as possible and that future problems are anticipated. ECOSOC is the advisory Economic and Social Committee, whose membership includes representatives of business and union organisations, via which these important interests are provided a regular avenue to express opinions and concerns. The *Committee of the Regions* was established after Maastricht in an attempt to provide at least some means by which distinct sub-national concerns could find a voice. It has yet to be seen whether it will play much more than a symbolic role: at present it has virtually nopowers[16].

Conclusion

European integration has transformed the politics of the continent. The countries of western Europe cooperate now in a manner virtually unthinkable fifty years ago, while those of central and eastern Europe queue up to join the European Union. The institutions established help to give order to a system of interactions between governments and across borders, without equal in terms of density or scale anywhere else in the world. This has been, by any standards, a remarkable achievement. Yet it is one unmarked by bold gestures to live long in the public mind. The evolving series of compromises have advanced European unity hesitantly, and, for example, created in the institutions of the EC a rather awkward structure with which all governments have been able to live, but in which none can rejoice. Many European citizens, thus, find the EU highly confusing and difficult to identify with, and this is no doubt one of the reasons why few among them currently celebrate the European citizenship which they now enjoy.

Endnotes

1. Zurcher, A. J. (1958): *The Struggle to Unite Europe 1940-1958*. (Westport, CT: Greenwood Press) P.6.

2. For an illuminating discussion of the Marshall Plan and the events surrounding it, see Ellwood, D. (1992): *Rebuilding Europe: Western Europe, America and Postwar Reconstruction*, (London: Longman).

3. The requirement that member countries be democracies has become a firm, although unwritten, rule of the integration process. Thankfully, the EC has never had to face the issue of what it should do were a member to revert from democracy to dictatorship. There is no provision in the founding treaties, or in subsequent amendments, for a country being removed from the Communities against their will. EC states appear to believe, or at least hope, that this is a problem which they will never run into.

4. An excellent 'insider' account of Delors, his strategy, and his efforts to achieve it, is given in: Ross, G. (1995): *Jacques Delors and European Integration* (Oxford: Oxford University Press).

5. Denmark held two referendums to ratify the Treaty. In the first, held in June 1992, a wafer-thin (50.7% to 49.3%) majority voted against the TEU. After the Danish government had re-negotiated elements of the deal, it was out to the Danish people in May the following year, this time successfully (56.8% to 43.2%). A plebiscite was also held in France in September 1992, where the public approved the Treaty by barely a 1% margin

6. The best historical account of the development of European integration is given in: Urwin, D. (1995): *The Community of Europe* (London: Longman). Other excellent overviews are given in: Dinan, D. (1994): *Ever Closer Union? An Introduction to the European Community* (Boulder, CO: Lynne Reiner); Nugent, N. (1995): *The Government and Politics of the European Union*, (Durham, NC: Duke University Press); Watts, D. (1996): *Introducing the European Union*, Sheffield: Sheffield Hallam University Press; as well as in: Arter, D. (1993): *The Politics of*

European Integration in the Twentieth Century. (Aldershot: Dartmouth Publishing).

7. The meeting will also generally be attended by the Commission member responsible for the particular policy area. In addition, the Minister will usually be supported by several officials sitting behind him ready to proffer advice and information. Translators are also present, although often working in booths some distance from the main conference table.

8. This has been argued to place an onus on the proposals which the Council receives. In particular, it has been suggested that the ability to make proposals which it is easier for the Council to pass than to amend gives a degree of 'agenda-setting' influence to the Commission and the Parliament. More technically-minded readers might wish to explore some of the literature in which this argument is developed: Tsebelis, G. (1994): The Power of the European Parliament as a Conditional Agenda-Setter, *American Political Science Review*, vol. 88, pp. 128-142; Garrett, G. and Tsebelis, G. (1996): An Institutional Critique of Inter-Governmentalism, *International Organisation*, vol. 50, pp. 269-299; Moser, P. (1994): The European Parliament as a Conditional Agenda Setter. What Are the Conditions? A Critique of Tsebelis, *American Political Science Review*, vol. 90, pp. 834-838; Tsebelis, G. (1996): More on the European Parliament as a Conditional Agenda Setter: Response to Moser, *American Political Science Review*, vol. 90, pp. 839-844; Crombez, C. (1996): Legislative Procedures in the European Community, *British Journal of Political Science*, vol. 26, pp. 199-228; Scully, R.M. (1997): The European Parliament and the Co-Decision Procedure: A Re-Assessment, *Journal of Legislative Studies*, vol. 3, forthcoming.

9. The opposite can also be the case, however: Mrs Thatcher appeared to loathe many of her European counterparts the more she saw them!

10. Useful further discussions of the Council of Ministers and the European Council can be found in: Wallace, H. and Hayes-Renshaw, F. (1996): *The Council of Ministers*, (Basingstoke: MacMillan); Nicholl, W. (1993): Representing the States, in Duff, A. and Pinder, J. and Pryce, R. (eds), *Maastricht and Beyond: Building the European Union* (London: Routledge); and Westlake, M. (1995): *The Council of the European Union* (London: Longman).

11. The number 20 is arrived at by the fact that each country is allocated one Commissioner, except for the five largest states (UK, France, Italy, Germany and Spain) which receive two. Proposals to reduce the number of commissioners were rejected at the Amsterdam talks.

12. The male 'his' is invoked because, thus far, all Commission Presidents have indeed been men.

13. The Commission in fact employs fewer than 20,000 people, including research staff, translators and basic clerical workers.

14. Useful sources for further reading on the Commission include Edwards, G. and Spence, D. (eds.) (1994): *The European Commission*, (London: Longman); Nugent, N. ed. (1997): *At the Heart of the Union: Studies of the European Commission*, (Basingstoke: MacMillan); and Fitmaurice, J. (1993): The European Commission, in: Duff, A. et al.

15. Good readings on the European Parliament include: Corbett, R. and Jacobs, F. and Shackleton, M. (1995): *The European Parliament* (third edition), (London: Longman); and Westlake, M. (1994): *A Modern Guide to the European Parliament*, (London: Pinto).

16. The European Court of Human Rights is attached to the Council of Europe, and sits in judgement over the compliance of Council of Europe members with basic human rights standards.

17. Useful further discussions of the Court of Justice can be found in: Bradley, K. and Sutton, A. (1993): European Union and the Rule of Law, in: Duff, A. and Burley, A. and Mattli, W. Europe

Before the Court: A Political Theory of Legal Integration, *International Organisation*, vol. 47, pp. 41-76.

18. Brief further discussions of these institutions can be found in: Dinan and Nugent.

THE EUROPEAN UNION AND EUROPEAN CITIZENSHIP
CHAPTER 3
Andreas Sobisch

Introduction

What exactly is meant by 'citizenship' and what does it mean in the context of the European Union? In fact, the terms citizen and citizenship are somewhat elusive as they are used in many different contexts and with varying connotations. There are British, French, and Italian citizens, as well as American and now, apparently, European citizens; we can even hear occasional talk of 'world citizens'. There are also good citizens, active citizens, and ordinary citizens. Further, there are citizen rights and citizen action' groups; there is a book on citizen politics[1]; and there is even a Citizenship Foundation. Finally, and very relevant for our purposes, many countries have specific programmes for citizenship education.

It is therefore sensible for this book to define the term 'citizenship' in such a way that its multiple meanings and uses can be differentiated and properly understood. We will do so by developing a simple conceptual framework that will help orient the reader in the terminological maze. We will also relate citizenship to Europe and the European Union. As explained in the previous chapter, since the Treaty of European Union (TEU), better known as the Maastricht Treaty, came into effect in November of 1993, it has been officially possible to speak of 'European citizens'. We will discuss what precisely is entailed in this concept and how it differs from traditional 'national' citizenship.

The Meaning of Citizenship

While there have been a number of useful attempts to 'model' the various types of citizenship[2], none of these models is based on functional criteria. Yet it seemed to this author that a framework based on functional considerations would be most useful to readers who, it is assumed, are generally unfamiliar with this concept. Therefore, we will discuss the term citizenship with respect to three distinct applications: (1) political-legal, (2) normative, and (3) psychological.

(1) Political-Legal: This is the most important and probably most common use of the term. We need to distinguish two separate, albeit related, categories of political-legal citizenship: (a) nationality and (b) citizens' rights[3]. Citizenship is often used as a synonym for nationality, i.e., when we speak of British, German, or French citizens. Citizens in this sense of the term are simply persons who possess the nationality of a particular country, the outward symbol of which is the passport. Occasionally persons may even hold 'dual' nationality, although many countries explicitly prohibit their nationals from holding a 'foreign' passport[4]. Nationality is one of the most important concepts in domestic and international law, and it is akin to membership in a political community, that community being a *state*[5]. Nationality is acquired either through 'blood', i.e., the nationality of one's parents (ius sanguinis) or, in some cases,[6] also by virtue of having been born within a given state's territory (ius soli). In addition, each state can award nationality through naturalisation, as specified by its domestic law. In international law, the key principle with respect to nationality is the 'right of abode', that is, the right of nationals to live in their country of nationality[7].

As a national of a given state, a citizen enjoys specific rights and is subject to certain obligations. Among the latter are such things as obeying the law, paying taxes, and performing military service, where required[8]. However, as with the rules regarding nationality and naturalisation, these rights and obligations are almost exclusively a matter of domestic law[9]. Hence, states differ greatly with respect to the rights they grant their citizens as well as in the degree to which these rights are constitutionally entrenched[10]. Moreover, states vary in the extent to which they make distinctions, for the purposes of rights and obligations, between their own nationals and foreign residents[11].

In general, it is useful to distinguish three types of rights under domestic law: civil, political, and social[12]. The origin of each of these types of rights is associated with particular historical periods. In most countries, *civil* rights constitute the oldest individual rights of the modern era. In Britain these began to emerge during the 18th century[13]. Civil rights concern the freedoms of the person and nowadays include the freedoms of conscience, speech, assembly, religion, property, contract, etc, as well as the freedom from arbitrary arrest, search and seizure, and others associated with the criminal justice system. The key principle is that of the 'rule of law'. Civil rights are thus the heart of the liberal conception of citizenship[14]. *Political* rights concern the freedom of the individual to participate in the political process. They began to appear during the 19th century and include the rights to vote, to stand for office, and to oppose the government, including the right to form political parties. The key principle is that of 'popular sovereignty'[15].

Social rights did not arrive until the 20th century, and even then only gradually. They are linked to the emergence of the modern welfare state and generally include public education, health care, and the various social welfare services associated with guarantees to a minimum standard of living (e.g., housing, nutrition, and income maintenance). Social rights are usually considered 'rights' not only because they often constitute legal entitlements in the context of modern welfare states (and thus have quasi constitutional status), but probably more importantly because they are seen by their defenders as essential to a meaningful enjoyment of civil and political rights[16]. Yet whether or not social rights should be considered 'rights' at all is hotly debated. Unlike civil and political rights, they are highly contingent on economic resources and thus often beyond the control of a specific government or judicial system (which may be asked to 'enforce' a social right). Moreover, social rights, where explicitly stated, tend to be vague so that they may be of little more than symbolic importance in a polity[17]. Social rights are also problematic because of the inherent tension between them and civil rights, particularly the right to property. It must be said, however, that such tension also exists among civil and political rights.

The above discussion has shed some light on the question why citizenship and nationality are so closely related, at least in the public mind. Rights, to be meaningful, are dependent on a polity, where they can be claimed by individuals via the judiciary, and where judicial decisions can be enforced by the executive. However, nationality and rights are not synonymous: as we have seen, non-nationals also have rights in most states, and nationals may have rights against their own governments outside the sphere of domestic law (i.e., the ECHR). However, they have these rights only because the state of their nationality and/or residence has voluntarily surrendered exclusive jurisdiction over these rights to the European Court of Human Rights. And even then a decision in favour of a plaintiff, and against the state, can be enforced only by the domestic administrative system. Nevertheless, the ECHR represents a major step away from the exclusive association of citizenship rights with nationality. As we will see at the end of this chapter, the European Union, especially in the context of the Maastricht Treaty, represents a further, though hardly unequivocal, step away from the connection.

(2) **Normative:** Citizenship in the normative sense of the word refers to those personal qualities which are associated with a 'good

citizen'. Unfortunately, as with all normative issues, there is no agreement as to what these qualities ought to be. Broadly speaking, we may distinguish two traditions of theorising about the good citizen: the *civic-republican* and the *liberal*[18]. The republican tradition, embodied in the classics of Plato, Aristotle, Machiavelli, and Rousseau, endured from the time of the Greek city-states until about the French Revolution. Its conception of *civic virtue* was based more on duties than on rights, and foremost among these duties were loyalty to the state and altruism toward the community. The civic-republican tradition, as Peter Riesenberg put it, was 'moral, idealistic, spiritual, active, participatory, communitarian, and even heroic'. But it was also 'culturally monolithic, hierarchical, and discriminatory', though not despotic[19]. Rather, it was based on *mutual* obligations between citizens and state. The state's obligations were, at least in the Greek and Roman traditions, comparable to the modern principle of rule of law: government was based on law and all *citizens* were equal before the law[20]. They also had participatory rights. While not democratic in the modern sense of the term, the civic-republican tradition was a far cry from the model of the New Socialist Person aspired to by communist regimes during the 20th century.

In recent years this civic-republican notion of citizenship has been revived by the *communitarian* school, associated perhaps most prominently with the American sociologist Amitai Etzioni[21]. This perspective maintains that individual rights must be tempered by a spirit of personal and civic responsibility, moral community, and (national) purpose. The allegedly excessive stress of the liberal tradition on individual rights leads, according to the communitarians, to selfishness, moral decay, and, eventually, to social breakdown. Modern communitarians, similar to their republican predecessors, emphasise the role of institutions such as the family, neighbourhood, churches, and schools as transmitters of values and as realms for communal activities.

The liberal tradition of citizenship, by contrast, stresses *individual* rights and *individual* morality. This tradition not only downplays civic duties and responsibilities, but is deeply suspicious of them: at best they are paternalistic and intrusive, at worst they serve as an excuse for authoritarian or even totalitarian oppression. But as Stephen Macedo[22] has pointed out, liberalism need not be devoid of civic virtue. For one thing, the enjoyment of individual freedoms necessitates respect for the rights of others: my freedom to swing my arms ends where your nose begins. Freedom also demands vigilance in its defence, not only against external enemies, but against domestic ones as well (e.g., an overbearing state). However, unlike other traditions and ideologies, liberalism does not pursue a particular vision of the good society - other than one that respects individual rights. A liberal society is pluralistic: progress is not ordained from above, but rather it emerges from the free competition of ideas and interests. Therefore, it requires a 'willingness to 'live and let live', to subordinate personal plans and commitments to impartial rules of law, and to persuade rather than coerce'[23].

Nevertheless, the liberal and civic-republican traditions of citizenship may not be as incompatible as it might appear at first glance. Both combine political and civil rights with certain obligations. According to Oliver and Heater, the key questions concern the nature of these obligations: which ones can citizens legitimately be expected to perform, how can these be justified, and how may citizens be motivated to perform them? They suggest that

> a good citizen is one who enjoys freedom and is vigilant to defend it against the abuse of power; and participates as effectively as possible in public affairs, especially in the local community[24].

This minimal definition, they suggest, should be acceptable to all traditions and therefore could serve as the starting point for a meaningful definition of good citizenship. But this definition still leaves open the issue of motivation. It is to this that we will turn in the next section.

(3) **Psychological:** Derek Heater in his model distinguishes two dimensions of citizenship[25]: 'status' and 'feeling'. The former encompasses civil, political, and social rights, whereas the latter refers to civic virtue. One component of Heater's model occupies an ambiguous position, embracing elements of both status and feeling: *identity*. Identity as a status refers to nationality: a person holding a British passport is a British national, endowed with all the rights (and duties) that this status entails. But what if this person happens to be a Catholic resident of Ulster? Would this person *feel* British[26], be *loyal* to Her Majesty's government, and, if called upon, defend the country against foreign or domestic enemies? This example illustrates that 'true' citizenship may involve more than just a legal status: it is also a state of mind.

But we should first briefly define the concept 'identity'. By identity we mean a sense of belonging to a collective body of people, bound together by some commonality, be that kinship, religion, region, ethnicity, language, nationality, class, or even gender[27]. It is generally accepted that identity is a response to conscious or unconscious social and psychological needs. Such identification may help citizens 'feel at home', infusing them 'with a sense of purposefulness, confidence, and dignity'[28]. However, it may also be a response to a feeling of danger or threat[29]. Identification with a group, in turn, will tend to inspire *loyalty* and *allegiance*.

Identity can serve several purposes. First, as implied by the definition in the previous paragraph, it may boost one's overall quality of life by strengthening a sense of satisfaction, comfort, security, pride, harmony, friendship, and happiness. Second, identity can strengthen the sense of civic obligation. As the previous section had argued, in a liberal society the very idea of obligation is controversial. Therefore, civic obligations should, as much as possible, be voluntary. A healthy sense of identification with the community, or nation, may arouse feelings of responsibility, empathy, or altruism that could motivate people to act on their obligations. Third, identity may enhance the *legitimacy* of a particular political regime. By legitimacy is meant the voluntary acceptance of that regime and its policies by its citizens. A sense of identity may help build up a reservoir of popular support that is, at least in part, independent of the satisfaction of specific material needs. A regime that has not built up such a reservoir of popular support may have a difficult time surviving an extended economic crisis[30].

The issue of legitimacy is also relevant in the context of our previous discussion of citizenship rights and nationality. Clearly, in order for rights to be meaningful, their legal basis must be accepted by the vast majority of the population of a given polity[31]. And there is no reason why this should not be so for rights that are of non-domestic origin. This point has particular relevance for the European Union. It would be an untenable state of affairs if, say, the right of a French resident of London to vote in municipal elections there was obstructed by London authorities and/or citizens. Likewise, if Greek employers defied their non-Greek employees' rights under that Social Chapter of the Maastricht Treaty, this would make a mockery of EU legislation in social affairs[32]. A strong sense of European identity would clearly help legitimise such rights. The last section of this chapter will deal with this issue in greater detail.

But identity need not be monolithic or exclusive. As Derek Heater has shown in chapter 1, dual and multiple identities are not only possible, they have existed throughout history. In fact, all of us possess dual, or multiple, identities as we are simultaneously members of various ethnic, religious, social, regional, or national groupings. And, at times, these identities may be in conflict with one another as, for example, when a French-Canadian is torn between his/her desire for greater autonomy for Quebec and the wish to maintain the unity of Canada. The concept of dual/multiple identity (and citizenship) is acutely relevant in the context of the European Union, which, with the Maastricht Treaty, inaugurated a new form of citizenship: European Citizenship. In the following section we will attempt to illuminate what this new type of citizenship entails.

European Citizenship

What precisely is European citizenship? The distinguished French sociologist Raymond Aron once said: 'There are no such animals as 'European Citizens'. There are only French, German, or Italian citizens'[33]. Nevertheless, many books and articles have been published on the subject in recent years, some of them cited in the endnotes to this chapter. Talk about something akin to a European citizenship is actually not new. At the time when Aron made his oft-quoted statement, the Paris Summit established a working group to study the conditions 'under which the citizens of the Member States could be given special rights as members of the Community'[34]. Over the next decade a number of reports were issued by the Community, calling for the granting of specific civil, political, and social rights to member state nationals. At the Rome Summit in 1990 it was decided that a 'European Citizenship' should be included, and thus formalized, in the Treaty of European Union, which was signed at Maastricht in December of 1991.

Yet even before Maastricht, member state nationals had certain political, civil and social rights in a wider European context[35], although these were usually not designated 'citizenship' rights. To begin, all EC member states are signatories to the 1950 European Convention on Human Rights and Fundamental Freedoms (ECHR), and several of them have incorporated the Charter into domestic law (so that it is enforceable through domestic courts). However, the ECHR is not an institution of the European Community[36] nor is it a polity. Nevertheless, as a precedent the ECHR is very important because it confers specific individual (mainly *civil*) rights upon Europeans in two novel ways: (1) in their own country they have rights protected by an international body; and (2) as foreign nationals they have these rights in the host state, provided it is a signatory to the Treaty. In fact, the rights under the ECHR are not limited to nationals of signatory states. In this sense it connotes a highly advanced notion of 'citizenship', going even beyond the Maastricht provisions.

Since the very beginning of the EC, member state nationals have also been represented - after 1979 via direct election - by the European Parliament, an institution whose role and influence within the EC has gradually increased over the years (see chapter 2). The Parliament is the only institution granting EC nationals *political* rights in the context of a supra-national body. Finally, EC member state nationals have enjoyed a number of important economic and social rights in the areas of free movement of labour and capital, social security, employees' rights, and non-discrimination, to mention but the most important ones[37]. These rights were strengthened by the Social Charter of 1989 and by the Social Chapter of the Maastricht Treaty.

Given the ambiguity surrounding the term European Citizenship, it is perhaps best defined ex negativo, i.e., by what it is not. First and foremost, the TEU 'does not establish a nationality of the Union, but rather a complementary citizenship' to that of a member state[38]. This is so because (1) the EU is not a sovereign state in the proper sense of the term, and (2), according to O'Keeffe, the 'legal bond' and 'genuine connection', as required by the ICJ's **Nottebohm ruling**[39], is simply not strong enough. Furthermore, the TEU does not include a full catalogue of (civil and political) rights and duties found in normal constitutional documents, but rather a fairly limited set of rights[40]. Nationality thus remains fully within the purview of member states: they have the exclusive right to determine who their nationals are, and only member state *nationals* qualify for rights under the EU citizenship provision. The 'European' passport that is now available is thus at most symbolic: as a document of nationality (of a would-be European polity) it has no legal force under international law.

Second, the 'rights' granted by the TEU are not only limited in scope, they are also highly qualified. The Treaty, in Articles 8-8e, specifically enumerates seven rights to be conferred upon everyone holding the nationality of a member state: (1) The right to free movement; (2) the right of residence; (3) the right to vote/stand in municipal elections in any member state of residence; (4) the right to vote/stand in EP elections in any member state of residence; (5) the right to diplomatic and consular assistance by any member state; (6) the right to petition the European Parliament; and (7) the right to apply to the newly created office of Ombudsman. In addition, the Treaty commands the Union, in Article F, to 'respect' 'as general principles of Community law', not only the ECHR, but also the 'constitutional traditions' of the Member States[41]. Finally, as a hedge against excessive centralisation and bureaucratisation in the Union, the Treaty establishes the *'subsidiarity principle'*, according to which all political decisions should be taken at the lowest possible level.

However, the rights enumerated above are not absolutes by any stretch of the imagination. Nor is it clear what concrete implications the broad principles outlined in the Treaty have[42]. The rather limited nature of the rights under Articles 8-8e is exemplified by the fact that: (1) the rights to free movement and residence apply to EU citizens as *economic* actors only and are subject to a number of restrictions, as specified by both EC and domestic law[43]. These include requirements that citizens residing in another member state not become a 'burden on the social security system of the host'[44]. Moreover, family members who do not possess the nationality of a member state are excluded from the provisions of Article 8; (2) With respect to voting rights in municipal elections, Article 8b(1) does not define 'municipal' and so potentially leaves much discretion to the host state[45]; (3) The right to diplomatic and consular protection, Art.

8c, only applies in a 'third state' where the citizen's state of nationality is not represented, and, in any event, this right is contingent upon successful negotiations with third states to set up the necessary arrangements. This may be more difficult than anticipated given **Nottebohm's** 'genuine link' requirements[46]. In general, a number of the provisions in Article 8 appear to be poorly drafted so that much litigation to clarify these rights can be expected in future years.

However, none of the above mentioned qualifications repudiates the fact that some of the rights enumerated in Article 8 are, at least symbolically, meaningful additions to the rights of European citizens. True, the rights to free movement and residence and the right to petition the European Parliament are not at all new. But this is not the case with respect to the rights of EU nationals to vote and stand for office (in municipal and European elections) in any member state, as well as the right to appeal to the Ombudsman, which - uniquely in the TEU - is also shared by third country nationals. According to O'Keeffe, the most significant aspect of the TEU with respect to citizenship is its dynamic character[47]. Article 8(e) specifically allows provisions 'to strengthen or add to the existing citizenship rights', with the Commission retaining the right of initiative. Moreover, the language in Article 8(e) would seem to allow only *additions* to, and no *restriction* of, existing EU citizen's rights, even though the Amsterdam treaty of 1997 did not contain any new provisions regarding European Citizenship. Furthermore, given the ECJ's jurisdiction over most, though not all, EU citizenship rights, and in light of its highly activist role in the integration process over the past four decades, an expansive tendency of these provisions would not be unexpected[48]. On the other hand, this 'optimistic'[49] view must be tempered somewhat by the Danish insistence that Council decisions under Article 8e would be considered a 'transfer of sovereignty' and therefore subject to special majorities, a view given some credence by the two European Council declarations to the effect that citizenship of the Union in no way 'takes the place' of national citizenship[50].

Conclusion

What, then, may we conclude about the nature of European citizenship? This chapter had begun by defining 'citizenship' on the basis of functional criteria. Accordingly, it makes sense to revisit our classificatory scheme now to see how European citizenship fits into it.

(1) Political-Legal: European citizenship clearly represents a legal status, although not in terms of *nationality*[51]. Rather it has legal force only in the political context of the Union and its member states. As such, European citizenship confers upon EC nationals specific *political*, *civil*, and *social* rights. Political rights include those of voting and standing for office, both in the domestic context (European Parliament) and as EU nationals in an EU host state (municipal and European Parliament)[52]. It is a bit more difficult to delineate civil from social rights, not only because they overlap, but also because it depends on one's precise definition of these two terms. Most citizenship rights in the context of the EU pertain to EU member state nationals as *economic* actors, e.g., the right of free movement. These could be interpreted as both civil (equal protection) and social (the ability to make a living). However, if one were to take a more restrictive view and define social rights purely in terms of the entitlement to welfare benefits[53], then social rights accruing from European citizenship status would, at best, include only those arising from the Social Chapter of the Maastricht Treaty as well as from earlier Community provisions[54]. Another ambiguous category would be the right to 'workplace democracy', as specified in the Social Chapter. The right to 'equal treatment' of men and women, on the other hand, unequivocally belongs in the 'civil' category.

(2) Civic-Virtue: The normative aspect of European citizenship is probably the weakest. Not only does the Maastricht Treaty not spell out any specific duties connected to European citizenship, but there are few, if any, opportunities for Europeans to carry out civic obligations in the context of the Union. There is no Union-wide military service[55], nor are there any laws, including tax laws, that apply directly to individuals. It is therefore difficult for European citizens to symbolically 'perform their duties'. Further, there are few Europe-wide institutions in which they can participate or to which they can donate their time and money. In short, it is very difficult to be a 'good European'.

(3) European Identity: Meehan has expressed the optimistic view that 'growing numbers of people say that they feel European as well as national' and that 'there is popular support for closer links in Europe' as well as for more common standards, social policies, and 'stronger democracy in the common institutions'[56]. How much of this is true or whether Aron's caution that the 'issue [of European integration] simply fails to interest the electorate' holds is still unclear and will concern us in much greater detail in chapters 5 and 6 of this book. At a minimum, however, it cannot be denied that the potential for the development of a truly European identity - especially one that co-exists with, rather than supersedes, domestic identities - is considerable given the increased interaction and interdependence among Europeans.

Education for Citizenship

While the next chapter will deal with this issue in far greater detail, it may be useful to briefly note the relevance of all three functional aspects of citizenship - political-legal, normative, and psychological - in the context of citizenship education, especially education for European citizenship. The three aspects correlate rather nicely with the three domains - knowledge, attitudes, and skills - identified by Derek Heater[57]. Accordingly, Europeans should be aware of their rights as EU citizens; they should have a basic *knowledge* of the history and relevance of the European Union and its institutions, as well as of the other EU member states, their histories, cultures, and political and economic systems. They should possess the requisite *skills* to participate meaningfully in the European environment, not only as political citizens, but also as workers, students, scholars, consumers, entrepreneurs, and tourists. This would include proficiency in one or more EU language other than their own. Finally, in the *attitudinal* domain, they should be encouraged to develop a European identity, not as a replacement for their own national identity, but rather as a complement to it - corresponding to the idea of multiple citizenship outlined by Heater in chapter 1. Clearly this is only a very minimal catalogue of learning objectives. The point here is not to be exhaustive, but simply to highlight the relevance of education in the context of the aspects of citizenship outlined in this chapter.

Endnotes

1. Dalton, R. (1996): *Citizen Politics: Public Opinion and Political Parties.* (Chatham, NJ: Chatham House)

2. See: Bellah, R. N. et al. (1985): *Habits of the Heart: Middle America Observed.* (London: Hutchinson); Turner, B. S. (1986): *Citizenship and Capitalism.* (London: Allen & Unwin); Heater, D. (1990): *The Civic Ideal in World History,* (London: Longman); Porter, A. E. (1993): Impoverished Concepts of Citizenship in the Debateon the National Curriculum, In: Gundara, J. S. and Porter, A. E. *Diversity, Citizenship and the National Curriculum Debate.* (London: Institute of Education). All are summarised in: Oliver, D. and Heater, D. (1994): *The Foundation of Citizenship.* (London: Harvester-Wheatsheaf).

3. These categories correspond to what Soledad Garcia calls the 'formal' and the 'substantive' meanings of citizenship. Garcia, S. (1993): *European Identity and the Search for Legitimacy.* (London: Pinter), p.22. See also: Hammar, T. (1990): *Democracy and the Nation State.* (Aldershot: Avebury). However, it is important to note that 'formal' citizenship (nationality) is not without

substance: it is also associated with specific rights under international law (see below).

4. Strictly speaking, a passport is not an entirely reliable indication of nationality. In case of dual (or even multiple) nationality, not all of them may be equally valid. As decided by the International Court of Justice (ICJ) in the famous **Nottebohm** case (*Liechtenstein v. Guatemala*, [1955] ICJ, 15:23), a 'genuine connection' between the individual and a state must exist before nationality can be claimed.

5. Statehood, in turn, is a coveted status in international law as it permits the state to enjoy the rights and privileges of sovereignty. According to the Montevideo Convention, statehood depends on having a defined territory, a permanent population, a government, and the capacity to enter in relations with other states. See: Menon, P. K. (1994): *The Law of Recognition in International Law.* (Lewiston, NY: Edwin Mellon Press).

6. Ius soli tends to be associated more with classic immigration countries such as the United States. EU Member States, such as France and the UK, have only limited provisions for citizenship through ius soli.

7. Oliver and Heater, p.53. However, the right of abode was originally not an individual right. Rather it resulted from obligations of states to each other. Now, however, it is also contained in both the European Convention on Human Rights (ECHR) as well as the International Covenant on Civil and Political Rights and can therefore be considered an individual right (See: Oliver and Heater, p.54).

8. There is some dispute over the issue of whether or not citizens do in fact have any duties or obligations, but that issue is irrelevant here. (See: Oliver and Heater, pp.81-89).

9. Exceptions are international treaties and conventions to which individual states may be a signatory. But even then it might still

be difficult for an individual to successfully claim such a right against his or her own government. For example, in the 1975 Helsinki Declaration of the Conference for Security and Cooperation in Europe (CSCE) all East European Communist states solemnly declared to respect various kinds of individual rights. On the other hand, under the ECHR, British (and other West European) nationals have won a number of cases against their own governments in recent years.

10. Whereas some states have strong 'bills of rights' that are protected by the judiciary and difficult to amend through the political process (e.g., the United States and Germany - although the former more so than the latter), in others basic civil and political rights are expressed only indirectly (France) or left to common law or are otherwise uncodified (UK).

11. Britain, for example, grants Irish nationals who reside in Britain the right to vote in national elections and, in general, makes very few distinctions between nationals and legal residents in terms of civil and social rights.

12. This classification goes back to the work of Marshall, T.H. (1950): *Citizenship and Social Class and other Essays.* (Cambridge: Cambridge University Press). For more detail on the contemporary debate, see various chapters in Oliver and Heater; Steenbergen, B. v. (1994): *The Conditions of Citizenship.* (London: Sage); Meehan, E. (1993): *Citizenship and the European Community.* (London: Sage); and Blackburn, R. (1993): *Rights of Citizenship.* (London: Mansell).

13. In fact, some of them can be traced back not only to the Bill of Rights (1689), but even to the Magna Carta (1215).

14. Most civil rights, unlike political rights, pertain to all residents, even to visitors, of a particular state. Thus, a tourist being suspected of having committed a crime in, say, the United States of America, would also have the rights to due process (Fifth &

Fourteenth Amendment), a jury trial (Sixth Amendment), and equal protection under the laws (Fourteenth Amendment) granted by the constitution. In that sense civil rights are not directly tied to nationality.

15. It is useful to remember not only that both civil and political rights appeared only gradually - in Britain, for example, the establishment of universal male suffrage took three reform acts covering a period of some fifty years - but also that they did so rather unevenly: women (and, often, racial and ethnic minorities as well) did not come to enjoy the full rights of citizenship until well into the 20th century. In fact, there is still a debate, even in liberal societies, over whether or not women do in fact enjoy equal rights with men.

16. Wilson, W. J. (1994): Citizenship and the Inner City Ghetto Poor; and Adriaansens, H. (1994): Citizenship and Citizenship, Work, and Welfare; both in: B. v. Steenbergen; Dahrendorf, R. (1988): *The Modern Social Conflict: Essays on the Politics of Liberty.* (New York: Weidenfeld & Nicholson); Friedman, K. (1981): *Legitimation of Social Rights and the Western Welfare State.* (Chapel Hill: University of North Carolina Press).

17. For example, what exactly does it mean to have a right to education? Does it include the right to study for an advanced degree or to an unlimited number of career changes, all at public expense? A right, in the constitutional sense, could clearly be taken to imply that. This problem renders social rights essentially unjusticiable, unless one wishes to bestow quasi legislative powers upon the judiciary. This however, would put into question the principle of popular sovereignty. Thus many argue that social rights are better left to politics, not constitutional law. (See:Oliver and Heater, chapter 5).

18. See: Taylor, C. (1989): The Liberal-Communitarian Debate, in: Rosenblum, N. L.: *Liberalism and the Moral Life,* (Cambridge,

Mass.: Harvard University Press). Also: Habermas, J. (1994): Citizenship and National Identity; in: v. Steenbergen; Oliver and Heater, especially chapter 6. The last two authors distinguish among four traditions, two of which, the classical-republican and the communitarian, they combine into a single one, the civic-republican tradition. They also describe 'active citizenship', which has been popularised lately by the Conservative Party's Citizens' Charter. Since it is of fairly recent origin, 'active citizenship' does not yet deserve to be called a tradition. Similarly: v. Gunsteren, H. (1994): Four Conceptions of Citizenship, in: v. Steenbergen.

19. Riesenberg, P. (1992): *Citizenship in the Western Tradition.* (Chapel Hill, NC: University of North Carolina Press), P. xviii.

20. Very few, of course, were entitled to that status.

21. Etzioni, A. (1994): *The Spirit of Community.* (New York: Simon & Schuster); and (1995): *Rights and the Common Good.* (New York: St. Martin's Press).

22. Macedo, S. (1990): *Liberal Virtues.* (Oxford: Clarendon).

23. Macedo, S. quoted in Oliver and Heater, p.123.

24. Oliver and Heater, p.130.

25. Heater, D. (1990): *Citizenship: The Civic Ideal in World History, Politics, and Education.* (London: Longman).

26. Strictly speaking, a citizen of Northern Ireland is of course not British, but a citizen of the United Kingdom of Great Britain and Northern Ireland.

27. Although the examples of Switzerland and the United States show that this common bond need not be based on the sharing of such tangible cultural traits. In these countries it is rather the specific political culture that has inspired a 'constitutional patriotism' which serves as the glue that holds the nation together. See: Habermas, J. p.27.

28. Keane, J. (1994): Nations, nationalism and citizens in Europe, *International Social Science Journal*, vol. 46,2; pp. 169-84.

29. See: Picht, R. (1993): Disturbed Identities: Social And Cultural Mutations in Contemporary Europe, in: Garcia. Picht distinguishes between 'regressive' and 'progressive' identities: the former is defensive and thus restrictive, designed to close off outsiders; whereas the latter is expansive, including ever larger numbers of people. The European Union possesses aspects of both: it can be designed as a 'Fortress Europe' (regressive), or as source of a new cosmopolitan identity (progressive).

30. While most of such 'diffuse' support should be based on the system's democratic nature, a strong sense of identity would help the chances of surviving even political crises. Clearly, the 'Troubles' in Ulster result at least to some extent from a lack of identification of the Catholic population with the 'British' authorities.

31. After all, one person's right may be another one's obligation. This is especially so in the case of social rights, where one person's benefit may mean higher taxes for someone else.

32. In fact, the Social Chapter of the Maastricht Treaty (not to be confused with its predecessor, the 'Social Charter' signed in 1989, and having no real legal force) even gives nationals social rights in their own country.

33. Aron, R. (1974): Is multinational citizenship possible? *Social Research*, vol. 41, no. 4, p.653. See also Meehan, especially pp. 1-10. As Meehan shows, Aron's conception of citizenship is a very limited one, based solely on the principle of nationality. But as this chapter has argued, there is more to citizenship than nationality. And, as will be seen below, even political rights are no longer inconceivable outside of the realm of the nation-state.

34. Bulletin EC 12-1974, point 111, quoted in O'Keeffe, D. (1994): Union Citizenship, in: O'Keeffe and Twomey, *Legal Issues of the Maastricht Treaty*. (London: Wiley Chancery Law).

35. See Oliver and Heater, chapter 7, for more detail on this issue.

36. Although Article F on the TEU states that the 'Union shall respect fundamental rights, as guaranteed by the [ECHR] ...'. Quoted in Oliver and Heater, p.141. This issue will be discussed further below.

37. See Meehan, E. chapter 5

38. O'Keeffe, p.91.

39. See note 4 above

40. In addition, the Treaty does not impose any specific duties at all, although the **Nottebohm** case requires 'reciprocal rights and duties'. O'Keeffe, p.32.

41. Quoted in Oliver and Heater, p.141.

42. See: Twomey, P. M. (1993): The European Union: Three Pillars Without a Human Rights Foundation, in: Twomey and O'Keeffe. Twomey points out not only that Article F is legally unenforceable by the ECJ, but also that the European Union is not bound by the ECHR and that the Human Rights Court in Strasbourg does not have jurisdiction to hear cases of alleged violation of the ECHR by Community institutions. He thus concludes that the failure to incorporate stronger human rights provision in the TEU represents a 'lost opportunity' for the Union. Carlos Closa, on the other hand, seems to take a less pessimistic view, stating that 'there seems to be no solid foundation to the claim for incorporating [human rights] into the concept of citizenship of the Union', since these are already part and parcel of the domestic legal systems of all Member States, and EU citizenship, in any event is 'additional' to national citizenship. Moreover, under domestic legal systems

human rights granted by the ECHR are available to all persons, not just nationals. Closa, C. (1993): Citizenship of the Union and Nationality of Member States, in: O'Keeffe and Twomey.

43. O'Keeffe, p.93.
44. Oliver and Heater, p.138.
45. O'Keeffe, p.97.
46. O'Keeffe, p.100. It needs to be remembered in this context that diplomatic protection is governed by international law, which allows only the diplomatic protection of nationals
47. O'Keeffe, p.102. See also: Closa, C. (1992): The Concept of Citizenship in the Treaty on European Union, *CML Review*, vol. 29, pp. 1137-69.
48. On this point see also: Meehan, chapter 5.
49. Depending, of course, on one's point of view.
50. See Closa, pp.114-5.
51. Although the right to diplomatic protection, being a right under international law, mimics the status of nationality to some extent.
52. The right to petition the EP could also be considered partly political, since the EP is a political body.
53. See: Oliver and Heater, p.94.
54. Examples include the 'right of elderly people to receive an income that guarantees a decent standard of living'; the right to 'social protection'; and the right to 'vocational training' (quoted from the Social Charter, which now forms the basis of the Social Chapter). A key question in this context would be whether these rights, such that they now exist, can properly be labelled 'rights'. At present they merely represent broad commitments to be implemented via specific domestic legislation. For more detail, see: Meehan, chapters 4 & 5.

55. Although the WEU may provide such an opportunity in the future.
56. Meehan, p.10.
57. Heater, D. (1992): Education of European Citizenship, *Westminster Studies in Education*, vol. 15, pp. 53-67.

EDUCATION FOR EUROPEAN CITIZENSHIP: A REVIEW OF SOME RELEVANT DOCUMENTATION

CHAPTER 4

Ian Davies

Any attempt to understand the development, current status and likely future paths of education for European citizenship must include analysis from at least three perspectives. Firstly, there is the form of education emerging from initiatives by the institutions of the European Union. Secondly, there will be those efforts made by governments of individual European countries. For those countries who are already members of the Union those efforts are in part to prepare for European citizenship which has become a legal reality since at least the Maastricht Treaty and has been seen as a significant feature for some time before that. For other countries who are currently outside the Union there may or may not be an intention to join with possible implications for the nature of the educational initiatives which are being developed. Thirdly, there are the forms of education for citizenship and wider political education generally that are promoted (in principle or in fact) by transnational agencies such as the Council of Europe and by projects organised by semi-autonomous agencies which cross borders such as the Baltic Sea Project which may add, directly or indirectly, to the nature of education for citizenship in Europe.

These three dimensions perhaps provide the minimum framework for any evaluation of the initiatives associated with education for European citizenship. It is not, however, suggested that they will all be covered adequately in the space of this chapter, nor for that matter anywhere else in the near future. Perhaps there will be more knowledge available in the near future. A new £4.5m 'research on youth' programme in the United Kingdom funded by the Economic and Social Research Council aims to illuminate a number of features of contemporary life including political and social participation and citizenship. This research is very necessary as there is obviously a huge potential difference between the aims of an educational programme designed to develop citizenship capability and its effects. Further illumination is possible through a research programme announced by the European Commission in 1996 which would:

> provide a pragmatic analysis and a practical demonstration of the present contribution that Community action programmes in the fields of education, training and youth are making to the development of citizenship with a European dimension'.

Before the results of this research are known there can be very little certainty about what is occurring within the European Union and even less about work beyond it. Within the EU it would be unrealistic to give simplistic undifferentiated perspectives. There are very significant and explicit differences between as well as within the nations of the European Union. There would be some debate, for example, whether the degree of difference in the orientation of the education policies relating to European citizenship between France and Denmark, is as great as the differences between Scotland on the one hand and England and Wales on the other which together are seen as a unified body for the purposes of providing information on education to some transnational bodies. In this chapter the information that is presented is subject to a very large degree on the provision of accounts by officials in various European institutions and in the member states of the EU. This is, of course, not the same as saying that there is a full account of what is actually occurring in those countries[2].

The best current general understanding that is available of the overview of all educational trends within the EU is that supplied by EURYDICE (1995). That organisation suggests that the following is occurring across Europe:

> the decentralisation of administrative and financial arrangements with more responsibility for management at institutional level; regional or local responsibility for training linked to economic and social development; efforts to extend the period of schooling by lowering the compulsory school entry age, raising the leaving age or by providing incentives for young people to stay on beyond compulsory schooling; efforts to expand or extend pre-school provision; common general education, normally coinciding with the period of compulsory schooling, which usually ends after the lower stage of secondary education; the introduction or reintroduction of more formal assessment procedures during schooling; a diversity of options and routes in (post compulsory) secondary education and in vocational training; attempts to improve the status of vocational qualifications as compared with academic qualifications; the development of post secondary and advanced vocational education and training; the introduction of modular courses in secondary education, training and higher education; efforts to improve the diverse forms of initial teacher training[3].

Thus, according to the above quotation, education is an increasingly important part of all people's lives even if only in terms of the longer periods of time to be spent within institutions. There is little explicit consideration of political education but a strong emphasis on the relationship between the economy and education through vocational courses. This shows the significance of political factors and the need for a professional form of political education. This political dimension in the context of a lack of explicit attention to political matters needs to be considered carefully.

Significantly, a recent letter from EURYDICE to the author asserted that 'We have not so far produced specific information related with this subject' (i.e. education for European citizenship). Furthermore the strong trend towards decentralisation means that it will be difficult to make general judgements.

In an attempt to provide at least a partial understanding of the state of education for European citizenship, information was gathered from a number of sources. The main bodies of the European Union (for example, the Commission, the Parliament), as well as all those whose purpose is to provide information on education (e.g. EURYDICE) were targeted with requests. Secondly, all government offices responsible for education in the fifteen member states and in the members of the European Economic Area were contacted with a request for information about the nature of education for citizenship in those particular countries. Thirdly, transnational bodies, a large number of educational projects or semi-official offices that had declared themselves in the literature on education for European citizenship as being concerned with these issues were asked for samples of materials. Finally, the existing literature giving accounts of issues and initiatives in the field of education for European citizenship was explored leading to a better understanding of some of the issues raised by the respondents referred to above, and also allowed for consultation with a limited number of experts on the meaning of those initiatives which has been useful to the construction of this chapter and to other parts of the book.

Educational Initiatives Sponsored by the European Union

For some "the nation state has become a cognitive trap in times of peace and a death trap in times of war"[4]. The perceived need to develop a new form of education is strong and the intention is that 'Education and training represent European citizenship in the bud' encouraging the free movement of ideas and individuals and the creation of a common identity and the recognition of common values[5]. Within the relatively narrow boundaries of citizenship as defined by the European Union there is nevertheless a long list of required educational action. These requirements have been summarised by Dekker and Portengen from EU documentation as follows:

> knowledge of European co-operation and integration in general (its historical development and institutionalisation), knowledge of the EU (its establishment, development, goals, functioning, institutions, bodies, decision making, multicultural characteristics, place in Europe and the world), and knowledge of the EU member-states (their historical, cultural, social, economic, political aspects).

> EU citizens are also expected to believe that co-operation among the member states and co-operation between the EU and the rest of Europe and the world is of high significance to believe in the advantages and 'challenges' of a greater economic and social space and to believe that the foundations of the EU are democracy, social justice and respect of human rights. The individual is also expected to have a feeling of belonging to a European community, a strong sense of European 'identity' and an appreciation of the other Europeans living at the other side of their national frontiers. The individual is also expected to share the values of democracy, pluralism, tolerance, friendship between peoples, social justice and respect of human rights. Finally they are expected to be willing to participate and to vote in the elections for the European Parliament[6].

The European Union's involvement with educational matters started from an extremely low base. One of the first initiatives (from

1953 and so prior to the Treaty of Rome) was concerned with European Schools mainly for the children of European officials. This clearly affected few people and has on occasion been challenged as providing inappropriate specialist allowances for a restricted group of migrants. However, there has been an increasing emphasis on the implementation of policies which either directly or indirectly have a potentially huge impact on the nature of education for European citizenship. Those policies attempt to maintain the two key principles of respect for linguistic and cultural diversity and a respect for the fundamental powers of the member states in matters of general educational policy[7].

A number of good guides to the development of the European Union's educational policies already exist[8]. It is necessary here only to give a few key points to describe those policies and initiatives and to illustrate the ways in which they have come about. The Treaty of Rome makes reference to vocational training but not to education and it was not until 1971 that the Ministers of Education of the member states resolved to explore the means of greater co-operation in education. The 1973 Janne Report recommended harmonisation within education and the Commission responded positively to this report in 1974. Two years later in 1976 an Action Programme was established and following the Report of the Adonnio Commission (which had been set up in 1984) an agreement was reached for widespread co-operation in fields such as language training and exchanges. The Resolution of May 1988 is particularly important as it encouraged member states to take a wide range of actions with the goal of strengthening the European dimension in education. This is given much greater force by article 126 of the Maastricht Treaty which encourages co-operation and sets the following target areas for Community action:

- developing the European dimension in education, particularly through the Treaty and dissemination of the languages of the member states

- encouraging mobility of students and teachers, inter alia by encouraging the academic recognition of diplomas and periods of study
- promoting co-operation between educational establishments
- developing exchanges of information and experience on issues common to the education systems of the member states
- encouraging the development of youth exchanges and exchanges of socio-educational instructors
- encouraging the development of distance learning[9]

The area that has probably attracted most attention in the fields noted above is that which relates to exchanges of students and staff. Of those programmes (which were introduced mainly during the 1980s) the most well known include ERASMUS, LINGUA, PETRA, and ARION. There were initially some disputes about the legality of the programmes but now it is clear that the scope of educational policy has been immeasurably strengthened.

The Commission has recently published the White Paper *Towards the Learning Society* which provides an analysis of the consequences of economic, social and technological change for education and training in Europe and proposes five areas for action:

- encourage the acquisition of new knowledge
- bring schools and the business sector closer together
- combat exclusion
- develop proficiency in three community languages
- treat capital investment and investment in training on an equal basis

The three current action programmes are Leonardo da Vinci (vocational education and training), Socrates (general education), and Youth for Europe III (non-formal youth education and activities). While vocational education is relevant to education for

European citizenship, the details supplied by the Commission for Socrates and Youth for Europe III is more explicitly relevant and those two programmes will be briefly summarised.

Socrates allows for the establishment of transnational projects, the mobility of teachers, students (although not school pupils) and educational staff, and exchanges of information.

This will be done through three chapters. Chapter one is known as ERASMUS and encourages transnational co-operation between universities and the mobility of students. Chapter two, Comenius, relates to school education with a focus on multilateral school partnerships, the education of the children of migrant workers and other initiatives associated with intercultural education, and updating and improving the skills of educational staff. The third chapter deals with horizontal measures which focus on languages, open and distance learning, adult education, exchanges of information, study visits for decision makers, and recognition of academic qualifications.

Youth for Europe III has five actions which seek to promote and assist:

- intra-community activities directly involving young people
- youth workers
- co-operation between member states' structures
- exchanges with non-member countries
- information for young people and youth research

The impact of these initiatives cannot be judged with any degree of certainty. The scale of involvement by member countries is impressive. However, it is wise to adopt a degree of caution. The first of the specific objectives for the Socrates programme, for example, aims :

to develop the European dimension in education at all levels so as to strengthen the spirit of European citizenship, drawing on the cultural heritage of each member state.[10]

It is important to note that the main objective seems to be to develop the European *dimension* rather than education for *citizenship*. The *spirit* of European citizenship is highlighted as opposed perhaps to something more tangible. The need to draw upon the cultural heritage of each member state is emphasised and is perhaps a sign of a perceived need to deflect any possible accusations of interfering with the socialising functions of individual countries. Throughout the literature of the various European programmes (and even in the Youth for Europe III documentation which is more explicit than others) there is a lack of consistency in the way in which the word 'citizenship' is used and at times it is ignored altogether in favour of terms which seem to imply that a somehow neutral collection of data or movement of people for vocational purposes is all that is required.

Two questions must remain: how far is the European Union interested in education for citizenship; and, even if it is so interested, how much confidence may we have that the programmes outlined above are likely to be effective?

Education for European Citizenship in the Member States of the European Union

All fifteen member states of the European Union together with the three members of the European Economic Area were contacted with a requests for information about the educational initiatives which supported the development of education for European citizenship. Contacts were made normally with the government office located within the member state itself, as well as the government office located within the UK. At times there were other contacts based on correspondence with colleagues at universities in those countries of the EU and EEA. Some of the literature which relates to education for European citizenship in specific countries was explored. Of course, a complete picture was not gained. Much depended upon the individual who replied to the enquiry and, as noted before, there will be too many differences between the official response and what is happening on the ground for easy assumptions to be made.

However, a number of points can be made on the basis of the replies received. It is clear that, despite the rhetoric of Europeanism and the range of initiatives which have emerged from the European Union, this area is not receiving a great deal of attention by national bodies. Some countries sent no material at all and when pressed by telephone calls to government offices usually replied that no documentation on education for European citizenship was yet available. Greece and Austria, for example, sent no material. In the case of Austria this could be explained by that country's relatively recent entry into the EU[11]. Others sent general documentation about the educational system within a country and, at times, there was little or no connection that could be drawn between these descriptions of, for example, the ages at which pupils transferred from primary to secondary school, that could be deemed in any real way to explain that country's position on education for European citizenship. Countries who came into this category included Sweden and Belgium as members of the EU and Norway and Iceland as members of the European Economic Area. Others who sent some materials that could relate more directly to education for European citizenship still did not present an entirely enthusiastic picture. The Netherlands, for example which is a country which at least superficially one would imagine to be somehow more European than others (due to its many international links, the widespread use of European languages, its geographical position), sent some general materials about the educational system, as well as promotional leaflets which seemed to be designed to recruit overseas students. Although the responses from some semi-official bodies were more positive (which will be discussed below) the point remains that in the Netherlands a study carried out in 1990 revealed that there was:

very little interest in internationalisation and Europeanisation in primary and secondary education[12].

Very generally, Eire[13], Italy[14], Portugal[15], Scotland[16] and Spain[17] sent documentation which showed them as being more enthusiastic than others to stress positive approaches to Europe (although, of course, even in these cases this does not necessarily imply that there is enthusiasm for education for European citizenship). It would be impossible to find a completely coherent explanation which would show any common features which would lead to greater support, on paper at least, from these countries for Europe. It is tempting to portray them simplistically as representatives of the geographical fringes of mainland Europe, and of 'new' democracies which have been politicised and are benefiting from EU investment.

There are a number of different ways in which Europe is characterised in national documentation. Firstly, there are some documents that make little real distinction between a person and a citizen. At times there is an idea that the individual is all that matters; at others there is a rather vague internationalism rather than a European approach. Generally, this approach can lead to some uncertainty. For example, following some statements which fail to make clear the nature of citizenship a 1991 report from Denmark asserts that:

> most teachers and authorities agree that 'Europe' should in one way or another be integrated in the education of different subjects and at different levels. But exactly how this should be implemented and what the content should comprehend have not yet been decided[18].

Secondly, there seems to be a stress placed on economic factors. This was apparent in some of the conversations I held with colleagues in the Netherlands where again an international approach was seen to be more realistic than one that was merely European. This economic approach can also be seen in Sweden where 14 of the 16 national programmes are described as being vocationally related[19].

Thirdly, there are various ways in which an intercultural approach is stressed. This could include the attempt to establish citizenship as a way of developing co-operation within a single country. This emphasis on a single country occurs in a number of different ways as seen by reference to documentation supplied from Luxembourg, France and Scotland. Luxembourg declared that 'neither in primary or in secondary education are there any special courses dealing with that subject matter' (i.e. education for European citizenship) and then went on to say that there were courses taught in French and German as well as the home language[20]. In a slightly different way the emphasis on a single country can be seen by referring to the example of France. Here the republican tradition in education has been asserted by a number of commentators[21] and could mean that there is rich potential for the development of education for citizenship.

However, emphasis is usually given for learning about France rather than others. Hopkins notes that:

> It was significant that senior officials at the French Department of Education were not at all discommoded at being unable to report any particular ways in which the 1988 Resolution had prompted any changes in their education system[22].

It is of course possible that no changes occurred because the French were already fully promoting education for European citizenship but this seems unlikely.

A final way in which this emphasis on a single country can be seen is in Scotland which is markedly more enthusiastic than England in its attitude towards Europe. There are a number of Scottish publications which declare very clearly a commitment to European ideals and provide case studies of practical work with a European theme. It may not have been the intention of the authors of these policies and activities to define themselves more separately from England and yet that seems to be one way of interpreting their effect[23].

Another form of intercultural approach but which is not based on a single country can be seen by reference to the Nordic Council of Ministers. In February 1995 a report (Nordic Co-operation in a New Era) discussed co-operation against the background of the results of the referendums held in Finland, Norway and Sweden on accession to the EU. It was felt that:

> measures in the fields of culture and education should have a distinct Nordic profile, should reinforce Nordic networks and the general public's perceptions of the Nordic region as a single entity in terms of culture, education and research[24].

When Europe is mentioned it is assigned a limited function or perspective:

> [there should be work to] reinforce the Nordic dimension in European co-operation on education and training.

Other ways of stressing an intercultural approach can be seen in the responses from Eire and Germany. In the former the 1995 White Paper argues that a number of issues are relevant:

> major changes in eastern Europe, concern about an apparent resurgence of racism, violence and xenophobia in many countries and the focus on conflict resolution in the island of Ireland serve to underline the importance of education in areas such as human rights, tolerance, mutual understanding, cultural, identity, peace and the promotion of co-operation in the world among people of different traditions and beliefs...

> As Ireland approaches the 21st century a strong sense of European citizenship increasingly complements a robust Irish identity.

Similarly the German statements adopt a positive approach to the political and affective dimensions of European citizenship. There is some debate about the strength or coherence of the German position on Europe but the most significant guidelines (produced in 1978, 1983, 1988, 1990 and 1992) include such statements as:

- the willingness to reach understanding so as to overcome prejudice and to be able to recognise mutual interests whilst at the same time affirming European diversity
- support for freedom, democracy, human rights and justice and economic security
- the will to maintain peace in Europe and throughout the world[25]

Some of the above obviously relates directly to what is done as well as to why education for European citizenship is considered important, but the next section of this chapter concentrates more narrowly on the question of implementing relevant work. The form of implementation varies between and within countries. For some, the establishment of structural reform of the national education system is one way of demonstrating a positive commitment to Europe. Documentation received from Italy, for example, includes the comment that:

In the last few years a number of major reforms has involved almost every level of school in order to bring the Italian system in line with a European model.

However, great caution should be expressed in light of the points made earlier about the increasingly decentralised European educational systems. If the way in which systems are becoming similar relates only to the extent to which they adhere to a generally diffuse national framework then perhaps it is possible only to speak of individuation rather than any coherent and consistent approach[26]. For some critics these structural factors are weak even in relation to those areas, such as creating equivalencies for qualifications, which have been targeted for relatively long periods by the European Union.

The bachillerato in Spain has not retained the standing of the French and German equivalents, the Swedes abandoned their final certificate in 1977, in Germany, France and Italy the abitur, the baccalauréat and the maturita do carry rights to enter higher education, but within the UK this is not the case with the 'A' level and there is no real equivalent to the GCSE. Generally, it has been argued that:

> equivalencies across the EU are now more difficult to achieve than in the 1960s[27].

The most obvious way in which schools could demonstrate their commitment to education for European citizenship would be through the curriculum. It is possible to establish a number of different curriculum models which would show the level and type of involvement. A particularly good example of these possible models is provided by Adelman and Macaro[28]:

1. promoting citizenship; active involvement in the principles of democracy, social justice rights and obligations; debating political issues within the European context; involvement in intra-European school projects examining the media for bias; analysing the various levels to see where decisions are best made; a European dimension in every school subject and/or specific course in a PSE programme.

2. examining the institutions for their effectiveness; making judgements about speed of unification; discussing pros and cons of federalism; a European dimension in all relevant school subjects.

3. historical perspective of the EU (circa 1950-92); understanding of the workings of institutions; keeping abreast of EU developments; school trips to other European countries for cultural awareness and cultural comparisons; language learning in a cultural context; a European dimension in vanguard subjects: History, Geography, and languages.

4. school trips for language learning; language learning for jobs, business and tourism.
5. historical and geographical knowledge of Europe.

There are, of course, issues about the extent to which these levels show an appropriate account of differential commitment, and the documentary evidence that I have gathered is certainly not strong enough to make firm claims about the placing of countries into such a framework. Nevertheless if the framework is used it does not lead to particularly encouraging interpretations. Adelman's and Macaro's assessment of the positions of Italy and England are that levels 4, 5 and occasionally 3 apply to the former, while levels 4 and 5 apply to the latter.

The documents sent by national governments do not lead me to suggest that radical or in-depth preparation is occurring. It is true that there are, as outlined above, some very positive statements from some countries about the aims of school work in relation to Europe.

This though does not seem necessarily to translate into action for education for citizenship. There seems to be three main overlapping forms of activity: language learning; investigations into a common cultural heritage; and the establishments of partnerships between schools which could arise through work in the mainstream curriculum or in out of class contexts. The latter is very strong with such work now being made much easier by the use of new forms of technology[29]. There is, of course, much involvement in the programmes of the EU with Comenius already popular. But outside that framework there is significant activity with, for example, in 1990 in France over 6000 partnerships between colleges and schools; and in Denmark 'the head of a folkeskole told us that his local council had no less than 25 international twinning arrangements and that his school and his pupils benefited from exchange visit programmes linked with them'[30]. Although the different education systems and timetables occasionally hinder matters there is still enough potential to make for good work with special programmes allowing for teachers to undertake in-service work in other countries (e.g. the Plato programme in the Netherlands). The work of the European clubs in Portugal is felt to be particularly positive. Language programmes are very common and in mainland Europe there is an everyday demonstration of the effectiveness of that work and the cultural environment that makes it possible with people often being able to operate in two or three languages. The work on a common cultural heritage also takes place in History, Geography and other areas. This work allows some, such as the staff of the Europees Platform in the Netherlands, to argue that Europe in the curriculum is no longer an aim but a criterion and that schools will be judged on the extent to which they take account of preparing people for life in the new Europe.

However, this sort of work while obviously valuable clearly shows that there are some omissions. There is little attention to the political aspects of Europe. Concerns over the democratic deficit will not be addressed in classes which focus on language learning. At the very least there is the possibility for Europe to be seen merely as a new context which provides new information but without anything fundamentally different happening. Will pupils be learning how to cope with the responsibilities and rights of European citizenship through such work? It seems more likely that they will only learn how to use certain skills in Europe.

The Work of Transnational Agencies and Independent Projects in the Development of Education for European Citizenship

It may be in the actions taken by autonomous or semi autonomous projects and organisations that one can see the most clearly focused efforts to promote a form of education for European citizenship. The brief comments made here will not do justice to their work. These organisations can profit from the lack of restraint imposed by governments who will, of course, at least at times, perceive Europe solely or mainly through the prism of the nation state. They also are relatively free standing from the formal machinery of the EU (although many have forged strong links with national governments and the European Union).

However, this detachment from bodies with significant legislative and economic influence may, of course, mean that there are organisations and projects which are simply less important and less able to act even although the actions that they aspire to are more directly related to education for European citizenship.

Some of those organisations, though, are extremely, important and the most significant is the Council of Europe. The Council's programmes on education and culture are managed by the Council for Cultural Co-operation (CDCC). It is assisted by four specialised committees on education, higher education and research, culture and cultural heritage. There are also regular conferences of specialised ministers. The Council aims to:

> promote human rights and fundamental freedoms and strengthen democracy...bring the peoples of Europe closer together and help to understand greater mutual understanding and confidence in Europe...help governments and citizens of Europe to meet the challenges facing our societies[31].

A number of current Council of Europe projects include 'Adult education for democratic citizenship'; 'Democracy, human rights and minorities: educational and cultural aspects'; 'History teaching in schools'; and 'Europe at school: the European Schools' day competition'. The outcomes of the Council's work are normally in the form of reports prepared by experts although there is work taking place with a very concrete impact on the education of pupils. The work of the Council has already been well reported in its own many publications and in associated publications on particular themes[32].

There are a host of other projects managed by organisations which are far smaller than the Council of Europe. A few of the most prominent at the moment include: the Baltic Sea Project and the Blue Danube Project which focus largely on transnational environmental issues; and the Orvava Project and the Civic Education Project (Odessa) which seek to develop democratic understanding in the countries of eastern Europe.

The American Federation of Teachers Educational Foundation has an Education for Democracy/International Database which in an eighty five page printout lists hundreds of educational associations, many of which are European, concerned with education for citizenship.

There are examples of particular approaches to learning and to assessment which attempt to develop common approaches and equivalences within Europe. The most well-known of these approaches is the International Baccalaureat which is taken by increasing numbers of students.

At the moment it is not possible to develop a coherent view of the work which is emerging from these projects. The members of the Council of Europe may have a different view of citizenship from the EU; the projects located in countries of the former eastern Europe may have a different approach and different concerns than those held by projects based elsewhere. There is some need to establish some research work into the aims and effectiveness of these different initiatives.

Conclusion

The range of activity which relates to education for European citizenship is staggeringly diffuse. This chapter has done no more than point to some of the statements that are being made and some of the initiatives being promoted by organisations and individuals. Education for European citizenship is now being spoken of and worked towards by more people than ever before but even in the institutions of the European Union there is a great deal of hesitancy. We may still be at the stage in which it is possible to speak only of education about Europe and in Europe. There is the possibility, given the number of opportunities for education in other countries and as workers of all kinds move more frequently, that some sort of civic society of education could develop. This would mean that students and teachers would move to gain more qualifications, improve their income and generally aim for a better quality of life. This is, in some ways, to be welcomed. But we must not assume that it would be the same as having provided an education for European citizens. As always, there is a reluctance to face the obvious: a society which fails to educate its citizens for democracy may not be democratic.

Endnotes

1 European Commission (1996): Terms of Reference. General invitation to an open tender number XXII/29/96 relating to the contribution of Community action programmes in the fields of education, training and youth to the development of citizenship with a European dimension. Brussels, European Commission. Quotation from page 3.

2 See Ryba, R (1992): Towards a European Dimension in Education: intention and reality in European Community Policy and practice. *Comparative Education Review* vol. 36, no. 1, pp.10-24.

3 EURYDICE (1995): *Structures of the Education and Initial Training Systems in the European Union.* 2nd edition. Brussels, European Commission. Quotation from introduction (no page numbers).

4 Farrell, B. (1995): The EU: a democratic development of the nation state. pp. 167-168 in *Political Education Towards A European Democracy.* A European conference held at Maastricht 8-11 October 1995. Bundeszentrale für politische Bildung and Instituut voor Publiek en Politiek. Quotation from page 168.

5 Commission of the European Communities (1994): *Guide to the European Community Programmes in the Fields of Education, Training and Youth.* Luxembourg, Office for Official Publications of the European Communities.

6 Dekker, H. and Portengen, R. (1996): European Citizenship: policies and effects. Pp 176-186 in W. Friebel (Ed.) *Education for European Citizenship: theoretical and practical approaches.* (Freibourg: RIF 1). Quotation from pp. 178-9.

7 McMahon, J. A. (1995): *Education and Culture in European Community Law.* (London: The Athlone Press).

8 For example, Neave, G. (1984): *The EEC and Education.* Stoke on Trent, European Institute of Education and Social Policy and Trentham Books. Also McMahon (1995): *Education and Culture in European Community Law.*

9 Lam, S. (1993): Education Before and After Maastricht. *European Information Service* number 143, September, pp. 14-17.

10 European Commission (1995): *SOCRATES: vademecum.* (Brussels: European Commission). P. 13.

11 Morawk, E. (1995) Legal framework of Civics education in Austria. pp. 76-79 in Political Education Towards a European Democracy.

12 Hopkins, K./Howarth, M./Le Métais, J./Parry, I./Smith, D./Strath, I./Willis, M (1994): *Into the Heart of Europe: the education dimension.* (Slough: National Foundation for Education Research). P. 103.

13 Department of Education (1996): *Charting Our Education Future: white paper on education.* (Dublin: The Stationery Office). See also Department of Education (1992): *Education for a Changing World.* Green paper. (Dublin: The Stationery Office).

14 Information from Biblioteca di Documentazione Pedagogica, Firenze. An undated paper titled 'The European Dimension of

Teaching' sketches some recent reforms at "almost every level ... in order to bring the Italian system in line with a European model".

15 Information supplied by Ministério da Educação, Gabinete de Assuntos Europeus e Relações Internacionais.

16 Scottish Consultative Council on the Curriculum (SCCC) (1993): *Thinking European: ideas for integrating a European dimension into the curriculum.* (Dundee: SCCC). See also SCCC (1995): *Sharing Responsibility: ideas for integrating a key aspect of the European dimension into the curriculum.* (Dundee: SCCC).

17 Ministry of Education and Science (1994): *Education: national report.* development of Education, National Report on Spain given at an International Conference on Education, 44th meeting, Geneva. (Madrid: Ministry of Education and Science).

18 Danish Ministry of Education (1991): *Report on the European Dimension in Education.* 6 March 1991. (Copenhagen: Danish Ministry of Education).

19 Information from the Ministry of Education, Sweden and forwarded by the Swedish Embassy. Some of the documents supplied from the Netherlands as a result of my request for information on programmes relating to education for European citizenship showed the economic imperative clearly e.g. *Study in the Netherlands: small countries have to be smarter.* This is the Asia edition of a magazine which seems to aim to attract overseas students.

20 Information from Ministere de l'education nationale et de la formation professionelle. Service de coordination de la reserche et de l'innovation pédagogiques et technologiques. Grand-Duché de Luxembourg.

21 See Starkey, H. (1992): Education for Citizenship in France. In Baglin Jones, E. and Jones, N. (Eds.) *Education for Citizenship:*

ideas and perspectives for cross curricular study. (London: Kogan Page); Ben Amos, A. (1994): Civic Education in France. Paper given at the University of Graz, Austria at the conference. The European Legacy; Vigouroux-Frey, N. and Convey, F.(1994): France, In Brock, C. and Tulasiewicz, C. (Eds.): *Education in A Single Europe*. (London: Routledge).

22 Hopkins et al (1994): *Into the Heart of Europe*

23 It is interesting that the Scottish publications refer positively to the UK government's statements on the European dimension in education and as this chapter deals not with the substance of what is happening but rather with official statements then it must be noted that there exists the possibility of misrepresenting the English perspective. However, it should be noted that many official documents from the Department for Education and Employment for England and Wales do not refer positively to Europe and recent publications argue that very little attention is being paid (see Morrell, F. (1996): *Continent Isolated: a study of the European Dimension in National Curriculum in England and Wales*. (London, The Federal Trust); Spencer, D. (1996): Concern as Europe slips off the map. *Times Educational Supplement*, 23 February).

24 Information from the Nordic Council of Ministers with various papers including *Nordic Education and Research Co-operation: present priorities* (1994); and Nordic Co-operation in a New Era (1995). It is from the latter that the quotations used in the text are taken.

25 Sekretariat der Ständigen Konferenz der Kultusminister der Länder in der Bundesrepublik Deutschland (1990): *Europa im Unterricht*. Bonn, KMK. Quotation from p. 16.

26 Hoelman, L. and Ester, P. (1994) *The Ethos of Individualism in Cross Cultural Perspective: exploring the European values data*. Paper presented at the 4th ISEEI conference at the University of Graz, Austria.

27 McLean, M. (1995): The EU and the Curriculum. *Oxford Studies in Comparative Education*, vol. 5, no. 2, pp. 29-46. Quotation from p. 39.

28 Adelman, C. and Macaro, E. (undated): *Curriculum Theory and Citizenship Education: a comparison between England and Italy*. Unpublished paper.

29 Austin, R. (1995): Using Electronic Mail in Initial Teacher Education To Develop European awareness. *Journal of Information Technology for Teacher Education*, vol. 4, no. 2, pp. 227-235. An innovation by the Politics Association 'Education for Democracy Initiative On the Internet' is also relevant here (see http://www.teleschool.org.uk)

30 Hopkins et al (1994): *Into the Heart of Europe*, p. 7.

31 Council of Europe (1996): the Council of Europe: achievements and activities. Publishing and documentation service, Council of Europe, Strasbourg.

32 For example, Starkey, H. (ed.) (1991): *The Challenge of Human Rights Education*. (London: Cassell and Council of Europe); Osler, A. (ed.) (1994): *Development Education: global perspectives in the curriculum*. (London: Cassell, Council of Europe); Slater, J. (1995): *Teaching History in the New Europe*. (London: Cassell, Council of Europe(.

SECTION 3
EUROPEAN CITIZENSHIP: APPROACHES

INTEREST IN, KNOWLEDGE ABOUT, AND SUPPORT FOR THE EUROPEAN UNION

CHAPTER 5

Andreas Sobisch

Introduction

European citizenship, whether in a political-legal, normative, or psychological (identity) sense, requires for its development not only a basic awareness of the European Union itself, but also a substantial amount of support for its political institutions and functions[1]. This first one of two empirical chapters will try to ascertain the extent to which such awareness and support exist today. Specifically, it will reveal how much (or how little) Europeans, and especially UK citizens, know about the EU[2], its institutions and purposes, and the extent to which they are even interested in EU affairs. It will further attempt to uncover how far a psychological identification with Europe has developed to this point. As the product of forty years of cooperation, such identification may serve as the basis for closer political and social integration in future.

However, we will begin by asking the question of how much public support for European integration there is at present. We will trace the levels of support over time, analyse its variation across the EU member states, and briefly discuss some of the causal factors that are behind the varying levels of support. The answers to these questions will not only help us understand the deficits that remain in terms of building a genuine European polity, but also identify the task that lies ahead for educationalists in terms of devising strategies and programmes to help alleviate these deficits.

The data upon which the following analysis is based are taken exclusively from the Eurobarometer survey series, which has been sponsored by the European Commission since the early 1970s[3]. The Eurobarometers are an exceptionally rich and reliable data source and therefore very popular with social scientists throughout the world. The tables and figures below represent only a small fraction of the types of questions asked of the over 14,000 respondents in each survey.

Support for 'Europe'

Figures 1 and 2 provide a comparison, over time, of agreement with two somewhat different statements in both the United Kingdom and the European Union as a whole[4]: (1) being in favour of European unification in general (with the meaning of the term 'unification' left open); and (2) supporting one's country's membership in the EC/EU. Several things are readily apparent.

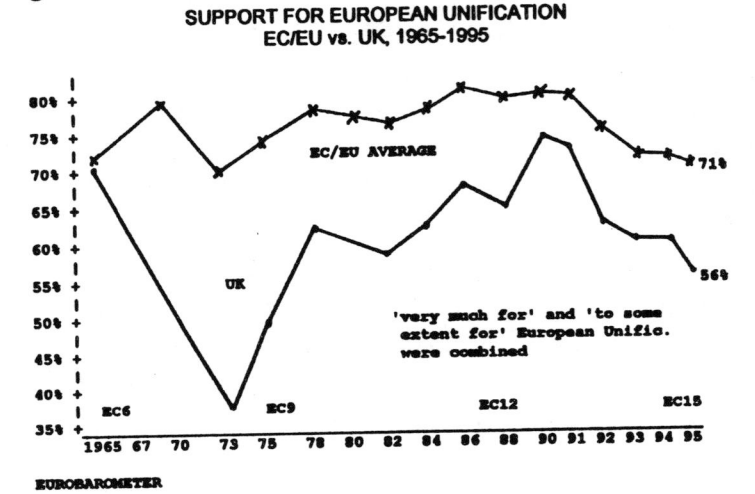

Figure 1

SUPPORT FOR EUROPEAN UNIFICATION
EC/EU vs. UK, 1965-1995

'very much for' and 'to some extent for' European Unific. were combined

EUROBAROMETER

Figure 2

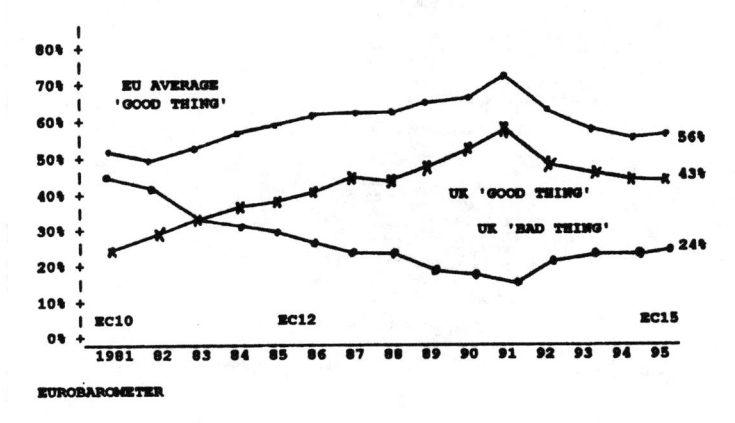

**SUPPORT FOR EUROPEAN UNION
MEMBERSHIP - UK
1981-1995**

```
80% +
     |
70% +    EU AVERAGE
     |   'GOOD THING'
60% +
     |                                                          56%
50% +
     |                                          UK 'GOOD THING'
40% +                                                           43%
     |
30% +                                          UK 'BAD THING'
     |                                                          24%
20% +
     |
10% +
     | EC10              EC12                              EC15
 0% +
       1981 82 83 84 85 86 87 88 89 90 91 92 93 94 95
EUROBAROMETER
```

First, the United Kingdom consistently trails the European average, regardless of which question is asked. However, certainly since the mid-1980s the difference is not always as large as one might expect (typically between ten and fifteen percent), and even in the UK a consistent majority is in favour of at least the basic idea of a 'unified' Western Europe, whatever that may specifically mean to each individual respondent. More importantly, since the mid-1980s the number of UK respondents who believe that UK membership in the EC/EU is 'a good thing' far surpasses that of those who believe it to be 'a bad thing'. Clearly there has been a 'conversion' of UK citizens, at least in terms of their feelings about the UK's membership in the EU: this group now comes close to majority status, while fewer than one in four are explicitly opposed.

Figure 3

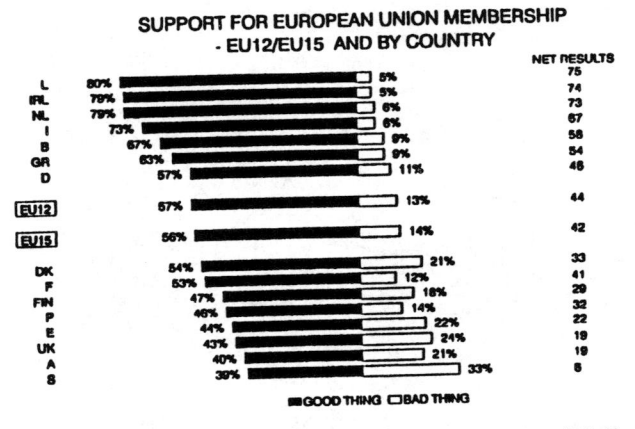

SUPPORT FOR EUROPEAN UNION MEMBERSHIP
- EU12/EU15 AND BY COUNTRY

Country	Good Thing	Bad Thing	Net Results
L	80%	5%	75
IRL	79%	5%	74
NL	79%	6%	73
I	73%	6%	67
B	67%	9%	58
GR	63%	9%	54
D	57%	11%	46
EU12	57%	13%	44
EU15	56%	14%	42
DK	54%	21%	33
F	53%	12%	41
FIN	47%	18%	29
P	46%	14%	32
E	44%	22%	22
UK	43%	24%	19
A	40%	21%	19
S	39%	33%	6

■ GOOD THING □ BAD THING

*percentage 'neither/nor', 'don't know' not shown

EUROBAROMETER 43.1

Figure 4

SUPPORT FOR EUROPEAN INTEGRATION
AND THE EC/EU - UK
1981-1995

UNIFICATION — 56%
MEMBERSHIP — 43%
BENEFIT — 38%
REGRET DISSOLUTION — 24%

EUROBAROMETER

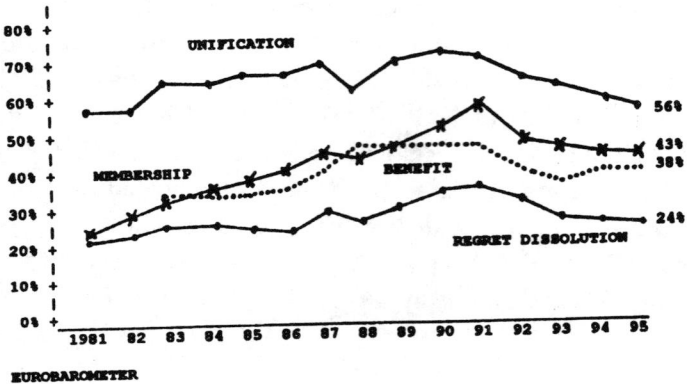

Figure 3 confirms the comparatively low levels of support for EU membership in the UK. In 1995 only the Swedes were more likely to be opposed to EU membership, and in terms of 'net support'[5] the

UK actually lagged considerably behind Denmark, the UK's traditional 'partner' in the 'Euro-sceptical' camp[6]. Figures 1, 2 and 4 further show that the degree of support for 'Europe' depends on exactly what is being asked: the more specific the question, the more guarded the support. While in 1995 almost sixty percent of UK respondents favoured efforts 'to unify Western Europe' (down from a high of over seventy percent in 1990/91), and forty-three percent favoured the country's EU membership (down from well over fifty percent), only slightly more than a third believed that the UK 'benefited' from such membership and even fewer, one in four, would explicitly regret the EU's dissolution (Fig. 4)[7]. This 'law of diminishing abstraction'[8] reminds us that surveys must be interpreted cautiously and cannot simply be taken at face value. This is especially the case when the questions are rather general, abstract, or 'painless'. However, when confronted with concrete and perhaps painful choices, especially if national sovereignty seems to be at stake, people do not necessarily choose Europe[9].

Figures 1, 2 and 4 also reveal substantial fluctuations, especially in the short term. While much of the short term fluctuation is probably due to chance[10], clear trends are also discernable. Without question, there has been a rather dramatic decline in support - on every question - since 1991. The conventional explanation is that this downturn reflects the public's disillusionment over the unfulfilled promises of the Single European Act[11], the acrimony over Maastricht and its successor treaty[12], as well as the impotence demonstrated by the EU in the Balkan conflict. It is uncertain as of yet whether this downward trend will continue or whether it has already bottomed out, although there are signs that it has, especially in the UK. Figure 4 indicates that the percentages of UK respondents who feel that UK membership in the EU is a good thing and those who believe that the country has benefited from such membership has remained fairly stable, or even recovered somewhat, since about 1993. Whatever the case may be, we must not forget that the EU has faced crises before and that it has always emerged from them stronger and more unified than before[13].

As already mentioned, within the UK there has been a substantial long term increase in the level of support for EC/EU membership - from about twenty-five percent in the early 1980s to over fifty percent only ten years later. Interestingly, neither the more general statement concerning European unification, nor the more specific one about the UK having benefited from EC/EU membership show similar levels of increase, and the one about regretting the EU's dissolution is even more stable. This suggests not only that UK citizens over the years have become rather used to their country's EC/EU membership, but, more importantly for our purposes, that at least some of that support for membership no longer is contingent upon the experience of concrete benefits that such membership might entail, e.g., lower prices, better access to foreign goods and markets, EU investment in the UK, etc. In fact, during the early 1990s we could observe a positive difference of almost ten percent between support for membership and the claim that such membership is beneficial to the UK. As explained in chapter 3, it is important for any political system, the EU included, to maintain public support that is independent of direct considerations of economic or other material benefit.

Nevertheless, it is undeniable that support for European integration, and in particular the European Union itself, is to a considerable extent driven by utilitarian (cost/benefit) considerations. This is demonstrated not only by the obviously close correlation between the 'support' and 'benefit' curves in Figure 4, but also by a substantial body of social science research[14]. While it is beyond the scope of this chapter to review that literature in detail, as a rough estimate one could say that between half and two-thirds of the support for integration is directly dependent on cost-benefit considerations, while only about one-third of it seems to be driven by other, including 'cognitive', factors. These include cosmopolitan attitudes brought about by urbanisation and increased levels of education as well as the simple adaptation to the Community and its institutions over the course of more than forty years[15]. Figure 5 nicely illustrates the sensitivity of support for European integration to economic fluctuations, be that in terms of changes in aggregate employment or in terms of respondents' subjective perceptions of the state of the economy[16].

Figure 5

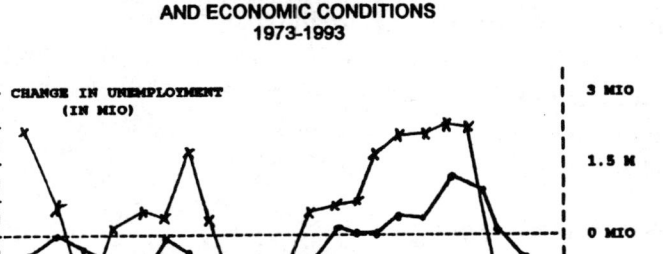

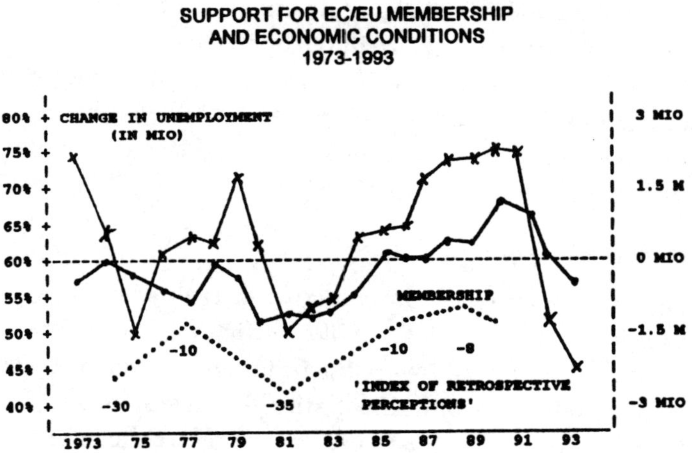

SUPPORT FOR EC/EU MEMBERSHIP AND ECONOMIC CONDITIONS 1973-1993

While supporters of the European Union may be disappointed by the actual levels of support for that institution, especially in the UK, we must not overlook the fact that 'hard core' anti-European feelings appear to occur more infrequently still. In the United Kingdom, fewer than one in four respondents explicitly consider membership in the EU to be a 'bad thing' even though almost twice as many (1995: 43%) consider it no longer beneficial for the country (see Figure 2). And in both the UK and the EU as a whole only about a third of those who oppose the Maastricht Treaty or the Single Market, including the Social Charter, are also opposed to their county's membership in the Community (not shown). People thus seem capable of distinguishing the different aspects of the EU and are quite selective in their support or opposition[17].

To summarise our initial findings then, we might say that while there is substantial support, even in the UK, for European integration in its various forms, this support is to a considerable extent contingent upon the perception of (primarily economic) benefits that such integration is expected to provide. At the same time, the extent of outright hostility to the EU and its policies is far smaller than public rhetoric (in the UK) would seem to suggest. It remains to be seen, however, whether the current quarrel over Maastricht II, the Single Currency, and perhaps even the Social Chapter might swing that balance in the opposite direction, especially in the UK. Recent history, however, would suggest that this is not very likely, at least in the short term. And, as is the case with political systems in general, the longer they last, the greater their chances of continued survival.

Interest and Knowledge

Beginning this chapter with observations concerning levels of support for integration might seem like putting the cart before the horse: to last, support must invariably be based on a relatively solid foundation of knowledge and information. Knowledge and information, in turn, at least partially depend on public interest. However, there would have been little point in going on, had we found little or no support for even the idea of a more integrated Europe. Having established that such support does exist - even if it is inconsistent and qualified - we can now consider a domain where educationalists can make a definite contribution: the state of interest in, and knowledge of, EU affairs and institutions.

Table 1 indicates that the self-declared interest in EC affairs is modest at best, especially when one considers that this type of self-reporting is likely to be somewhat inflated[18]. However, interest in domestic affairs is, on average, about the same, and in some countries, notably France and Italy, even lower (not shown)[19]. More interesting, perhaps, is the negative correlation, at least in the aggregate, between interest and support for European integration: the Danes are most interested in European affairs but among the least supportive of integration, while the Germans and the Dutch

Table 1
Interest in and Knowledge about the EU

	Fra	Bel	NL	Ger	Ita	Lux	DK	Ire	UK	Gre	Spa	Por	EU12[1]
Interest in EU Politics[2]													
% a Great Deal	8	4	5	5	6	12	19	6	10	11	6	4	8
% Some	31	25	22	25	30	41	40	32	34	36	32	25	30
% Little or None	61	69	72	69	63	47	40	62	55	51	60	71	61
Feeling Informed About EU[3]													
% Very/Quite Well	29	41	31	30	21	50	42	34	24	21	25	22	30
% Not Very/At All Well	70	58	67	67	76	46	58	63	71	77	72	73	68
Knowledge about the TEU[4]													
% A Lot/Fair Amount	17	12	21	12	19	17	43	27	12	21	6	5	14
% Little or Nothing	83	85	75	84	66	82	56	72	85	72	87	84	80
Identifying EU Members[5]													
% All 15	14	13	6	16	7	30	21	6	4	18	8	13	11
% 12-14	41	39	34	36	28	40	42	27	17	33	25	19	31
Remember Date of Election[6]													
% Yes: Year and Month	21	41	23	41	39	57	20	25	6	40	25	14	29
% Year Only	18	22	27	32	18	21	19	13	10	18	13	21	20
Location of Eur. Commission[7]													
% Correct Answer	71	90	80	78	73	84	90	78	62	63	68	63	75
% Incorrect Answer	17	6	13	11	8	9	7	9	15	11	10	7	10

[1] Unweighted Average
[2] Eurobarometer 42 (Autumn 1994)
[3] Eurobarometer 42
[4] Eurobarometer 39 (Spring 1993)
[5] Eurobarometer 43 (Spring 1995)
[6] Eurobarometer 42
[7] Eurobarometer 39
Note: for exact question wording, see Appendix

tend to be quite supportive but show much less real interest. Curiously, at the individual level this relationship is the exact opposite, and thus more in line with expectations: the more interested respondents are in EU affairs, the more likely they are to support the various aspects of integration (not shown).

This apparent paradox can be 'resolved' by remembering that levels of interest are likely to be high in Denmark because of the two referendum campaigns regarding the ratification of the Maastricht Treaty. In this case, the controversial nature of the Treaty (and the EU in general) seems to have pushed up interest. Conversely, in countries where support is generally high (Germany, Netherlands), and were the EU is fairly non-controversial, the public is relatively bored by the topic. In general, however, the individual level relationship would seem to be more important, because it suggests that higher levels of interest may generate support. However, at this time we cannot exclude the possibility that the causal arrow actually points in the opposite direction, with greater interest in EU affairs being generated by higher levels of support for it. Whatever the case may be, the wide variation with respect to interest in EU affairs seen in Table 1, from a low of twenty-seven percent in the Netherlands[20] to a high of fifty-nine percent in Denmark, indicates that interest can be mobilised under certain circumstances. Whether such interest can be generated through the schools by way of a 'European' curriculum is an open questions, but the possibility for this certainly exists.

Since interest in EU affairs is generally modest, it comes as no surprise that levels of information and knowledge can be even lower - although here it depends very much on the specific issue or question at hand. Table 1 shows that, on average, only one in three Europeans *feels* informed about the EC, and in only one country, Luxembourg, do more people feel informed than uninformed. On specific issues, such as the Maastricht Treaty, the (subjective) state of knowledge is even lower: eighty percent (EU average) admit to knowing little or nothing (UK: 85%). Interestingly, on average only about a third (UK about 40%) *fail* to offer an opinion concerning the Maastricht Treaty (not shown). This finding raises some doubts about the reliability of the various indicators of support for specific EU policies, even the EU itself: much of it may be based on only a flimsy understanding of the issues involved. Of course, it works both ways: opposition to the EU may stand on equally shaky grounds. The situation can be even be more precarious when we consider 'objective' knowledge: in Spring 1995 only eleven percent of EU respondents (UK: 4%) could correctly identify all fifteen EU member states, and fewer than a third (UK: 17%) could identify at least twelve of them[21]. Similarly, only half of the respondents (UK: 16%) knew, in 1995, that there had been a European election during the previous year. On the other hand, certain facts do seem to stick in the public's mind. For example, three quarters of the EU public (UK: 62%) knew the location of the European Commission - perhaps no big surprise given that Brussels is very much the centre of attention of Community business. On the other hand, only about a quarter (UK: 9%) knew the location of the European Court of Justice (not shown).

We are therefore left with the following conclusion: if explicit opposition to European unification is relatively small, while, at the same time, support for it is based on a relatively weak foundation of interest and knowledge, the large 'grey area' in between those two positions might render a sensible and well designed educational programme rather useful and effective. As the Danish case illustrates, interest and knowledge do not necessarily translate into support. However, support that is buttressed by actual knowledge (and perhaps interest) is more valuable than support that is based on only a casual understanding of the issues involved.

We conclude this chapter by presenting evidence concerning the development of a European identity[22]. Such identity might one day serve as the foundation of a European polity, whether federal or not, and thereby protect it against the vicissitudes of both the political and the economic business cycles. Table 2 clearly shows that up to this point in time only a small number of de jure European citizens actually feel as such in a psychological sense. While fifty-nine percent (UK: 49%) feel that European citizenship is a 'good thing', only fifteen percent (UK: 11%) report to 'feel

European' often, and fifty percent (UK: 68%) state that they 'never' feel this way. On the other hand, thirty-four percent (UK: 19%) feel European at least sometimes, and forty-eight percent (UK: 36%) feel very or fairly 'attached' to Europe. In addition, twenty-four percent (UK:11%) claim pride in the European flag[23].

These percentages clearly do not reveal an overwhelming sense of European identity that is in any way challenging their national (or local/regional) identities. But, as Derek Heater points out in chapter 1 of this volume, it may be wrong to see identity as a zero-sum issue. Certainly most respondents do not see it that way. Thus, almost half (UK: 39%) see the EU as a protector of national identities, almost two-thirds (UK: 52%) see no conflict between European and national identity, and a majority (UK: 43%) expect both identities to coexist in future. Thus, while as of today a strong sense of European identity has failed to develop, there are signs that this may happen in future. For once, 'Europe' is generally seen in a positive light. As this chapter has shown, a majority of Europeans favours European unification, most see European citizenship/identity as compatible with their own national citizenship or identity, and few explicitly reject their country's membership in the EU. More tellingly perhaps, given the law of self-fulfiling prophecies, in 1992 only about a third of Europeans (UK: 51%) believed that citizenship would be exclusively of the national variety in the near future. Most seem to think that some combination of national and European citizenship would be the norm. Euro-enthusiasts may consider this finding quite satisfactory.

We must now turn to two further questions: (1) what might serve as the basis of such a common identity should it ever develop, and (2) what evidence is there to support the hypothesis that a European polity can cohere even in the absence of a strongly developed sense of identity but independent of calculations of mere economic advantage? It is to these issues that we shall turn in the following chapter.

Table 2
National vs. European Citizenship

	Fra	Bel	NL	Ger	Ita	Lux	DK	Ire	UK	Gre	Spa	Por	EU12[1]
Europ. Citizenship Evaluat.[2]													
% A Good Thing	62	59	56	53	73	48	28	65	49	73	78	71	59
% A Bad Thing	10	7	16	16	4	23	54	12	29	7	3	4	16
Europ. Citizenship Feeling[3]													
% Often	15	14	10	7	17	22	16	14	11	22	23	16	15
% Sometimes	38	40	32	27	40	41	35	22	19	38	35	49	34
% Never	46	43	57	62	41	35	48	62	68	39	38	33	50
Attachment to Place[4]													
% Town/Village	81	82	64	89	88	81	84	89	80	93	93	94	85
% Region	81	81	73	93	86	80	92	89	88	97	94	91	87
% Country	74	13	81	87	89	92	98	95	89	97	89	94	89
% EC/Europe	47	39	30	44	65	54	52	35	36	51	56	44	48
Pride in European Flag[5]													
% Proud	29	28	11	19	43	24	11	38	11	28	22	34	24
% Somewhat Proud	61	62	66	58	49	44	45	49	52	49	62	50	55
% Not Proud	10	11	23	23	8	33	44	13	38	23	16	16	22
EU as Threat or Protection[6]													
% Threat	34	24	33	32	18	28	45	35	42	29	25	19	30
% Protection	48	52	40	42	60	39	32	36	39	43	47	50	46
Compatability?[7]													
% Yes	66	64	69	58	71	62	66	50	52	62	64	63	62
% No	27	20	16	22	13	28	29	32	38	20	15	18	23
Future Citizenship Feeling[8]													
% National Only	23	31	34	33	26	18	48	39	51	46	36	42	36
% Natl. and European	53	44	51	46	57	55	44	52	35	48	54	51	48
% European and Natl.	12	15	9	14	13	14	4	6	8	4	5	4	9
% European Only	11	11	6	8	5	12	3	3	7	2	5	3	6

[1] Unweighted Average
[2] Eurobarometer 35 (Spring 1991)
[3] Eurobarometer 37 (Spring 1992)
[4] Eurobarometer 34 (Autumn 1990)
[5] Eurobarometer 37
[6] Eurobarometer 38 (Autumn 1992)
[7] Eurobarometer 38
[8] Eurobarometer 42

Note: for exact question wording, see Appendix

Endnotes

1. See also: Garcia, S. (1993): *European Identity and the Search for Legitimacy*. (London: Pinter).

2. Throughout this and the following chapter, the terms European Union (EU) and European Community (EC) appear to be used as synonyms. However, this is not the case. The EU came into existence only in November of 1993 so that it is improper to use this term when referring to the Community before that date. Moreover, and contrary to popular belief, the European Community continues to exist. Strictly speaking, the EU consists of three pillars': (1) the **European Community (EC)** and its institutions (Commission, Parliament, etc.), (2) a **Common Foreign and Security Policy (CFSP)**, and (3) cooperation in **Justice and Home Affairs (JHA)**. The last two pillars are primarily intergovernmental, rather than supranational, and EC institutions play a reduced role in that area. See: Wood, D. and Yesilada, B. (1996): *The Emerging European Union*, New York: Longman. While it has become common practice to use EU instead of EC, the reader should be aware of the distinction.

3. Individual surveys, now carried out and published twice each year, are available from all major European social science data archives, including ESRC, located at the University of Essex. All of the tables and figures reported in this chapter display national aggregates and either have been taken directly from the summary reports published for each study by the Commission's Directorate-General for Surveys, or are based on computer analysis of Eurobarometers 35, 37, 39, and 42. For further detail, including information on the sampling method used, please see Appendix or contact the author directly.

4. The precise question wording is as follows: (Fig.1) 'In general, are you for or against efforts being made to unify Western Europe' (Fig.1 combines answers 'very much' and 'to some

extent'); (Fig.2) 'Generally speaking, do you think that our country's membership of the European Community is a good thing, a bad thing, or neither good nor bad'?

5. Net-support is calculated by subtracting the percentage who say EU membership is a bad thing for their country from the percentage who claim it to be a good thing. Net support would then be +24% for the UK and +33% for Denmark. By comparison, the respective percentages are +46% for Germany, 41% for France, +67% for Italy, +73% for the Netherlands, and 74% for Ireland (see Figure 3, right column)

6. If the new members of Sweden and Austria (as well as Finland) undergo the same process of adaptation as other new members before them (including the UK and Denmark in the 1970s), opposition to EU membership in those countries will soon fall considerably, leaving the UK once again as the trailer in terms of support for membership.

7. Exact question wording as follows: 'Taking everything into consideration, would you say that on balance our country has benefited or not from being a member of the European Community'? And: 'If you were told tomorrow that the European Community had been scrapped, would you be very sorry about it, indifferent, or very relieved'?

8. Immerfall, S. and Sobisch, A. (1997): Europäische Integration und Europäische Identität. Die Europäische Union im Bewuätsein ihrer Bürger. *Aus Politik und Zeitgeschichte*, B10/97

9. For example, in 1994 three quarters of Europeans were in favour of a 'common defence' (as specified by the Maastricht Treaty). However, when specifically asked to choose between national and EU competence in 'defence policy', only half of those respondents favoured 'joint EU decision making' in that policy area (not shown).

10. Within individual countries, including the UK, fluctuations of up to six percent between adjacent years are not terribly unlikely (due to sampling error). Small fluctuations from year to year can therefore generally be ignored. However, trends that continue for two or more years should be considered 'real'. Finally, the combined EU sample includes up to 14,000 respondents and is thus virtually free of sampling error.

11. The now infamous Cecchini-Report, issued in the mid 1980s, had forecast additional economic growth of at least four percent per year. Instead today unemployment has reached record levels in several EU countries

12. On issues such as the Single Currency and the admission of new members, European governments share widely diverging opinions

13. Pertinent examples are de Gaulle's 'empty chair' policy during the mid 1960s, as well as Mrs. Thatcher's demands for a substantial refund of the UK's contribution to the EC in the early 1980s.

14. Anderson, C. and Kaltenthaler, K. (1996): The Dynamics of Public Opinion Toward European Integration, 1973-1993. *European Journal of International Relations*, vol. 2, pp. 175-199; Dalton, R. and Eichenberg, R. (1992): A People's Europe: Citizen Support for the 1992 Project and Beyond. In D. Smith and J. Ray (eds.) *The 1992 Project and the Future of Integration in Europe*, (New York: M.E. Sharpe); and (1994): Economic Perceptions and Citizen Support for European Integration. Revised version of paper presented at the Annual Meetings of the American Political Science Association, Washington, D.C., 1993; Eichenberg, R. and Dalton, R. (1993): Europeans and the European Community: The Dynamics of Public Support for European Integration. *International Organisation*, 47, pp. 507-534; Patterson, W.D. and Sobisch, A. (1994): Materialism, social

values and attitudes towards European Integration. *History of European Ideas,* vol. 19, no. 1-3, pp. 253-260; Gabel, M. and Palmer, H. (1995): Understanding Variation in Public Support for European Integration. *European Journal of Political Research,* vol. 27, no. 1, pp. 3-19.

15. See: Inglehart, R. (1970): Cognitive Mobilisation and European Identity. *Comparative Politics,* vol. 3, pp. 45-71; and (1971): Changing Value Priorities and European Integration. *Journal of Common Market Studies,* vol. 10, pp. 1-36; and (1970): Long Term Trends in Mass Support for European Unification. *Government and Opposition,* 12, 150-77. Janssen, J. (1991) Postmaterialism, Cognitive Mobilisation, and Public Support for European Integration. *British Journal of Political Science,* vol. 21, pp. 443-68. Patterson, W.D. and Sobisch, A. (1993): Materialism, Social Values, and Attitudes Toward European Integration: Re-Assessment. Paper presented at the Annual Conference of the Southern Political Science Association, Savannah, GA, November 4-7. Wildgen, J. and Feld, W. (1976): Evaluative and Cognitive Factors in the Prediction of European Unification. *Comparative Political Studies,* vol. 9, pp. 309-34.

16. In Fig. 5 the 'index of retrospective economic evaluations' averages respondents' assessment of their country's 'general economic situation' as well as their own 'personal financial situation' during the year prior to each survey.

17. Stated somewhat differently, only about ten to fifteen percent of UK respondents give consistently 'Euro-negative' answers, while over thirty percent give consistently 'positive' answers.

18. It has long been recognised by social scientists and survey researchers alike that many respondents overstate (understate) self-reported behaviour whenever such behaviour is considered socially important (unacceptable). For example, the percentage of respondents who claim to have voted in 'the last election' routinely exceeds the actual turnout by some five to ten percent.

The opposite would be the case if we were dealing with 'immoral' or illegal behaviour. This is known as the 'social desirability effect'.

19. In 1990 the difference between interest in EC affairs and domestic affairs was as follows: France (+15%), Italy (+9%), Germany (-6%), Denmark (-10), *UK (-13%)*, Netherlands (-14%).

20. If 'some' and 'a great deal' of interest are combined.

21. The respondents were given a card with the names of all European countries, from which they had to pick those belonging to the EU.

22. See also: Reif, K. (1993): Cultural Convergence and Cultural Diversity as Factors in European Identity, in: Garcia.

23. Based on the highest three categories of a ten-point scale.

THE SOCIAL BASIS OF EUROPEAN CITIZENSHIP
CHAPTER 6
Andreas Sobisch and Stefan Immerfall

Introduction

In the early 1970s Lindberg and Scheingold[1] introduced the concept of the *'permissive consensus'* into the EC vocabulary. By this they meant the tacit (as opposed to explicit and enthusiastic) support that European political elites enjoyed in building the European Community. This tacit support was 'permissive' (i.e., allowing integration to proceed) as long as integration did not seriously threaten domestic concerns and interest groups. This, in turn, was unlikely as long as integration was primarily 'negative', that is concerned with the removal of (mainly trade related) barriers[2]. However, certainly since the mid-1980s the European Community has gone well beyond being merely a 'Common Market'. The Single European Act (SEA), the Schengen Agreement, and the Maastricht Treaty (TEU) represent important steps toward a more intensive, or 'positive', form of integration, transforming the structure of the Community and turning it into a powerful political actor in its own right. Positive integration, however, also creates greater controversy as the costs of integration to particular countries, regions, or social groups increase[3].

This is not to suggest that the 'permissive consensus' is now irrelevant. On the contrary, the previous chapter has shown that it is still very much alive. For example, noted that support for the basic idea of a more united Europe is still quite strong and that the incidence of 'hard core' anti-European feelings is relatively low: in 1995 only fourteen percent of Europeans (UK: 24%) thought that their country's EC/EU membership was a bad thing; and when we considered multiple negative responses, this anti-European minority shrunk even further. Put differently, despite considerable efforts recently at building stronger and more effective European institutions, and despite the fact that in almost every member state political entrepreneurs of various colours stand ready to exploit (actual or potential) anti-European sentiments, substantial and explicit public opposition is still relatively rare and, with the possible exception of Denmark, so far no major party in any one of the member states has bet its fortunes on a hard-core anti-Europe campaign. However, given the recent trends of decline in support for integration, and given the ambitious agenda of integrationists for the near future (e.g., the single currency), this complacency on the part of the public (and of political elites) cannot be taken for granted[4]. In any event, there can be no question that in the long run, if European integration is to move forward, the 'new' European Union must be based on a more solid foundation than the permissive consensus.

In fact, Karl Deutsch and his collaborators argued long ago that in order for the countries of Europe to integrate - to form, as they called it, a 'security community' - these countries would need to develop a strong 'sense of community'[5]. Naturally, such a community has to be based, in part, on the mutual compatibility of basic values. But more than that, it is also a matter of

> mutual sympathy and loyalty; of 'we-feeling', trust, and mutual consideration; of partial identification in terms of self-images and interests; of mutually successful prediction of behaviour, and of cooperative action in accordance with it - in short, a perpetual dynamic process of mutual attention,

communication, perception of needs, and responsiveness in the process of decision making[6].

Accordingly, in this chapter we will be concerned with the circumstances under which such a 'sense of community' might be created and sustained. Specifically, we will be concerned with the issue of European social integration. Social integration here is defined as the condition in which individuals are connected to each other and embedded in the society at large through increased levels of interdependence, communication, cooperation, and problem solving. We assume that European social integration is facilitated in part by long-term processes of political, social, and economic convergence at three levels[7]: the structural make-up of societies; their institutions and organisations; and the patterns of orientation of their citizens.

Why should social integration be so important for political integration? The history of European state-building would seem to suggest otherwise. Territorial consolidation was achieved from above, and the successful would-be state builder could care little about the social heterogeneity of the different regions and populations he controlled, as long as the heterogeneity did not obstruct his ability to exercise control[8]. However, the political context of today is clearly very different. It is not only practically inconceivable for integration to proceed without explicit popular consent, it would also be undesirable from a normative perspective: Europe today is, after all, democratic.

Social integration is relevant also because political, economic, and social commonalities are more likely to create common interests, which, in turn, would greatly facilitate intergovernmental cooperation as well as improve the prospects for supra-national institution building. For example, the persistence of social and economic inequality across member states will make it much more difficult to create a *'Social Europe'* based on the principle of social solidarity, as the economically more prosperous members would find themselves permanently subsidising the less prosperous ones. Social and economic inequalities also feed into the party systems, thereby inhibiting the formation of a genuinely European party system. Likewise, differences in economic performance will lead to different sets of priorities regarding fiscal, monetary, and industrial policies. Further, dissimilar patterns of associational life - the civil society - may affect the nature and quality of democratic politics in different ways across the member states, leading, perhaps, to different levels of citizen influence over the political decision making process. Finally, different value systems in the areas of personal freedom, gender relations, morality, etc. will make it more difficult to reach agreement on a common set of policies on the European level.

Our investigation will lead us to examine several areas - covering each of the three levels: macro, micro, and intermediate - where convergence would seem to be particularly relevant. These are: (1) political structures; (2) social stratification; (3) economic and fiscal performance; (4) demographic development and family values; (5) associational life, and (6) patterns of attitudes on the key dimensions identified by Deutsch: basic values, trust, expectations, as well as a greater sense of 'we feeling'[9]. The survey below, of course, is hardly exhaustive, but it will serve to highlight some current trends that may present some clues as to where European society is heading in the foreseeable future.

Trends in Convergence and Divergence of European Societies

1. Political structure: There are a number of political-structural commonalities across EU member states which, at least in combination, distinguish them from the other democratic societies of the western world. These include the Civil Law tradition and its manifestation in both the Napoleonic Code and the German Civil Code (the former used mainly in southern Europe, the latter in the north); the parliamentary system of government; and the party system, including the social structure upon which it is based[10]. Many of these structural commonalities are based on similar historical experiences, especially with respect to the impact of the industrial revolution and the relationship between church and state[11]. One important consequence of this common experience is the generally strong commitment to the *welfare state* - the social market economy, as the Germans call it. This commitment is partly reflected in the Social Charter (1989) and the Social Chapter of the Maastricht Treaty (see Table 1)[12]. Some analysts have even referred to a special 'European Capitalism' - based, among other things, on a well qualified work force; high wages; relatively high levels of state intervention in the economy; a strong social safety net; corporatist or quasi-corporatist industrial relations; and an emphasis on long term investment strategies[13].

Indeed, a number of studies have established the existence of marked differences among societies with respect to their attitudes toward the welfare state[14]. Compared to the 'New Nations' (USA, Australia, etc.), Western European societies, with exceptions such as Switzerland, do form a common cluster. They are much more critical of inequality, display a higher esteem of welfare solidarity, and tend to give more responsibility to the state. Table 1 provides quite convincing evidence of the overall strong public support for welfare state principles in the context of the European Union. Despite the controversy surrounding the initiatives that would have the EC take on greater responsibilities in social affairs[15], very solid, even overwhelming, majorities of Europeans in all member states support, at least in principle, the social aspects of both the SEA and the TEU. Asked concretely if they favour 'social rights' such as social protection, job training and safety, or protection of the disadvantaged, two-thirds of Europeans (UK: 64%) agreed with at least ten of the eleven suggested items. Beyond the welfare state, Europeans also agree on the need to protect the environment, with strong majorities everywhere, including the UK, considering it an 'immediate and urgent' problem rather than one that can be left to the future.

Table 1
European Capitalism?

	Fra	Bel	NL	Ger	Ita	Lux	DK	Ire	UK	Gre	Spa	Por	EU12[1]
Maastricht: Social Policy[2]													
% For	74	71	76	76	68	76	69	71	74	68	68	65	72
% Against	14	13	11	13	15	10	26	8	13	7	11	11	13
EC Social Charter[3]													
% Good Thing	56	56	76	60	70	50	54	67	68	80	61	63	64
% Bad Thing	5	4	3	5	2	4	19	3	8	2	2	1	5
Single Mkt. Social Dimension[4]													
% Good Thing	65	61	75	66	77	63	55	73	59	76	72	79	68
% Bad Thing	8	5	6	7	2	6	24	6	17	3	2	2	7
Protecting Social Rights[5]													
% In favour of 0 items	7	5	3	3	3	12	13	4	3	4	34	11	5
% In favour of 10 items	22	22	24	19	19	10	20	19	28	26	17	15	21
% In favour of all 11 items	42	46	36	45	44	46	21	62	36	48	57	51	44
Protecting the Environment[6]													
% Immediate & Urgent	80	85	84	90	91	83	87	70	82	97	82	73	84
% Problem for Future	17	11	11	8	7	12	10	19	10	3	12	14	11
% Not Really a Problem	0	2	3	1	1	1	3	8	3	0	1	1	2
Basic Right more important[7]													
% Freedom	46	51	57	39	37	42	70	46	59	62	40	48	50
% Equality	49	40	39	40	58	54	25	51	36	28	56	47	43
Environment and Economy[8]													
% Economy Priority	5	5	2	3	4	6	2	12	5	6	6	9	5
% Environment Priority	13	23	31	29	18	28	34	15	25	21	19	18	23
% Both Equal Priority	79	67	65	66	71	58	61	59	66	71	69	62	66

[1] Unweighted Average
[2] Eurobarometer 39 (Spring 1993)
[3] Eurobarometer 33 (Spring 1990)
[4] Eurobarometer 33 & 35 (Spring 1991)
[5] Eurobarometer 30 (Fall 1988); Germany: West Germany only
[6] Eurobarometer 37 (Spring 1992)
[7] Eurobarometer 30
[8] Eurobarometer 37

Note: for exact question wording, see Appendix

Convincing as this evidence may be, agreement with these items is relatively easy and 'painless', and when questions force respondents to choose among competing, or even mutually exclusive, alternatives, a number of intra-European differences emerge. For example, when asked which of the two rights, freedom or equality, was 'more important', the European public overall was nearly equally split. More importantly, several countries diverged significantly from the EU average. Whereas the Danes, British, Dutch and Greeks favoured freedom, the Italians, Spaniards, and, to a lesser extent, the Luxemburgers preferred equality[16]. On the other hand, very few European accorded the economy a priority over the environment, and in every country strong, though varying, majorities gave equal weight to both. Table 1 thus demonstrates that despite a broad consensus, Europeans are not monolithic. And it is precisely these differences in relative emphasis of competing goals (e.g., freedom v. equality) that give rise to profound disputes over social and other policies at the European level.

2. **Social stratification:** There has been much discussion, controversial both in matters of substance and methodology, about the extent and nature of social mobility and about the differences among countries in the patterns of social mobility. Proponents of different lines of arguments do agree, however, on some crucial points[17]. First, the rate of social mobility depends upon the changing patterns of occupation. Second, while there may or may not be a basic mobility pattern common to all advanced capitalist societies, even within a presumably standard pattern there appear to be definite differences among European societies. Evidence currently does not support the hypothesis that European societies will invariably converge into one type of society marked by similar disparities in wealth, income, and the amount of movement between social strata[18]. Where common trends prevail, such as in the growing importance of education and the shifting of jobs to the tertiary sector, significant differences in the make-up of the tertiary sector remain. These differences are related to factors such as the

type of welfare state, political institutions, and national trajectories of economic and social development[19].

Table 2
Social Stratification

	Fra	Bel	NL	Ger	Ita	Lux	DK	Ire	UK	Gre	Spa	Por	EU12[1]
Subjective Social Class[2]													
% Middle & Lower Middle	58	51	60	59	70	62	65	51	45	63	72	67	60
% Working Class	27	36	22	30	19	24	23	44	51	31	25	28	30
Trend 88/89 - 93/94[3]	+4	+1	-2	-4	+3	-11	-5	-2	+9	+11	-21	-12	-5
Income Inequality[4]	6.5	4.3	5.5	5.5	6.0	na	na	na	7.0	na	na	na	na
% "The Rich Get Richer"[5]	25	26	22	33	36	33	25	27	25	28	25		27

[1] Unweighted Average
[2] Average of Eurobarometers 30-42 (1988-1994)
[3] Trend = % Middle Class - % Working Class (pos. =gap increasing; neg. = gap declinging)
[4] Ratio of Income of Richest 20% of households to poorest 20%, latest year available
Source: **The Economist**, Nov 5th, 1994
[5] Eurobarometer 30 (Fall 1988); Germany: West Germany only
Note: for exact question wording, see Appendix

Nevertheless, some basic commonalities with respect to stratification are clearly visible across EU member states. As Table 2 shows, all European countries with the possible exception of the UK are now middle class societies. While the objective differences in standard of living and quality of life may still be substantial (see next section), *psychologically* speaking these countries seem to have overcome the narrow antagonism of class predicted by the Marxian analysis of capitalism. On average, twice as many (60%) respondents consider themselves 'middle class' as opposed to 'working class'. And overall this pattern holds fairly well across all member states with the exception being the UK and, possibly, Ireland. It even holds true for the economically less advanced nations of southern Europe. And even though data with respect to income inequality in Table 2 are incomplete, they do suggest that most EU member states belong to the same category: compared to the United States (11.0) and Australia (10.0), income inequality in Britain (the highest in the EU) is considerably lower and much closer to Germany and France.

However, Table 2 also suggests that the overall trend may be moving in the direction of increasing inequality. The negative trend values for subjective social class indicate that the gap between the size of the middle class and the working class is declining again, at least in some countries[20]. More ominously perhaps, a substantial proportion of Europeans (average: 27%) believes that the 'rich get richer while the poor get poorer'. And this perception by the public is indeed borne out by 'objective' data: income inequality has increased significantly in most countries during the 1980s. It is, however, still unclear whether this phenomenon is a temporary one - caused by prolonged economic recession and the structurally based loss of industrial jobs, or whether it is part of a long term trend toward increasing inequality[21].

3. **Economic and fiscal performance:** As spelled out in the Treaty of Rome, the European Union seeks to promote equal and equally improving conditions of employment (Art. 1). However, its economic accomplishments are a matter of debate. Franz Höllinger and Max Haller, for instance, detect no evidence of diminished divergence. In a recent study they found that for the whole of Europe the centre-periphery structures, defined in terms of economic and social indicators, have changed remarkably little in the last sixty or so years[22]. Countries like Belgium, Denmark, Sweden or Switzerland have performed well, with or without being in the EC/EU, whereas countries like Greece, Portugal or Spain, have been consistently relegated to the periphery.

However, on the basis of GDP per capita figures, both on the national and the regional level, Robert Leonardi claimed that convergence has taken place from 1950 onwards[23]. Since Leonardi does not compare his figures to non-EU countries and since his data indicates that the gap between the poorer and richer regions and countries has not further closed since the end of the seventies, it could be argued that economic convergence was at least as contingent upon worldwide economic conditions as on the pursuit of regional development in the EU. If so, the economic convergence that has occurred may very well be reversible. At any rate, large differences in both social and economic conditions and in the subjective quality of life remain[24].

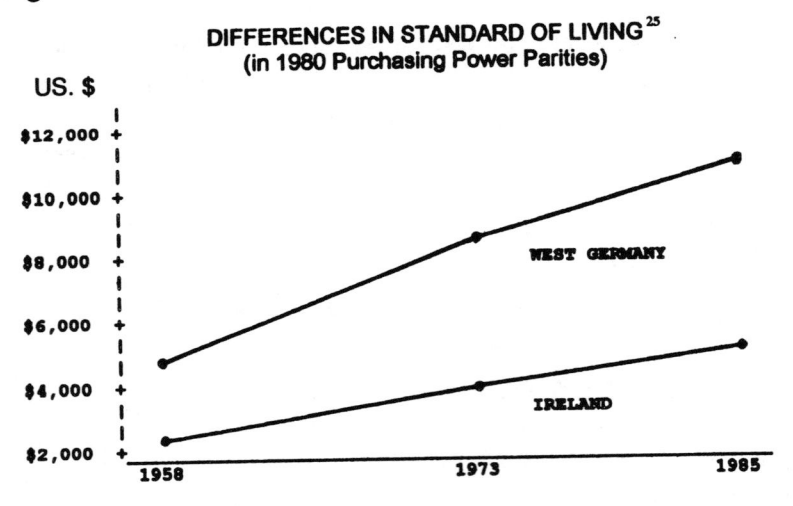

Figure 1

DIFFERENCES IN STANDARD OF LIVING[25]
(in 1980 Purchasing Power Parities)

```
US. $
$12,000 +
           |
$10,000 +
           |                                              • WEST GERMANY
$8,000  +
           |                      •
$6,000  +
           |                                              • IRELAND
$4,000  +  •                      •
           |
$2,000  +_____
          1958                  1973                1985
```

Another important aspect of economic convergence is wage income. In several steps, legal barriers to labour mobility have been eliminated by the EU, and EU nationals are now entitled to employment on equal terms with citizens of any other member country (see Chapter 3). Flanagan, however, does not find evidence of a major decline in intra-Community wage dispersion[26]. Figure 1 supports that conclusion: the gap between one of the poorest EU member states, Ireland, and one of the richest, Germany, has remained fairly constant over the years, regardless of whether both countries were in side of the EC (1973-1985) or not. The first

'Cohesion-Report', issued by the European Commission in November of 1996, also presents a mixed picture with respect to the reduction of regional disparities. Differences in income were about as large in 1993 as they had been in 1983, while the regional disparities in unemployment have increased significantly. On the other hand, as a whole between the mid 1980s and the mid 1990s the poorest countries of the Union - Greece, Spain, Portugal, and Ireland - were able to close the gap to the other member states, in terms of income, somewhat. Part of the problem apparently is that much of the structural aid provided by the richer members states inevitably returns to these as most investment commodities are produced there.

The persistence of inequality across the EC/EU contrasts sharply with the situation in the United States, where geographic economic inequality was sharply reduced since its peak in 1880. The US reduction of economic regional inequality (over an - admittedly - much longer time span) was not unleashed by institutional reforms but by geographical migration. In the European situation, incentives generated by wage-differentials between countries are apparently thwarted by the language barrier More convergence has been reached on the fiscal level. Although the EMS broke up in 1992-93, there is less divergence in the inflation rates now than there was in the 1960s and 1970s. All countries, more or less, voluntarily or forced, have adopted a certain amount of fiscal discipline. There is particular convergence in the credit quality of the core countries of the planned EMU[27]. Still, as the current discussions about a common currency aptly demonstrate, the prospects for monetary integration continue to be unpromising and uncertain.

Attitudes toward the economy seem to be more related to business fluctuations and economic cycles than to deep-seated convictions and values. In all western countries, concerns about unemployment and inflation change with expectations of future economic performance and are thus more closely tied to the security of one's workplace and to the economic situation in general[28]. It would therefore be difficult to establish systematic differences in basic economic values across the member states. In fact, as Table 1 has shown, there is strong support in all countries for the basic institutions and policies of the modern welfare state. Still, there are some differences in the preference order of economic goals. It is well established, for example, that, due to their experience with hyper inflation during the 1920s, Germans and the German economic policy system (especially the Bundesbank) are particularly concerned with monetary stability.

4. Demographic Development and Family values: Demographic trends seem to be the ones which are converging most marketly. All West European countries have passed through the second stage of the demographic transition - the dramatic decline in the birth rate. In fact, Ireland is the only West European nation where the birth rate is above population replacement, and even there it is rapidly decreasing. Family values have also changed to some extent. While, contrary to prevalent belief, marriage is not considered an outdated institution by West Europeans, attitudes towards divorce, premarital cohabiting, and children without/before marriage have been relaxing in the last decade in the socially more conservative countries of southern Europe. At the same time, there has actually been a swing back in the conservative direction in the most permissive countries[29]. In that sense a certain amount of value convergence has definitely occurred. Overall, however, Peter Ester and his collaborators, in their survey of values between 1980 and 1990, noted rather inconsistent, and even unexpected, patterns of value change and they had to conclude that, at least for the period of the 1980s, there was almost as much evidence of value divergence as of convergence.

Differences in family patterns remain as well. Drawing on a wide range of indicators, Riitta Jallinoja argues that gender relations still differ among the countries of Western Europe[30]. These differences are partly reflected in female labour force participation rates, where

Table 3

Family Values

	Fra	Bel	NL	Ger	Ita	Lux	DK	Ire	UK	Gre	Spa	Por	EU12[1]
A Woman's Job is at home[2]													
% Agree	26	38	17	36	30	28	17	32	24	41	25	42	30
% Disagree	57	37	70	44	52	49	75	56	66	42	55	47	54
Man at home is not good[3]													
% Agree	27	41	16	40	40	25	23	37	24	64	28	66	36
% Disagree	52	41	70	35	41	54	64	48	57	24	58	26	48
Homosexual Rights (favour)[4]													
% To marry	32	35	57	24	23	32	59	22	30	15	42	18	32
% To adopt children	25	23	47	17	12	13	17	8	13	8	34	12	19

[1] Unweighted Average
[2] Eurobarometer 42 (Fall 1994)
[3] Eurobarometer 42
[4] Eurobarometer 42
Note: for exact question wording, see Appendix

countries such as Germany or the Netherlands display a low, and the Scandinavian countries a high participation rate[31]. However, Karlheinz Reif notes a definite convergence in the attitudes towards women in politics: whereas in 1973 thirty-seven percent of Europeans stated that 'politics should be left to men', in 1991 only twenty-three percent felt that way[32]. Tables 3 and 4 provide further insight into the social values and beliefs of the European public and the question of how much convergence has taken place. While with respect to gender roles, for example, a majority of Europeans now disagrees with the statement that 'a woman's place is at home', significant differences remain across member states with respect to this question. Three countries are quite unequivocal on this issue, with two thirds or more disagreeing (the Netherlands, Denmark, and the UK), while four others (Belgium, Germany, Greece and Portugal) are more circumspect: agreement and disagreement are in rough balance. This pattern is repeated on the other questions in Table 3. Whether the issue is male gender roles or homosexuality, the difference between the most 'progressive' and the most 'conservative' states is close to fifty percent. Most interestingly, the cross-national pattern only approximately follows the predictable north-south axis: Germans are considerably more conservative than the Dutch or the Danes, while Spaniards are not only more liberal than the Greeks and the Portuguese, but more liberal than the Germans as well. In any event, it is clear that there remains substantial potential for disagreement on social and family policy.

Table 4

Religiosity[1]

	1994	1993	1992	1991	1990	1989	1988	Trend[2]
France (%)	46	40	46	45	52	54	50	down
Belgium	59	59	61	63	63	64	60	stable
Netherlands	50	46	51	53	55	44	49	stable
Germany	49	52	51	56	57	54	58	down
Italy	82	84	84	83	83	86	87	stable
Luxemburg	69	62	62	67	70	70	68	stable
Denmark	53	51	55	52	52	54	52	stable
Ireland	71	68	72	73	73	82	83	down
UK	52	55	53	54	56	62	60	down
Greece	93	91	90	70	89	87	85	up
Spain	66	68	67	92	73	73	69	down
Portugal	89	91	90	86	86	88	87	stable
Average[3]	65	64	65	66	68	68	67	stable

[1] Average of Eurobarometers 30-42; percentages are those respondents who describe themselves as "religious"
[2] Average 1988/89 v. Average 1993/94
[3] Unweighted Average
Note: for exact question wording, see Appendix

Table 4 shows substantial, and not entirely unexpected, differences across member states in terms of religiosity. This table also provides a better assessment of the temporal dimension, even if the evidence is far from conclusive since the time period is rather short. While religiosity overall is roughly stable from 1988 to 1994, it is clearly in decline in almost half of the EU countries, with only Greece contradicting the trend. Table 4 thus supports the general assumption of the secularisation of western, or at least European, society. Table 5 is consistent with this conclusion as it shows church attendance to be in decline in five countries as well as overall. This finding is also in line with those of Ester and his colleagues.

Table 5

Church Attendance[1]

	1994	1993	1992	1991	1990	1989	Trend[2]
France (%)	31	36	34	32	37	38	down
Belgium	43	46	43	48	48	52	down
Netherlands	32	35	37	37	37	37	down
Germany	31	41	34	36	53	52	down
Italy	72	76	75	75	77	77	stable
Luxemburg	57	53	62	62	61	58	stable
Denmark	39	32	36	33	38	34	stable
Ireland	85	89	85	89	90	92	down
UK	35	36	30	35	34	36	stable
Greece	88	86	84	84	81	74	up
Spain	55	58	54	58	57	54	stable
Portugal	66	64	64	63	67	65	stable
Average[3]	51	51	51	52	56	55	down

[1] Average of Eurobarometers 31-42; percentages refer to those respondents attending church at least " a few times per year"
[2] Average 1989/90 v. Average 1993/94
[3] Unweighted Average
Note: for exact question wording, see Appendix

5. Associational life: Since the days of Alexis de Tocqueville, the mosaic of intermediary linkages and group life below the state organisation has been considered paramount for the stability of democratic societies. As a prerequisite for democratisation and development in post-communist and third world-countries, this civil society is once again at the centre of scholarly attention[33]. The civil society is also important in the context of West European integration, specifically for the creation of a cross-European political space.

While there is a lack of data, particularly on informal groups that forge linkages within or even across nations, the scattered data available suggests significant variation in the social behaviour of everyday life. West Europeans differ in the number of friends they have, in the category of people they turn to for help, and in their interaction patterns. Interestingly, however, the differences within continental Europe seem to be smaller than the differences between Western Europe as a whole and the USA[34]. The role of the so-called 'third sector' also varies by a wide margin[35], as does the inclination of West Europeans to join voluntary organisations, which may pose a barrier to cross-European political and civic organisations[36]. Finally, while about a quarter of Europeans over the age of fifteen does voluntary work, half of them on a regular basis, there is much cross-national variation in the extent and content of volunteering[37]. All of this is likely to pose a barrier to cross-European political and civic organisations and to a 'civic Europe' as a whole. Table 5 is certainly consistent with that finding, even if church attendance is at least as much an expression of religious beliefs as of social behaviour.

Yet despite the pessimistic assessment in much of the scholarly literature on this issue, the evidence contained in Table 6 is actually quite mixed. The differences in interpretation may in part be caused by the absence of precise criteria for 'convergence.' For example, if we use the 'ten percent rule'[38], Europeans would be remarkably similar with respect to arguing politics with friends and reasonably similar (only four countries outside the range) in terms of political interest and conventional participation[39]. If our criteria were stricter, permitting, say, only a five percent divergence in either direction, we would find much less convergence. But even then on only two items (political interest 1988/9 and conventional participation: never done) would more than half the countries fall outside of the permissible range[40]. Either way, European countries would be quite similar with respect to both 'unconventional' and 'violent' participation. However, given the paucity of longitudinal data, we

Table 6
Political & Associational Life

	Fra	Bel	NL	Ger	Ita	Lux	DK	Ire	UK	Gre	Spa	Por	EU12[1]
Interest in Politics[2]													
% Very/Some (1994)	43	29	45	40	42	52	72	44	55	41	37	26	43
% Very/Some (1988/89)	46	36	56	57	29	51	70	46	59	51	35	10	46
Try to convince friends[3]													
% Often	15	13	25	10	25	17	23	13	16	16	17	13	16
% From time to time	45	48	53	45	39	50	43	39	36	54	40	41	44
Conventional Participation[4]													
% Never done	38	50	46	68	51	57	63	63	31	41	61	71	53
% Done one thing	32	26	35	17	24	25	20	24	48	31	18	13	26
% Done two or more things	31	24	20	15	25	18	17	13	21	28	20	16	21
Unconventional Participation[5]													
% Never done	80	92	93	98	90	95	89	93	89	89	90	98	91
% Done one or more things	20	8	7	3	10	5	11	7	11	11	10	2	9
Participated in Violence[6]													
% Never done	97	99	99	99	99	99	99	99	97	99	99	99	
State Suppression of Protest[7]													
% Approve of none	52	55	17	32	57	46	15	40	32	70	63	71	45
% Approve of one	22	24	24	22	24	28	17	19	20	15	18	15	20
% Approve of two	16	12	35	18	13	16	34	22	22	10	10	5	18
% Approve of two or more	11	9	25	27	10	10	33	19	26	6	9	10	18

[1] Unweighted Average
[2] Eurobarometer 42/Average Eurobarometer 37 & 39 (Fall 1994)
[3] Average Eurobarometers 30-39
[4] Eurobarometer 31/Spring 1989 (participation in: citizen action group; demonstation; boycott; signing petition)
[5] Eurobarometer 31 (Rent-tax strike; wildcat strike; occupy buildings; block traffic)
[6] Eurobarometer 31 (violence against things; violence against persons)
[7] Eurobarometer 31 (using police against protesters; sentences to protesters; prohibit demonstrations; troops to break up strikes)
Note: for exact question wording, see Appendix

still cannot infer the dynamics of the evolution of an all-European civil society with any degree of certainty.

The biggest differences among countries can once again be detected on the attitudinal level. There is considerable variation with respect to attitudes toward state repression (e.g., prohibiting protest demonstrations or jailing protestors). Undoubtedly these variations are related to the different national experiences in that area. Thus the Greeks, Spaniards, and Portuguese - given their postwar history - are most reluctant to grant the state such powers, whereas the otherwise quite liberal Dutch or Danes appear more ready to do so in such circumstances.

Overall there certainly is sufficient reason to be sceptical about the possibility of a European 'imagined community'. But this is probably related as much to the lack of a transnational European public, which holds true even for the level of elites, where discussions between intellectuals still take place mostly within the confines of national philosophical traditions[41]. Moreover, there are no truly European political leaders and no European political parties. The current transnational political groups in the European Parliament are too unstable and too heterogeneous to serve as crucial links between voter choice and MEP behaviour. The multi-level decision system of the European polity adds to the lack of democratic accountability. Perhaps even more important is the fact that this is true for mass communication as well. The development of a European public opinion lags far behind the actual transfer of resources and jurisdiction to the EC's supra-national authorities (Commission, EP, ECJ), and the difficulties of forging a common European public opinion are likely to stay[42].

6. Patterns of Attitudes: Harmonisation and its possibilities and limits are clearly evident on both the structural and the attitudinal levels. Additional evidence of the impact of social processes common to all West European nations on attitudes may be seen in the decline of nationalism and the increase in trust among West

Table 7

Trust in Fellow Europeans[1]

Trust2 (in) (by)	Fra	Bel	NL	Ger	Ita	Lux	DK	Ire	UK	Gre	Spa	Por	USA	Jap	Rus
French (%)	-	85	71	66	49	82	69	59	49	46	67	57	47	36	27
Belgians	74	-	75	71	54	90	73	69	73	50	59	53	65	51	37
Dutch	71	92	-	74	43	90	83	65	77	50	60	60	80	62	42
Germans	73	73	73	-	53	76	74	57	67	49	57	46	67	59	33
Italians	70	57	59	56	-	83	51	41	53	40	60	37	73	61	34
Luxemburgers	69	76	80	63	60	-	71	60	68	52	63	63	76	53	39
Danes	73	85	91	84	47	83	-	76	92	53	58	53	79	68	43
Irish	63	58	61	52	49	54	60	-	66	38	51	44	71	47	34
British	44	63	73	49	52	58	69	66	-	51	53	52	70	49	43
Greeks	61	45	36	65	38	42	37	39	41	-	58	51	39	50	32
Spaniards	48	58	65	56	50	55	56	48	45	41	-	46	41	53	37
Portuguese	67	60	58	48	49	61	53	44	54	43	52	-	60	44	36
Average[3]	66	70	70	64	51	69	67	59	65	50	59	53	64	53	36

[1] Eurobarometer 39
[2] entries combine answers "a lot" and "some" trust
[3] Unweighted Average
Note: for exact question wording, see Appendix

European nations. Mattei Dogan, for instance, presents convincing survey data clearly indicating a decline of nationalism within Western Europe[43]. The feeling of national pride, the degree of confidence in one's army, the willingness to fight for one's country, and the mistrust of neighbouring countries are in retreat. Tables 7 and 8 summarise the evidence concerning the very crucial aspect of 'mutual trust' among Europeans.

Clearly, the level of trust among member state publics has increased even in the last decade (Table 8)[44], and it is currently at reasonably, though perhaps not extremely, high levels, especially among the core member states (the 'Original Six'). Moreover, levels of distrust seem to be related more to the lack of confidence in a country's economic prowess than any inherent lack of trustworthiness of its inhabitants. This would seem to be the most logical explanation for the relatively lower levels of trust in the southern states, which

Table 8
TRUST INDEX[1]

	1986[2]	1990[3]	1993[4]
French	1.60	1.77	1.73
Belgians	1.82	1.91	1.95
Dutch	1.93	1.93	1.97
Germans	1.74	1.79	1.65
Italians	1.51	1.61	1.53
Luxemburgers	1.89	1.97	2.01
Danes	1.96	1.95	1.94
Irish	1.60	1.64	1.68
British	1.60	1.57	1.66
Greeks	1.52	1.54	1.52
Spaniards	1.54	1.72	1.68
Portuguese	1.50	1.57	1.56
(Average)[5]	1.68	1.75	1.74

[1] entries represent weighted EC average
(0 = no trust ..... 3 = a lot of trust)
[2] Source: Karlheinz Reif (1993)
[3] "   "   "
[4] Eurobarometer 39
[5] Unweighted Average

would include Italy[45]. It would also explain the similarly high levels of trust in Americans (on par with Germany). However, one certainly should not pass over remaining differences among European mass beliefs. One is what Ulf Hedetoft called the 'mentality of war', that is, beliefs about when and why one's country should go to war[46]. This 'mentality of war' is radically different in Great Britain, West Germany, and Denmark, putting in question the viability of a common foreign and defence policy.

Karl Deutsch had written not only of the necessity to develop a greater sense of trust among member state citizens, but also of the importance of a greater sense of common identification or 'we feeling'. While the previous chapter had already indicated that a true European identity is still in its infancy, there is evidence that

Table 9

EUROPEAN VALUES

	Fra	Bel	NL	Ger	Ita	Lux	DK	Ire	UK	Gre	Spa	Por	EU12[1]
A European Culture?[2]													
% Mentioning 0 items	10	8	4	12	8	8	5	14	11	14	24	23	12
% Mentioning 1 items	18	19	21	17	25	20	15	21	26	15	31	19	21
% Mentioning 2 items	25	26	22	22	33	36	33	25	27	25	28	25	27
% Mentioning 3+ items	47	47	53	50	34	36	46	40	37	47	17	34	41
% "Doesn't Exist"	9	5	2	7	4	5	3	8	5	3	13	6	6

1 Unweighted Average
2 Eurobarometer 33 (Spring 1990)
Note: for exact question wording, see Appendix

the basis of such a common identity may already have been established in the minds of most Europeans. As Table 9 clearly shows, strong majorities in all EU member states believe that 'Europe' stands for more than just a geographical location. Asked to choose from a list of values they personally considered specifically European, only a handful of respondents failed to identify any. The list consisted of the items culture, peace, democracy, way of life, standard of living, and quality of life. The vast majority of respondents readily identified themselves with most of these values. While this evidence is only tentative, it is suggestive of at least the potential for the development of a European identity in future.

Conclusion

If we pull together all the scattered evidence assembled here, what is the conclusion? It is certainly a mixed bag. There are definitely pockets of European societal equalization, and levels of trust as well as of feelings of European 'distinctiveness' are at fairly high levels. But, as far as we can see, these trends do not amount to an unequivocal movement towards the social integration of Europe. Important differences remain, some of which could be linked to a persistent North-South divide, others to cultural clusters of particular nations, to historical patterns and institutional persistence, or to 'families of nations'[47].

The longer the time horizon, the more likely one is to find increasing similarities - at least in some basic aspects of industrialization and modernisation. This finding is consistent with the thrust of Harmut Kaelble's important - and more optimistic - social history of Europe[48]. Especially in terms of economic organisation, today's European societies certainly are more similar than they were a hundred years ago. Also, compared to other macro-regions like Russia or Japan, and to a somewhat lesser extent to the USA, common European patterns seem to have emerged. Nevertheless, when one looks at the European Union and its forty years of existence, it does not seem as if there is a uniform trend towards a single European society, even if European societies are in many ways differentiated from other equally advanced macroregions. On the other hand, we should not assume that in order for European integration to move forward, complete homogenisation is required. On the contrary, many multi-cultural and multi-ethnic societies are quite stable (e.g., Switzerland and the USA). However, these societies share very strong political and historical bonds, and they possess a strong socio-political consensus which, as we have seen, is still very much in its infancy in Europe. European institutions must first earn their legitimacy, and for this to occur greater levels of social, economic, and political convergence is probably required

If then, for the time being, there is no European society, what are the consequences for future political integration? One may speculate about at least two different outcomes. The first option would be to curtail any far reaching attempts for an integrated Europe in the sense that the founding fathers like Monnet, Schumann, de Gasperi, and Adenauer originally had envisioned. Instead, the EU would be limited to an utilitarian endeavor to supplement, bolster and, occasionally, restrict its member states. The deficit of a feeling of

Table 10

National or Common Policy?[1]

Primarily National Policy Areas	Education, Culture, Media, Health & Welfare, Workers' Safety
In Between	Immigration, Environment, Consumer Protection Defense Policy Economic/Industrial Policy, VAT, Currency
Primarily Common Policy Areas	Foreign Policy, Science & Technology Drugs, 3rd World, Human Rights

[1] Eurobarometer 42.

Note: Respondents were asked (For several policy areas) to state their preferences with respect to deciding policy at the national level or as a common EC/EU policy (see Appendix for exact question wording)

European unity and the absence of common interests created through social integration would still allow for incremental cooperation, either to tackle common problems such as environmental protection, security issues, or border-policing ('task-force-model') or to prop up the EU as a guarantor of further European wealth and prosperity ('insurance-model'). Close cooperation is especially likely in areas such as scientific research and foreign policy, where the pooling of resources would either make economic sense or allow Europe to speak with a louder voice (see Table 11). Similarly, in those areas where a common policy makes practical sense (immigration, the environment, defence, and even certain economic matters), the population is at least equally split on whether or not to proceed with national or common EU polices.

Yet, limits of cooperation are quickly reached. What about social and cultural policy? In these areas most Europeans still prefer to go it alone. Moreover, there are not only differences in the levels of social spending, but also in the structure of welfare institutions, all of which would make a social space rather unlikely. Even if the European public is strongly committed to the welfare state, and even if it realises that with completion of the European Single Market member states cannot control tax burdens on capital and firms, the aggregate seems to preclude any European solutions.

Table 11

The Future of Europe[1]

	Fra	Bel	NL	Ger	Ita	Lux	DK	Ire	UK	Gre	Spa	Por	EU12[2]
% Sovereign country	14	15	7	13	9	11	14	14	16	6	14	9	12
% Cooperation	38	32	34	35	35	22	49	47	46	31	37	45	38
% Common organisation	37	35	49	43	38	56	34	28	29	39	30	23	36
% European State	8	8	6	6	9	5	2	3	4	9	7	4	6
% Total 1 & 2	52	47	41	48	44	33	63	61	62	37	51	54	50
% Total 3 & 4	45	43	55	49	47	61	36	31	33	38	37	27	42

1 Eurobarometer 42 (Fall 1994)
2 Unweighted Average
Note: for exact question working, see Appendix

Table 11 reinforces the point about 'incremental cooperation'. While very few Europeans believe that each European country should mainly keep to itself and 'care only about its own affairs', even fewer currently believe in the model of fully shared sovereignty in a 'single common European state'. The vast majority prefers a solution somewhere in between those two extremes, about equally split between those who would like to see at least a 'partial transfer of sovereignty', and those who prefer cooperation without any loss of national autonomy (L'Europe de patries). Overall, slightly more people prefer for their nation to keep its full sovereignty than to relinquish all or parts of it.

An alternative scenario to both the task-force and insurance-models is that, out of motives of self-preservation, European elites may be tempted to manufacture consent through the creation of common enemies. The reinforcement of outside borders in order to strengthen internal homogeneity is a well known instrument of

Table 12

Immigration and Xenophobia

	Fra	Bel	NL	Ger	Ita	Lux	DK	Ire	UK	Gre	Spa	Por	EU12[1]
Foreign Population Quantity[2]													
% Too Many	55	57	47	40	45	23	41	8	43	64	27	30	41
% A lot but not too many	35	33	40	49	43	69	44	38	40	33	45	36	41
Disturbed by....[3]													
% People of other nation	14	13	10	11	8	9	16	4	11	35	6	7	12
% People of other race	19	21	7	12	11	5	17	7	13	20	8	8	13
Immigrants from EC countries[4]													
% Accept w/out restrict.	29	33	28	29	46	16	41	47	28	28	52	46	35
% Accept with restrictions	49	48	52	50	39	67	51	38	50	51	37	37	47
% Should not be accepted	18	16	16	16	10	9	7	6	18	19	5	5	13
Immigr. fr. south of Med.[5]													
% Accept w/out restrict.	10	10	12	15	22	8	6	21	10	9	25	24	15
% Accept with restrictions	50	54	62	56	58	68	63	58	62	56	57	55	58
% Should not be accepted	37	32	23	25	16	18	30	13	25	32	13	9	23
Immigrants seeking asylum[6]													
% Accept w/out restrict.	21	15	31	22	27	16	36	18	18	15	43	23	24
% Accept with restrictions	46	57	56	54	47	67	55	54	56	57	44	50	53
% Should not be accepted	30	25	11	21	18	11	8	16	19	24	7	11	17
Immigration Prob. Assessment[7]													
% A big problem	67	71	63	84	64	39	62	11	47	76	35	19	56
% Not a big problem	23	20	28	13	26	42	34	66	44	19	52	50	33
Non-EC population rights[8]													
% Extend	12	10	12	12	31	17	5	16	7	14	34	22	15
% Left as is	40	32	52	43	29	59	49	52	45	40	35	44	43
% Restrict further	40	48	29	38	28	19	43	17	41	35	14	16	32

[1] Unweighted Average
[2] Eurobarometer 42 (Fall 1994)
[3] Eurobarometer 42
[4] Eurobarometer 39
[5] Eurobarometer 39
[6] Eurobarometer 39
[7] Eurobarometer 39
[8] Eurobarometer 37
Note: for exact question wording, see Appendix

institution building. Many Europeans are already convinced that they live in an age of global competition and, in this sense, consider Japan and the USA as economic adversaries. A European Union purely based on utilitarian rationality and economic necessity may increasingly turn inward to defend its wealth. Coinciding with rising trust in one another, Europeans already, and increasingly, distinguish between 'good' EU foreigners residing in their countries and 'bad' asylum-seekers and immigrants[49]. A Europe along this line would not be a Europe as envisioned by the framers of the Treaty of Rome. Its common consciousness would then not be built on social commonalities accumulated across European societies, but on the degrading of others - other religions, ethnic groups, races. A Europe of exclusion, perhaps even excluding large parts of Eastern Europe, may contradict the best of Europe's enlightenment tradition.

If, given the ambivalent state of affairs of European social integration, this is a real, and rather bleak, possibility, would it then not be preferable to proceed along the lines of Charles de Gaulle's 'Europe de patries'? On a recent trip to Germany, former British foreign secretary Malcom Rifkind called for a Europe based on a partnership of nations, i.e., the democratic legitimacy of national parliaments rather than unloved European institutions. Rifkind scorned German Chancellor Helmut Kohl's headlong pursuit of European economic, monetary, and political union as a nightmare for Britain[50].

Yet even if possible, going alone hardly represents a tenable position for the European nations. Even the larger European countries look small in an era of interdependence and global markets. For better or worse, the 'small' European nations of today have to go together. While few take seriously Chancellor Kohl's warning that without political union - of which a single currency is a prerequisite - the Europeans risk perhaps even war, no one knows either how the financial markets would react to a collapse of the proposed monetary union. It may be true that, as Goran Therborn puts it, the best Europe can hope for its future is to be the world's Scandinavia[51]. But even this trajectory is predicated upon continuous political and social stability coupled with vigorous economic productivity. It is hard to imagine how Europe should remain competitive without continuous integration. It is in this context that the European identity questions continues to loom large.

Endnotes

1. Lindberg, L. and Scheingold, S. (1970): *Europe's Would-be Polity.* (Englewood Cliffs, NJ: Prentice Hall).

2. Dalton, R. and Eichenberg, R. (1992): A People's Europe: Citizen Support for the 1992 Project and Beyond, in: Smith, D. and Ray, J. (eds.), *The 1992 Project and the Future of Integration in Europe.* (New York: M.E. Sharpe).

3. See: Keohane, R. and Hoffmann, S. (1990): Conclusion: Community Politics and Institutional Change, in: Wallace, W. (ed.), *The Dynamics of European Integration.* (London: Royal Institute for International Affairs).

4. The British Conservative Party would appear to be a candidate for such a course, given its role in opposition since 1997.

5. Such a 'community' would then serve as the basis of diffuse support which, as we had argued in chapter 3, any political system needs to build in order to be able to overcome obstacles such as protracted economic crises. Clearly, this principle also applies to the European Union, and the last chapter had indeed uncovered evidence that such diffuse support for the EU already exists to some extent. For example, we noted the discrepancy between, on the one hand, respondents' support for (or opposition to) their country's membership in the European Union and, on the other, their assessment of the benefits of such membership.

6. Deutsch, K. et al. (1957): *Political Community and the North Atlantic Area.* (Princeton, NJ: Princeton University Press), p.36. The authors distinguished two types of a security community: (1) amalgamated and (2) pluralistic. The former comes about through a formal merger of two heretofore independent units, whereas in the latter the participating units retain their political independence. Needless to say, the social prerequisites for the former are much more stringent than those of the latter, but both types are relevant for today's (and tomorrow's) European Union..

7. A note of caution: the exact nature of the relationship of these three levels to each other is still quite poorly understood. We do not assume that convergence on one level automatically causes convergence on another. For example, two societies may have similar industrial structures, equivalent party systems, and similar family structures - and still pursue very different political goals. We merely assume that the greater the level of social integration - at any level - the easier it is to proceed with political integration. For detail on this macro-micro relationship, see Alexander, J. et al. (1987): *The Micro-Macro Link.* (Berkeley, CA: University of California Press).

8. Ironically, the history of the European Union was also an almost exclusively elite-driven process - so much so that many scholars until recently simply denied the relevance of public opinion in this process. As the prime example of this classic 'functionalist' school of thought, see: Haas, E. (1958): *The Uniting of Europe.* (Stanford: Stanford University Press). A more recent summary of neo-functionalist arguments can be found in: Nelsen, B. and Stubb, A. (1994): *The European Union: Readings on the Theory and Practice of European Integration.* (Boulder, Co: Westview).

9. Most of our evidence on points (1) through (5) will be based on survey data. We will thus discuss the attitudinal dimension throughout this chapter before we come to a conclusion under point (6) as well as in the final section of this chapter.

10. Admittedly, there are some important exceptions. The Civil Law tradition does not extend to England, Wales, or Ireland; France and Finland have a hybrid presidential-parliamentary system; and the Irish party system and social structure is rather unique in Western Europe. But all European systems share the legacy of class, religion, and/or ethnicity based mass parties. The next few years may provide more insight into the question of whether or not the UK fits into the continental model, depending a the Euro-policies of a Labour government.

11. Lipset, S.M. and Rokkan, S. (1967): Cleavage Structures, Party Systems and Voter Alignments: an Introduction, in: Lipset, S.M. and Rokkan, S. (eds.), *Party Systems and Voter Alignments*. (New York: Free Press).

12. The UK, of course, serves as a partial exception to this rule, especially with its opposition to a 'Social Europe'. However, this may change after the next election, and, in any event, by world standards the British welfare state clearly fits in much more with the European model than with the American or any other one.

13. Albert,M. (1992): *Kapitalismus contra Kapitalismus*. (Frankfurt: Campus). Immerfall, S. (1995): Sozialer Wandel und Soziale Angleichung: Das Europäische Modell im Globalen Wettbewerb, in Clausen, L. (ed.), *Gesellschaften im Unbruch*. (Frankfurt: Campus).

14. Immerfall, S. (1995): Der Vergleich europäischer Gesellschaften. Eine Übersicht über forschungsleitende Ansätze, ausgewählte Erträge and aktuelle Perspektiven, Unpublished Habilitationsschrift: Universität Passau, chapter 4.3.

15. Beginning in the mid 1980s with the negotiations concerning the Single European Act, which led to the Community Charter of Fundamental Social Rights of Workers, commonly known as the Social Charter, and which, in turn, served as the basis for the Social Chapter of the Maastricht Treaty.

16. One must be cautious not to overinterpret these differences, interesting and important though they are. They likely reflect differences in relative priorities much more than differences in fundamental commitment. As Ronald Inglehart has pointed out, there is likely to be a diminishing marginal utility to egalitarian policies: with increasing economic equality due to the policies associated with the modern welfare state, the social base of support for such policies gets smaller and smaller. See: Inglehart, R. (1990): *Culture Shift in Advanced Industrial Society.* (Princeton: Princeton University Press) especially chapter 8.

17. Erikson, R. and Goldthorpe, J. (1992): *The Constant Flux: A Study of Class Mobility in Industrial Societies.* (Oxford: Clarendon Press); Treiman, D. and Ganzeboom, H. (1990): Cross-national Comparative Status Attainment Research, *Research in Social Stratification and Mobility,* vol. 9, pp.105-127.

18. Davis, H. (1992): Social Stratification in Europe, in: Bailey, J. (ed.), *Social Europe.* (Harlow, Essex: Longman).

19. Scharpf, F. (1986): Strukturen der post-industriellen Gesellschaft, oder: Verschwindet die Massenarbeitslosigkeit in der Dienstleistungs- and Informations-Ökonomie? Soziale Welt, vol. 37; 3-24; Blossfeld, H.P. (1992): Is the German Dual System a Model for a Modern Vocational Training System? A Cross-National Comparison of How Different Systems of Vocational Training Deal with the Changing Occupational Structure, *International Journal of Comparative Sociology,* vol 33. no. 3-4, pp 168-181; Esping-Andersen, G. (ed). (1993): *Changing Classes. Stratification and Mobility in Post-Industrial Societies.* (London: Sage).

20. The positive value for the UK indicates that the working class is actually growing relative to the middle class, since the former is larger in that country.

21. What seems certain, however, is that governments in continental Europe are much more cautious and hesitant to embark on a

policy of social and economic deregulation than their Anglo-Saxon counterparts, the latest example of which is provided by New Zealand.

22. Höllinger, F. and Haller, M. (1995): Zentren und Peripherien in Europa. Eine Analyse und Interpretation der Verschiebungen zwischen dem ersten und dritten Viertel des 20. Jahrhunderts, in: Immerfall, S. and Steinbach, P. (eds.), Historisch-vergleichende Makrosoziologie: Stein Rokkan - der Beitrag eines Kosmopoliten aus der Peripherie. *Historical Social Research,* Special Issue No.2, vol. 20.

23. Leonardi, R. (1995): *Convergence, Cohesion and Integration in the European Union.* (New York: St.Martin's Press).

24. Noll, H.H. (1993): Lebensbedingungen and Wohlfahrtsdisparitäten in der Europäischen Gemeinschaft, in Glatzer, W. (ed.), *Einstellungen and Lebensbedingungen in Europe,* (Frankfurt/New York: Campus).

25. Figure 1 displays GDP per capita figures (in 1980 dollars) adjusted for purchasing power parities, i.e., the real value of money. In percentage terms, the gap between the two countries is virtually identical at the three time points in Figure 1: 100% in 1958, 106% in 1973, and 106% 1985. This pattern holds for nearly all countries. See: Summer, R. and Heston, A. (1988): Improved International Comparisons of Real Product and its Components, 1950-1980, *Review of Income and Wealth,* vol. 30, pp.207-62

26. Flanagan, R. (1993): European Wage Equalization Since the Treaty of Rome, in Ulman, L./Eichengreen, B./Dickens, W. T. (eds.), *Labour and an Integrated Europe.* (Washington, DC: The Brookings Institution).

27. *Neue Züricher Zeitung,* 29 August 1996, p.24.

28. Clark, H./Dutt, N./Kornberg, A. (1993): The Political Economy of Attitudes Toward Polity and Society in Western European Democracies. *Journal of Politics,* vol. 55, no.4, pp. 998-1021.

29. Ester, P./Halman, L./de Moor, R. (1993): *The Individualising Society: Value Change in Europe and North America*. (Tilburg, NL: Tilburg University Press).

30. Jallinoja, R. (1995): Centrality and Peripherality Upside Down? Gender Equality and the Family in Western Europe, in: Immerfall, S. and Steinbach, P.

31. See: Haller, M. and Höllinger, F. (1994): Female Employment and the Change of Gender Roles: the Conflictual Relationship Between Participation and Attitudes in International Comparison. *International Sociology*, vol. 9, no. 1, pp. 87-112.

32. Reif, K. (1993): Cultural Convergence and Cultural Diversity as Factors in European Identity, in: Garcia, S. (ed.), European Identity and the Search for Legitimacy. (London: Royal Institute for International Affairs).

33. See: Schmitter, P. and Karl, T.L. (1991): What Democracy is .... and is Not, *Journal of Democracy*, vol. 2, pp. 75-88.

34. Höllinger, F. and Haller, M. (1990): Kinship and Social Networks in Modern Societies: a Cross-Cultural Comparison Among Seven Nations. *European Sociological Review*, vol. 6, no. 2, pp. 103-24.

35. Kuhnle, S. and Selle, P. (eds). (1992): *Government and Voluntary Organisations: a Relational Perspective*. (Avebury, Vt: Aldershot/Brockfield).

36. See: Immerfall, S. (1997): Soziale Integration in den Europäischen Gesellschaften, in Hradil, S. and Immerfall, S. (eds.), *Die Westeuropäischen Gesellschaften im Vergleich*. (Opladen: Leske + Budrich).

37. See: Gaskin, K. and Smith, J. (1995): *A New Civic Europe? A Study of the Extent and Roles of Volunteering*. (London: Volunteer Centre UK).

38. That is, considering 'similar' everything within ten percent of the overall average.
39. Defined here as joining citizen action groups, signing petitions, or participating in protest demonstrations or boycotts.
40. Considering that sampling error is about +/- 3% for each individual survey, this would seem to be an unduly strict criterion.
41. Münch, R. (1993): *Das Projekt Europa: Zwischen Nationalstaat, regionaler Autonomie, und Weltgesellschaft.* (Frankfurt: Suhrkamp).
42. Gerhards, J. (1993): Westeuropäische Integration und die Schwierigkeiten der Entstehung einer Europäischen Öffentlichkeit, *Zeitschrift für Soziologie*, vol. 22, no. 2, pp. 96-110.
43. Dogan, M. (1994): The decline of Nationalism in Western Europe, *Comparative Politics*, vol. 26, no. 2, pp. 281-305.
44. For a more extended look at the evidence concerning mutual trust, see: Reif, K.
45. A lower level of familiarity may also be relevant, given that Greece, Spain, and Portugal have been members only since the 1980s. However, this would not explain why, on average, the Italians are much closer to the above three countries than to the other five of the original six.
46. Hedetoft, U. (1995): *Signs of Nations.* (Dartmouth: Aldershot).
47. For this discussion see: Castles, F. (ed). (1993): *Families of Nations. Patterns of Public Policies in Western Democracies*, (Aldershot, NH: Dartmouth Publishing); Hofstede, G. (1994): Images of Europe, *Netherlands' Journal of Social Sciences*, vol. 30, no. 1, pp. 63-82; Immerfall, S. (1995): *Einführung in den Europäischen Gesellschaftsvergleich. Ansätze - Problemstellungen - Befunde.* (Passau: Rothe); Therborn, G. (1995): *European Modernity and Beyond. The Trajectory of European Societies, 1945-2000*, (London: Sage).

48. Kaelble, H. (1987): *Auf dem Weg zu einer europäischen Gesellschaft.* (München: C.H.Beck).

49. Note the discrepancy, in Table 12, between EC foreigners and non-EC foreigners in terms of the right to immigrate with our without restrictions. Unfortunately, the data do not allow deeper analysis of the category 'accept with restrictions'. One may assume, based in the pattern found in the table, that most Europeans would impose greater restrictions on non-EC foreigners. On the other hand, Table 12 does not contain evidence that illiberal attitudes toward immigrants and asylum seekers are widespread at this point. For example, in no case do more than a third of Europeans (on average) advocate that harsher measures be taken against such individuals, although in some countries that percentage is somewhat higher (e.g., Belgium and Denmark). On this issue see also: Fuchs, D./Gerhards, J./Roller, E. (1993): Wir and die anderen. Ethnozentrismus in den zwölf Ländern der europäischen Gemeinschaft, *Kölner Zeitschrift für Soziologie and Sozialpsychologie,* vol. 45, no. 2, pp. 238-253.

50. *Financial Times,* Feb 20, 1997, p. 2.

51. Europas künftige Stellung - Das Skandinavien der Welt? in: Hradil S. and Immerfall, S. (eds.), *Die westeuropäischen Gesellschaften im Vergleich.* (Opladen: Leske + Budrich).

SECTION 4
EUROPEAN CITIZENSHIP: PRACTICAL APPROACHES

EDUCATIONAL PROJECTS FOR DEVELOPING EUROPEAN CITIZENS

CHAPTER 7

Ian Davies

This section of the book gives examples of work which may help pupils and students to develop knowledge, skills and attitudes or dispositions which will prepare them to deal effectively with the demands associated with living in a modern Europe. The chapters which follow are not designed to give a full and complete coverage of what can or should be done in schools which are determined to provide education for European citizenship. Rather, snapshots of very different projects are provided.

The need for such work is easily demonstrated. Recent studies have shown that although Europe is regarded as one of the most significant contemporary issues there is nevertheless widespread apathy among pupils and that negative feelings about a European identity may be strong in certain countries including England[1]. If education for European citizenship is to be anything more than an aspiration which is referred to in general terms in documents produced by civil servants and in the speeches of politicians there needs to be discussion of practical projects which may lead others to follow by developing their own ways forward. It is not suggested that the examples provided here should be slavishly imitated, but rather that they should be seen as an encouragement for others to take the debates forward.

The way in which work in the future takes place will thus depend on the interpretations that are made by readers of the following chapters in this book and from examples elsewhere. Those readings will generate a number of different questions and issues. Without wishing to restrict the nature of those interpretations and in an attempt to start a debate around some of the key issues I would like to offer a number of questions.

Question 1: What is the form of citizenship that relates to each practical project?

Here the best way forward will be to consider the issues posed by Derek Heater in the first chapter of this book. It should not be assumed that all the authors in this part of the book have a common understanding of the nature of European citizenship either because of disagreements over substantive issues or because of the different emphases that are brought to bear on particular issues. Ultimately we should be able to recognise the current frameworks (legal and otherwise) which provide the context for our thinking and actions in the field of education for citizenship as well as being able to develop a preferred model. And ultimately each person and group will be able (in a democracy in which education for citizenship is practised professionally and effectively) may arrive at their own version of a preferred model. This is not to say though that anything is acceptable. The most useful characterisation of the nature of a citizen given recently is that provided by Oliver and Heater[2] who note that:

> Individuals are citizens when they practise civic virtue and good citizenship, enjoy but do not exploit their economic benefits, do not allow any sense of national identity to justify discriminating or stereotyping of others, experience a sense of non-exclusive multiple citizenship and, by their example, teach citizenship to others (p. 8).

It is hoped that this book has already given some reasonably clear guidelines as to the nature of citizenship. There seem to the editors of this book to be essentially three key aspects of citizenship: membership in a defined community (e.g. a country) with certain rights and duties; a sense of belonging and loyalty to that community; citizenship skills including those of the good citizen (e.g. participation). But it would be wrong to present only those projects which have passed some sort of 'test'. As such, it is for the reader to consider the way in which those projects' intentions and realities (as described in the text) relate to a version of citizenship that is ideal or otherwise. This position itself raises major considerations. For example, will the development of education for European citizenship encourage in practise a homogeneous view of political life or does the very nature of democratic discussion mean that heterogeneity (within certain limits) will emerge and be regarded positively? Will the respective emphases placed by various authors on legally defined rights and responsibilities and more affective notions relating to identity and allegiance lead to variations within a theme or different themes? The question of whether multiple citizenships should or could also mean the existence of multiple meanings of citizenship has not been fully resolved in the presentation of these projects.

Question 2: What is the model for education for citizenship that is being presented in each project?

All the contributions included in this section of the book were commissioned from those who were clearly in a position of being expert on education for European citizenship. All the authors here would not necessarily agree with each other or with those who are in positions of power and authority in national governments and European institutions. The examples given are merely what a number of people currently perceive to allow for the development of education for European citizenship. It is clear in some of the following pieces that education for European citizenship emerges from a strong sense of a particular awareness of others and determination to promote opportunities to develop some shared ideas which will help develop tolerance rather than more narrowly - or, to state the idea more positively, more coherently - conceived notions of education for European citizenship. For some readers, some of the authors may have cast the net too wide and devoted too much attention to issues that are a necessary but insufficient dimension of education for European citizenship; for others this broader approach will be welcomed.

A number of research projects[3] have been concerned to know how teachers perceive political learning. It is possible to draw attention to at least four models of that political learning and as such it is important for the reader to be asked to consider which of those four (or which combination of models or which new model) relates to the projects described here. The four models which could be considered initially by readers are political literacy, global education, citizenship education and cultural studies. The divisions between those models are not always clear cut and it is immediately noticeable that the title 'education for citizenship' is only one way of characterising work in this area. In England and Wales 'education for citizenship' is simply the title that has been chosen by national agencies although there are signs both that that title competes for space with other titles such as 'values education'[4] and that some have chosen to use 'citizenship' as a means of justifying, at times rather untidily, their ongoing concerns. (One could draw attention here to the guidelines for education for citizenship devised by Manchester local education authority in 1992[5] which differ markedly from that produced by the National Curriculum Council in 1990[6]).

In light of the above little more than a crude overview can be given of the four models which I have highlighted but perhaps this may help illuminate the reading of the following chapters at least to a limited degree. This overview would be as follows:

citizenship education focusing on voluntary service in a society where knowledge and obligations are at least as important as rights

cultural studies focusing on enabling pupils to develop a critical understanding of the world and cultural environment in which they live

global education being characterised by affective learning and holistic approaches to world issues

political literacy being concerned with skills, issues and action and relating to a broad definition of politics

Question 3: What organisational model for education for citizenship does each project suggest?

There are fierce debates about the way education for citizenship should be developed in schools and colleges and universities. At times this debate draws attention simply to the practical business of getting things done and there is little real disagreement about the nature of the education that is being developed. However, it is also possible to see issues which are discussed superficially in terms of more or less effectiveness being in reality about a preferred type of education.

There are at least two levels on which this debate can be conducted: input measures and evaluation criteria. The former would raise issues associated with at least four main areas: the age at which people begin to receive a formal education for citizenship; a concentration on academic subjects through which education for citizenship is infused or an explicit consideration of relevant issues; the use of classroom learning or a stronger emphasis on the role of whole school learning; the involvement of learners in real world issues or in only simulated or imaginary contexts. Within these areas there will be many possible links. For example, some may argue that only that who are beyond the age at which compulsory education has finished are considered able to cope with real world issues and even then only in a context which is determinedly academic. There is extensive literature already available on each of these issues. Evaluation criteria are also important. By this I mean the ways in which judgements are made about the work of those (teachers and learners) involved in education for citizenship. How important is the role of knowledge; what sort of skills are valued and how are they assessed; are certain values to be respected more than others and are they procedural or substantive. (Although the debates are extremely complex and simplistic divisions between types cannot be made it can, very generally, be argued that procedural values are those which are concerned with processes and substantive values with specific goals).

One needs to ask about the ways in which one can begin to recognise the good work of teachers: is this to be judged in terms of the impact that students have upon the world (perhaps in the form of very personal and local effects) as good citizens or are these links too difficult to make? Generally, there are a number of extremely difficult issues which remain unresolved and it is hoped that the following chapters will give examples of the sort of approaches that some have found useful.

Question 4: What is the likelihood that a particular project or projects will be sanctioned or approved by those with the power to make change occur?

This question is perhaps the most important of all. If educational projects and thinking do not make things happen, if majorities are left unaffected while the talking continues, then little of immediate value will have been achieved. This is not to decry the value of theorising as the gap between theory and action is far less wide than many imagine. All have theories and rightly so. What really needs to occur is to target the space between actionless thought and thoughtless action (both of which do not exist in any literal sense), but which nevertheless are at times perceived to drive educational reform. The question of implementation is not, of course, free standing from the other questions raised in this introduction to the practical projects which follow. Fullan[7] has argued that key issues in relation to implementation include the perception of the need for change, as well as the clarity, complexity and quality/practicality of the proposed reform.

In order to consider the way in which any of the projects highlighted in the following chapters might be received and developed into wider programmes a number of factors need to be highlighted. Three broad questions are raised here. Who will react positively to these projects; for how long will those projects have an impact; and what sort of area will the project impact upon. Firstly, what are the likely reactions from different audiences? Is the project likely to lead to a positive reaction from learners, parents, local, national or international agencies? Do these audiences see the need for such work and do they feel that the project is clear and manageable? A proper assessment of this question can only be arrived at from a full consideration of all the issues in this book. Projects which aim to develop education for European citizenship will not be regarded positively unless there is evidence of widespread consideration of European issues. Secondly, will the project have a short or long term impact? It may be necessary to assess the distinction between the superficial elements of a project (such as perhaps its immediate subject matter, although this is of course not always a way to determine superficiality) and the structure or substance of the work. Some projects may choose to use study of, for example, a question such as 'should the countries of the former eastern Europe be allowed to join the EU'. This question will probably be of little interest in a few years time and yet the notion of developing pupils' thinking about the factors that relate to the contemporary world and the political future may be of long standing value[8]. Thirdly, on what will the project have impact? This issue overlaps with others mentioned above but is significant in its own right. Certain ways of thinking about Europe may be considered more positively than others. It will be necessary to reflect upon what those different characterisations may be and to consider the extent to which it is possible for any educational project merely to follow those trends or to set new goals. Each project has a particular emphasis. I have made the point above that there are different models both of citizenship and education for citizenship. The questions that needs to be addressed by readers when reading the following chapters not only relate to the validity of those conceptions but also their usefulness in the development of programmes within and between and across countries. Whether a programme has an overtly political or economic dimension, for example, may be extremely important.

Conclusion

The above questions are just some of those that may be used as a guide to reading the following chapters. The authors of these chapters are experts and would no doubt have their own questions and issues, and be able to pose more specific points. The litmus test of all educational work is the extent to which it makes any difference. I am painfully aware at this point that a hostage to fortune is being offered. A book cannot pretend to change much - if anything. And yet, all the authors are involved in the ways in which action can be taken.

In light of some of the examples shown in the literature of educational change which point to the dangers of regarding innovations (or, worse, policy statements) as ends in themselves, it is worth aiming a little higher. The reader will decide whether the following projects are likely to achieve those more ambitious goals.

Endnotes

1   Convery, A./Evans, M./Green, S./Macaro, E./Mellor. J. (1996): Pupils' perception of Europe: identity and education. (London: Cassell). Adams, T./Evans, M./Raffan, J. (1996): *A pilot study evaluation of UK co-ordinated SOCRATES: Comenius Action 1 school based partnership programmes.* University of Cambridge, Department of Educational Studies. Both reported in Evans, M.

(1996): Young Britain revealed as Euro-sceptic bastion. *Times Educational Supplement*, 8 November 1996, p.14.

2. Oliver, D. and Heater, D. (1994): *The Foundations of Citizenship*. (London: Harvester Wheatsheaf).

3. Project 'Modes of Political Learning' funded by the Standing Conference on Studies in Education. Publications include Bousted, M. and Davies, I. (1996): Teachers' Perceptions of Models of Political Learning. *Curriculum*, vol. 17, no. 1, pp. 12-23. The thinking for the development of the initial framework for the models of political learning shown here was assisted by Professor Ian Lister.

4. School Curriculum and Assessment Authority (SCAA) (1996): *Consultation on Values in Education and the Community* London, SCAA.

5. Manchester Local Education Authority (1992): *Education for Citizenship*. (Manchester: Manchester LEA).

6. National Curriculum Council (1990): *Education for Citizenship*. (York: National Curriculum Council).

7 Fullan, M. (1991): *The New Meaning of Educational Change.* (London: Cassell).

8 For good discussion and good practical classroom examples of how to teach about the future see Hicks, D.(1994) *Educating for the Future: a practical classroom guide.* (London: World Wide Fund for Nature).

FOREIGN LANGUAGE LEARNING AND CITIZENSHIP: ISSUES FOR LIFELONG LEARNING

CHAPTER 8

Hugh Starkey

Introduction

Unlike some parts of the world, Europe is demographically a relatively stable continent and the majority of its population is adult. Many of those living in Europe have memories of participating in and suffering the consequences of war between countries that are now member states of the same Union or Council. Very significant proportions of the adult population of Western Europe, possibly a majority at the time of writing, have reservations about the plans for European unity outlined in what has become known as the Maastricht treaty of 1992. Some electorates such as Switzerland and Norway voted to stay outside the Union. Others, such as France, managed only the narrowest of majorities when asked to vote in a referendum. However, the concept of Europe is not limited to the European Union based on economic and political considerations. The more than 40 members of the Council of Europe, founded on a looser association of educational and cultural co-operation and a Convention on Human Rights, represents a parallel and less exclusive vision. Whatever our definition of Europe, democratic and peaceful progress implies that citizens extend their range of identities to include European as well as national, regional, ethnic or religious. Whereas it is clearly important to educate the next generations in European citizenship, arguably the greater task lies in providing such education for the current adult populations.

This chapter looks at a particular formal course which offers English speaking adults the opportunity to improve their French. The 220 hour course studied over an eight month period was prepared and administered from the Centre for Modern Languages at the Open University. It attracted over 2000 students when first offered in 1995 and a similar number in each of the following years. Although students enrol on the course for a variety of reasons (mostly instrumental to do with work or leisure), and they may have no objectives other than to improve their level of linguistic skill, the course arguably provides them with an experience that is recognisable as civic education. Such education is certainly an appropriate, if modest, contribution to life-long learning. It is significant for the scale of the operation and its pedagogy based on each student receiving an identical multi-media package.

Given their previous experiences of language learning and their expectations of improving skills rather than learning specific content it is interesting to note the very positive attitude of students towards their perhaps unsolicited exposure to education for citizenship. Indeed students claim significant shifts in their perceptions of this group of their European neighbours.

Claims Made for Life-Long Learning

If we are to believe UNESCO, life-long learning is in itself and by its essence a major contribution to world peace and democracy.

> Thus the education of each citizen must continue throughout his or her life and become part of the basic framework of civil society and living democracy. It even becomes indistinguishable from democracy when everyone plays a part in constructing a responsible and mutually supportive society that upholds the fundamental rights of all[1].

The former President of the European Commission argues that without life-long learning citizens become the powerless victims of the economic forces of globalisation. Education is about understanding and adapting to changes and preserving individual freedom and choices, attributes essential to any concept of citizenship

> in a world in which the accelerated rate of change and rapid globalisation are transforming each individual's relationship with both time and space, learning throughout life is essential for people to retain mastery of their own destinies. Major transformations in the nature of employment are taking place in some parts of the world, undoubtedly to spread, that will involve a reorganisation of individuals' use of time. Learning throughout life can become, then, the means for each of us to establish an equilibrium between learning and working, continued adaptation for a number of occupations and for the exercise of active citizenship[2].

The content of the education presented in the context of life-long learning, so the International Commission on Education for the Twenty-first Century maintains, should include intercultural understanding. Like the construction of Europe, the growing global awareness needs to be more than economic, it has to be cultural with a common ethical basis of concern for humanity, a human rights perspective, for short.

> Knowledge of other cultures leads, then, to an awareness of the uniqueness of one's own culture but also an awareness of a heritage common to all humanity...

> Education must help to engender a new humanism, one that contains an essential ethical component and sets considerable store by knowledge of, and respect for, the cultures and spiritual values of different civilisations, as a much needed counterweight to a globalisation that would otherwise be seen only in economic or technical terms[3].

One way in which such education can be delivered is by flexible distance learning offered by universities that are no longer elite institutions essentially for young people.

> Each university should become an 'open' university, offering possibilities for distance learning and learning at various points in time....By calling on all universities to be places of culture and of learning open to all, the Commission....wishes to contribute to affirmation of a major task of the university - even a moral obligation - to participate in the major debates concerning the direction and future of society[4].

Language Learning for European Citizenship

The Delors Commission makes recommendations and observations which apply at a global level. On a regional level the Council of Europe's programme 'Language learning for European citizenship' makes the specific link between foreign language learning and citizenship issues. Objectives of the programme include promoting effective communication, developing intercultural competence and promoting responsible learner autonomy. This latter objective also links closely with concerns to promote life-long learning.

> The promotion of genuine multilingual and multicultural citizenship requires concrete steps to ensure that language learning is possible for all at each level of education in a life-long perspective so that citizens may have the opportunity to acquire adequate competence in at least two modern languages[5].

Programmes to promote language learning have not always prioritised intercultural or socio-cultural competence. The Council of Europe has taken the lead in encouraging the development of a theoretical underpinning for this aspect of language teaching. Language skills and communicative competence are seen as inadequate objectives in themselves. Learners also need knowledge and open minded attitudes.

In view of the increasing opportunity for personal contact in Europe, learners need to be prepared for intercultural communication.

Accordingly the traditional *civilisation* or *Landeskunde* approach, centred on the acquisition of knowledge about the foreign culture (much of which can be acquired independently of the target language), needs to be enriched by the acquisition of intercultural skills and an attitude reflecting openness to Otherness[6].

In a work commissioned by the Council of Europe, Byram and Zarate identify four types of socio-cultural competence. These are most easily expressed using the French concepts:

- *savoir* or knowledge
- *savoir-être* or the affective capacity to relinquish ethnocentric attitudes
- *savoir-faire* is about competencies and skills
- *savoir-apprendre* is the ability to learn[7]

These objectives put language learning in the mainstream of international thinking on the aims of education, as the Delors Commission defined a very similar four pillars of education, namely:

- Learning to know
- Learning to do
- Learning to live together
- Learning to be[8]

What I have referred to as international thinking might also be termed internationalist thinking on education. Socio-cultural elements, without a democratic, internationalist perspective can be made to help reinforce prejudice and serve ideology. Writing also for the Council of Europe, Neuner (1994)[9] gives the example of the GDR curriculum for elementary level English 1978 which maintained that: 'comparisons between the life of workers in our Republic, with those of certain other countries will strengthen the pupils' conviction of the superiority of socialism'. In this case, the relationship of the world of the authorities providing education to the target culture was one of great ideological difference and hence hostility. Whether explicitly, as in this case, or implicitly the choice of content in a language course reflects the socio-political relationship between those for whom the course writers are working and the institutional view of the target culture:

> The socio-political constellation determines the relationship of the learner's own world and the world of the target socioculture: it may be friendly, neutral or adverse; dominant, on equal terms or dependent. Consequently, the view of the world of the target language, the selection of topics and the interpretation of events will be influenced by the specific constellation of native and foreign worlds[10].

A concept of 'foreign language learning for citizenship' promoted by an international organisation committed to human rights and democracy, such as UNESCO or the Council of Europe, is consequently likely to emphasise aspects of teaching and learning such as the development of attitudes of mutual tolerance and interest. A nationalist version of education for citizenship through foreign language learning would stress the superiority of the home culture possibly by highlighting eccentricities and idiosyncratic elements of the foreign culture. It would highlight difference, possibly concentrating on folkloric elements and perhaps including material designed to be humourous at the expense of the foreign culture. It may be that a number of language courses produced in the UK in the past two decades would be considered to be at the nationalist end of the spectrum if analysed in this light.

If a nationalist foreign language course emphasises difference, then an internationalist and democratic one stresses similarities. Of course, by definition a foreign language and its culture are different from the native language and culture. This is not to say, however, that there are not considerable areas of similarity. A nationalist course might be said to be based on an either / or approach; either my culture or your culture. A democratic internationalist approach is based on both / and; both different and in many respects similar.

As an aid to syllabus construction for the socio-cultural element of foreign language teaching, Neuner has derived a list of universal areas of experience. A syllabus based on the following, he argues, will enable citizens of one nation or culture to identify to some extent with those of a foreign culture.

1. the experience of basic existence (birth, existence, the inevitability of death)
2. the experience of personal identity (personal characteristics)
3. belonging to a private sphere (small social community; family; we)
4. belonging to a social sphere (our street, city, nation etc.)
5. relationships (friends, lovers, you)
6. shelter (house, home)
7. environment beyond house and home (physical properties; nature; civilisation)
8. work (securing subsistence)
9. education
10. recreation / art
11. supply and provision (food, clothes etc.)
12. mobility (space)
13. past, present, future (time)
14. communication (sign systems / media)

15. health care (health / sickness / hygiene)
16. ethical norms and values

Learning a foreign language always invites comparisons. The nationalist perspective invites unfavourable judgements on the foreign culture. A democratic internationalist course will enable students to gain a new perspective on their own culture by comparing its features to those found elsewhere. The yardstick in this case is not the immutable traditions of a by definition superior home culture. Rather judgements are made by reference to internationally-validated ethical and legal norms, standards which can be encapsulated in the phrase human rights. A further Council of Europe study expresses this succinctly:

> Inventing a new world solidarity may be the highest aim of adult education, provided the global educational approach does not prove a new means of spreading uniformity and standardisation.
>
> A guarantee is given if universal awareness is added to the protection of human rights, again provided that the protection of human rights is understood in its full implications and with due regard to the exceptional diversity of those rights. Education can reconcile the universalist with the particularist approach. By being myself I am conscious of being part of far greater communities as well as being a product of them[11].

There is considerable evidence to suggest that foreign language learning of itself and even residence abroad as part of that experience are not sufficient to promote the development of inclusive extra identities such as a sense of being European. University language students returning from their year abroad have been reported to be less well disposed towards the inhabitants of the countries they had visited than they had been before their departure[12]. Research with some of my own former students led a colleague and I to conclude:

The experience of study abroad in another European country has enabled these future teachers to reflect on their personal identities, both national and European, and to examine critically their own attitudes and values. While for some this has confirmed their national identities, others have adopted a new European identity alongside existing identities. The experience of living and studying abroad has allowed a number of them to stand back from their own cultures and societies and assess their strengths and weaknesses. It has not necessarily challenged those from majority communities to recognise the pluralist and multicultural nature of individual states or to re-define national identity and citizenship in a more inclusive way. It would seem that it is largely those students who have had direct teaching and experience of human rights and democratic values within their own schooling who identify these as being at the heart of the European ideal[13].

The suggestion that the introduction of a human rights perspective into the disciplines of history and foreign languages, separately and in co-operation, should be a priority direction for research and development over the next few years appears in this light timely and well founded[14].

Foreign Language Learning and Political Education

We have noted that the socio-cultural content is an essential part of language learning.

> If language is considered as a system of signs, and signs are characterised by the fact that they are units of form and meaning, it is impossible to learn a language by simply acquiring the forms without the content.
>
> And as the content of a language is always culture-bound, any reasonable foreign-language teaching cannot but include the study of a culture from which the language stems[15].

The aim of foreign language teaching can then be said to be intercultural communicative competence, building on earlier work on communicative competence by bringing in contributions from intercultural pedagogy, theories of socialisation, ethnography and anthropology and political education. Doyé argues that foreign language teaching is therefore in a key position to promote international and intercultural understanding. This is education for international citizenship and the expression 'education for citizenship' corresponds exactly to what is called 'political education' in Germany[16].

The political nature of foreign language learning in an internationalist European context can be perceived in the sense of empowering the citizen through enabling them to gain access to information in excess of that available in a closed monolingual community.

> Access to media, not to mention informal personal conversation with individuals outside one's own and linguistic community, is a valuable source of empowerment against tendencies towards information management at a national level[17].

Some of the issues on Neuner's list above may also have a political, if not necessarily party political dimension. As common ground between political and cultural communities there is arguably a place for them in a foreign language teaching syllabus. Indeed the absence of such topics would in itself be a statement of political position.

> There are many groups in all the countries of Europe which are not political parties seeking election to government but whose activities are to be regarded as political in the sense that they are intending to exert an influence on the nature of life or some aspect of life in the polity as a whole...Organisations concerned with issues that transcend

national boundaries such as education and research, international relations, human rights, public health and the environment would seem obvious cases in point[18].

In many respects then, foreign language education, if it espouses a human rights perspective and international standards, is both citizenship education and political education. However, this fact is rarely made explicit so we may wonder if the students notice, and if they do, whether they mind receiving this unexpected extra dimension to their course. I decided to examine the recently developed Open University French course for adults, *Ouverture*. In the light of the above discussion it appears to conform to the highest expectations of discussions of life-long learning and also to be based on an internationalist and democratic perspective.

When I moved to the Open University in 1996, I was fortunate to have access both to those who made the course and a number of students who had studied it. Before outlining their reactions, it may be useful to provide a little more context.

The Centre for Modern Languages at the Open University

The Open University presented its first courses in 1971. As its name implies it is a university but one that is open to those who have not necessarily achieved any formal qualifications. It contributes to opportunities for life-long learning for adults in the UK and, increasingly, overseas. It has students in over 90 countries. It currently offers more than four hundred courses and packs to about 200 000 students a year, half of whom are studying for a BA or BSc degree. Over two thirds of its students remain in full time employment throughout their studies. Course material in the form of study books, videos and audio cassettes is produced by teams of academics supported by administrative, clerical and editing staff, and production and technical staff from the BBC for the audio-visual elements.

Students receive course materials for study at home and are required to submit regular assignments to their personal tutor by correspondence. Face-to-face tuition is also provided in the form of group tutorials or day schools. Many courses also have a week long summer school. Assessment is usually by formal examination and by coursework, credit being accumulated towards degrees, diplomas and certificates.

The Centre for Modern Languages was set up in 1991 and its first course was presented in 1995 when over 2000 students registered. Following this first French course, a second level French course was offered in 1996 and a third French course and the first German course in 1997, when total student numbers on language courses passed 5000.

The number of students studying languages with the Open University is very significant in national terms which means that the courses are probably the greatest single source of information for adult learners of European languages in the UK. In other words the messages about speakers of European languages and their cultures contained in the courses have the potential to influence the attitudes of people in all parts of the country and in all areas of economic activity.

The First French Course: Ouverture

The first French course had three explicit aims, to do with communication, study skills and cultural content. Communication skills are to be enhanced by giving students practice in the four skills of reading, writing, speaking and listening and enabling them to develop their expertise in practical situations of a general nature. The course is also specifically intended to equip students for life-long learning. As the course team put it:

> The course also aims to help you to learn *how* to learn a language. This will enable you to go on learning effectively long after you have finished studying the course materials[19].

The third aim is about socio-cultural competence:

> We also believe that you can't really understand or speak a language well unless you know something about the underlying culture: for this reason almost all the topics in the course centre on aspects of life in modern France. You'll be learning *about* France *through* the French language.

The course team particularly stress the importance of the videos in this respect.

> Video gives us an insight into French life and culture which would not be available if we were simply using text or audio-based material. Some of the *activités* therefore centre on what might be termed 'video portraits' - insights into the lives of French people, not only through sound but through image[20].

The choice of content for the first French course *Ouverture* is unlike any other course produced for learners of this level. Students receive eight books, each designed to support about a month's personal study. The books are designed to help students co-ordinate their study of the audio and video tapes that are also provided. The medium adopted gives the course team far more scope than would be available to producers of a text book or stand alone video package.

The Open University formula for languages was, at the outset, the production of a multi-media course with close integration of the video, the audio and the text elements. Given the participation of the BBC as the producers of the video and audio elements there was an expectation that the team would include documentary features in the BBC tradition. Thus, for book three of the course, where the topic for the month is communal living, the four case studies are a girls' boarding school and a prison on audio and, a barracks and a Trappist monastery on video. Clearly few non-French or even French adults would ever have the possibility to experience life in any of these four institutions, yet each of them has resonance in the French collective conscience and may be referred to in literature, art, songs or conversation. To this extent, at least, the offering of an opportunity to attain some understanding of and feeling for these institutions may be considered to be part of education for European citizenship and even, in the German conception, mentioned above, political education[21].

Linguistic Content and Socio-Cultural Content

It is likely that the main concern of the learners following this course is linguistic. However, the extent to which linguistic and socio-cultural content are interlocked is very significant. For instance, in the unit mentioned above, the grammar content is to do with the past tense and with rules (such as expressing can, cannot, must and ought).

> The main grammar associated with this book relates to the use of past tenses. Also, as you discover what members of the various communities like and dislike about their life styles and what they are allowed and forbidden to do by the rules of their institutions, you'll learn how to express your own likes and dislikes and to talk about obligation.

Practising past tenses implies a sense of history and continuity within institutions. Allowing and forbidding are to be studied by reference to rules. Members of communities have rights and duties, or obligations. For this reason the course team chose to visit rule bound institutions where they would be able to record examples of people using modal verbs such as must and ought. Although the decisions about the linguistic functions to be learnt at this stage in the course led to this content, the fact remains that rule governed institutions are so central to any society, that these linguistic functions permeate discourse. Modal verbs are essential for verbal interaction in society. The language is revealing of the extent to which our consideration of rules is often subconscious. By approaching the study of a culture through language, these implicit assumptions are brought to the surface.

Thus, judging by their choice of content, the course team would appear to be supporting civic mindedness. The introduction to book three could serve for any course on civic education or citizenship:

> The common themes running through the book are the constraints and restrictions communal life imposes on members of the communities, but also the advantages that such a life can bring[22].

The second part of the course, books five to eight, is perhaps even more revealing. It goes under the title *Valeurs* meaning values. The sequence moves from marketing and consumer issues in book five through issues of employment and unemployment, including the role of trade unions, in book six to what might be considered the hidden underside of French life in book seven. The topics covered are deprivation in the context of a rich European state, housing, hunger and life in what in Britain and the US are known as the inner cities, which in France are the areas outside the cities *les banlieues*. Real social problems are seen from the perspective of community organisations trying to tackle them. The final book of the course considers the good society, or what elements lead to quality of life.

Again, the content, perhaps particularly of book seven, is almost explicitly that of a civic education course:

> We look at different communities who may be said to be either excluded from society, or living on the margins of society. We visit charitable organisations, looking at some of the problems and some of the solutions that are being tried. In the second part of the book we study some aspects of life on a multi-ethnic housing estate, with its underlying violence, but also its creativity and vitality. The single theme that runs through the book is that of the fight against exclusion through charitable action, government measures, individual initiatives and cultural integration[23].

It is not unusual for foreign language courses even at school level to include material on social issues. Indeed, most courses include discussions of environmental issues and social questions such as racism and unemployment. It is perhaps one thing to discuss such issues with young people who are in the process of forming their opinions and who may wish to be informed. It is quite another to raise the same questions with adults who may already have very firm views on social and political issues. I explored this question with the chair of the course team and with a number of students.

The View of the Course Team Chair

In an extended interview, the course team chair, Marie-Noëlle Lamy, a French native speaker with considerable experience of teaching in British universities, insisted that the starting point for the syllabus design was linguistic. It was not cultural still less political.

Students were to be encouraged to practise expressing a point of view in the foreign language and were to learn specific skills of, for example, expressing likes, dislikes and needs, presenting information and arguments, agreeing and disagreeing. The audio and video elements of the course, made in conjunction with the BBC provide examples of French people expressing arguments, saying what they like and dislike about their situation. Students are encouraged to model their practice on the linguistic forms they hear. They are not, of course, obliged to agree with the speakers.

That said, choices had to be made about who would be interviewed and filmed. Some of the choices were pragmatic. The BBC producer advised that it would be easier to film in a medium sized city such as Nantes rather than in Paris. There was an expectation, both from the BBC and from the Open University that locations and interviewees would represent a range of backgrounds. In order to appeal to a wide range of potential students, there was a deliberate attempt to present interesting situations which would hold the interest of the course members. Hence there was an intention to 'get behind the scenes'

> We wanted to get away from the tourist perspective, to go behind the glossy brochure, behind the façade.

However the course does not provide specialist sociological information. It simply attempts to provide the opportunities to learn and practice the language necessary to engage with big issues, but without engaging with the issues themselves in any depth. That is left for a later course.

It is true that there is an emphasis on values. People who feature in the course material discuss their values but there is no attempt to impose values on students or take up particular positions on an issue. The course team were working in any case within the BBC tradition of balance and neutrality.

That said, the course team were concerned that the experience of language learning should be culturally enriching. Students should be encouraged to relate what they learn about France to their own situation:

> It is important to get students thinking about their own society. Students should be able to identify with what they see and hear in the course. The content should be seen as interesting and relevant.

> As linguists it is not necessarily our role to engage with issues in such a way as to get students to question their assumptions. On the other hand, the course team does try to widen perspectives of France and French people and to that extent is content to help students modify their perceptions.

In an attempt to ascertain whether students did indeed feel that their perceptions had been changed, I conducted interviews with twelve students from different parts of the UK and a geographically mixed group of 30 students also completed a questionnaire for me. The interviews and the questionnaire were based on an opportunity sample, namely students whom I had taught at summer school and who volunteered to help me with this research. The interviews were conducted and the questionnaire completed in August and September 1996. Most of the students were remembering their experience from their study of the course in 1995.

Student Reactions to the Course

The interviews confirmed that the choice of topics is perceived as being relevant and in particular they are able to identify with the people featured in the audio and video material. One student mentioned the interview with the nursery teacher who is working and studying another, a professional housing officer, recognised the situation of the young people on a run down housing estate. There is a feeling that the people and the situations are authentic and the diversity of voices and situations is appreciated.

The course team's claim not to be providing sociological data, nor attempting to promote particular values seemed to be vindicated by one student who maintained that immigrants in France are responsible for homelessness. It was clear that her essentially ill-informed opinion possibly based on racist prejudices went unchallenged by the course. On the other hand, students do feel better informed after studying the course and one made the claim that when he heard unfair criticism of the French in places where he socialised he now reacted confidently in defence of French people. The course had clearly provided this student with information and a capacity to empathise.

The questionnaire asked whether the course helped students to modify their view of France and French speaking people and most students emphasised a growing realisation of similarity as well as difference. This was entirely in keeping with the intentions of the course team. That said, it is perhaps the most significant finding in terms of developing a common European citizenship. The following quotations provide a flavour of these responses:

> It has confirmed the view I had already formed that modern French society shows many common features with England.

> A generation has become 'homogenous' Europeans, whilst older traditions emphasise the differences between us.
>
> Exactly the same issues as in UK. It is heartening to know that concerns are now at least European wide.
>
> Gave me a broader view of things I hadn't seen. Perhaps has shown more similarities than one would think.

The use of authentic case studies seems to have helped bridge the gap between cultures:

> Hearing ordinary people talk about their impressions and feelings I feel more sympathetically inclined to the country as a whole, probably because of seeing it through the eyes of its people.
>
> Increased my awareness of the richness of French life. I'm more fully aware of the wide range of people in France.
>
> It has shown to some extent the very mixed cultural society existing in France. A proportion of French people are neither white nor hold the views that are assumed to be French.
>
> I feel I comprehend the French viewpoint better when I hear it in the media. I feel able to see behind the tourist places I visit how the French way of life works.

Students were also asked if they felt that there was any bias in the materials and the way topics were presented. One student expressed some reservations on behalf of others:

> The course material has a very particular bias, which does not bother me because I probably share the same concerns and views, but which may annoy other students who have a different view of the world.

This not very clearly defined view was made more explicit by others who mentioned: 'very middle of the road middle class'; 'quite a strong feminist viewpoint'; 'just possibly too rosy a view'. It is clear from other feedback that the course team has received, including the excellent retention rate on the course, that the materials are not considered as political, even though, as we have noted, the course has many features of a civic and political education course. With such a broadly based student body, there are students who may be experts on most of the topics covered. One letter to the course team began: 'I have been in prison in France, so was interested in the section of the course on prisons'.

The development of a new identity, such as citizen of Europe, is more than a cognitive process. It demands essentially an emotional commitment. I tried to ascertain the extent to which students reacted with their feelings to the material. The comments above show that students identify with the French people featured. The questionnaires also showed that by far the most significant and memorable part of the course is that covering charities working with the poor and homeless.

Conclusion

The course team of *Ouverture* devised a course able to meet the aspirations of proponents of life-long learning and which appears to conform to the suggestions of Neuner regarding areas of common experience.

Whilst the course does not claim to provide significant sociological or political information as such, it nonetheless appears to help students to empathise with people speaking a different language living in a neighbouring state. Students maintain that they also come to reflect on their own society as a result of their studies. The outcomes for students, as well as enhanced communication skills, seem to be new perspectives on France and French speaking people. They are stimulated to reflect on the common experience of those living in Europe. Perhaps these modest achievements indicate a significant way forward in developing a feeling of European citizenship.

Endnotes

1. Delors, J. (1996) *Learning: the treasure within* (Paris: UNESCO). pp. 63.
2. Delors, p. 101
3. Delors, p. 50
4. Delors, p. 134
5. Sheils, J. (1996): The Council of Europe and Language Learning, p. 101 in *Evaluation and Research in Education*, vol. 10, no. 23, pp. 88-103
6. Sheils, J. (1996): *The Council of Europe and Language Learning*, p. 94 in Evaluation and Research in Education, vol. 10 (2 & 3) pp. 88 -103
7. Byram, M. and Zarate, G.(1994): *Definitions, objectives and assessment of socio-cultural competence* (Strasbourg : Council of Europe).
8. Delors, p. 86
9. Neuner, G. (1994): *The role of sociocultural competence in foreign language teaching and learning* (Strasbourg: Council of Europe CC-LANG (94) 2).
10. Neuner, p. 6
11. Gelpi, E. (1996): *Towards a democratic citizenship*, (Strasbourg: Council of Europe). P. 23
12. Meara, P. (1994): The year abroad and its effects, *Language Learning Journal*, vol. 10, pp. 32-38
13. Osler, A. and Starkey, H. (1996): *Teacher Education and Human Rights* (London: Fulton). P. 96.
14. Byram, M. (1996): Education for European Citizenship. *Evaluation and Research in Education*, vol. 10, no. 23, pp. 61-67. Quote for p. 65.

15 Doyé, P. (1996): Foreign Language Teaching and Education for Intercultural and International Understanding. *Evaluation and Research in Education*, vol. 10, no. 23, pp. 104-112.

16 Doyé, p. 108

17 Wringe, p. 75.

18 Wringe, p. 76

19 Centre for Modern Languages (1994a): *Ouverture Study Guide*, (Milton Keynes: Open University). P. 1.

20 Centre for Modern Languages, p. 38.

21 Doyé

22 Centre for Modern Languages (1994b): *Ouverture, Cadences livre 3*, p. 1 (Milton Keynes: Open University).

23 Centre for Modern Languages, (1995): *Ouverture, Valeurs livre 3* (Milton Keynes: Open University). P. 1.

EUROPEAN CITIZENSHIP AND EDUCATION FOR DEMOCRACY AND HUMAN RIGHTS
CHAPTER 9
Don Rowe and Jan Newton

Every Member of the Council of Europe must accept the principles of the rule of law and of the enjoyment by all persons within its jurisdiction of human rights and fundamental freedoms.

Statute of the Council of Europe 1949

One of the defining characteristics of modern European citizenship is its foundation on a common code of Human Rights which is designed to protect and preserve basic civil and political rights, democracy and the rule of law. This is a more inclusive definition than one restricted to citizens of the European Union. It extends human rights, at least in theory, to all citizens of the member states of the Council of Europe. Therefore, promoting these rights and values should be seen as central to the project of educating for a common European citizenship. Indeed, member states have an obligation to promote knowledge and understanding of the content of the European Convention on Human Rights (ECHR) and its significance both for national communities and individual citizens[1]. The single idea underpinning the Convention is the belief in the inviolability of human dignity which is to affirm that, irrespective of people's legal rights as citizens, they possess a number of fundamental moral rights as human beings. Therefore teaching about human rights must be complemented with teaching which encourages respect for those rights and the social mechanisms which embody them. This inevitably raises several important pedagogical issues which we discuss in the first half of this chapter, outlining the principles on which we have tried to base our curriculum development work. In the second half, we offer some practical examples of how we have attempted to apply these principles in practice.

The Pedagogy of Human Rights Education

Firstly, we think it important to distinguish human rights per se from the international codes. Not all human rights breaches encountered in daily life contravene international law nor are all of the rights in the international conventions immediately relevant for school students. Therefore, it is important that human rights education (HRE) is not overly constrained by the language, form or the content of the international codes. Some published materials for young children have presented human rights as simplified versions of the international codes. In one exercise of this type, for example, children are asked to match certain statements of rights, with their corresponding number in the ECHR and, in another, they look at pictures to identify the appropriate human right (such as matching a picture of a bus with the right to travel). We question the value of such exercises because they fail to help children understand the real meaning of these rights in their human context. This can lead to 'disembedded' thinking about rights, divorced from any moral obligations, purpose or context - and human rights are never encountered in this form.

Human rights education should aim to influence behaviour and promote students' moral development. Both Piaget[2] and Kohlberg[3] identified the development of moral cognition as a shift from externally imposed behavioural norms to internally generated moral norms. Young children, on this account, understand rights to be entitlements embodied in rules and laws, rather than morality.

As they grow older, they should be encouraged to see that these norms have intrinsic value and thus to internalise them. Human rights teaching should promote the view that violating the rights of others is not wrong because it is against international law, but that it is against international law because it is wrong. Kohlberg claimed that techniques such as perspective taking, role play, and discussion of moral conflicts (for example, when one right is in tension with another) encourage progress towards moral maturity. Other writers, such as Gibbs[4] and Hoffman[5] have suggested that empathy development should also be regarded as an equally important component of moral growth. Human rights education should therefore be characterised by an integration of both cognitive and affective approaches, because whilst it is undoubtedly the case that by means of cognitive processes one becomes more empathically aware, it is equally true that unless there is a basic empathic response towards other people, then there is little motivation to act positively in support of their rights.

Attention must be paid both to the form and the knowledge content of human rights courses. We believe that the formal content of a human rights curriculum should be determined by a combination of factors and should attempt to answer the question: what light can be thrown on issues of rights, responsibilities and justice in view of pupils' existing social understanding and their present circumstances and needs? We developed a matrix of sociomoral concepts which provides a focus for much of the formal content of our material and this is described in more detail in the second section. Integrated into this knowledge/content model is a concern that the methodology must be equally consistent with these concepts in that it should respect students' rights, and demonstrate, or model, a concern for justice and democracy. If the maintenance of democracy is an aim of the ECHR, then education for European citizenship will be most effective when it promotes democratic discourse in the classroom. Democratic discourse not only assumes the existence of value pluralism, it embraces it as contingent on the fundamental right to freedom of belief and expression. Citizens differ radically as to the kind of society they wish to advance.

Democracy is not about abandoning or suppressing these differences, but about providing an optimum framework within which these competing social goals can co-exist. It assumes a willingness to use reason and argumentation to resolve the tensions between competing interests and ideals and we believe it is not too strong to claim that schools are the primary location for the development of democratic dispositons. Recent research into the nature of talk in the classroom is relevant here. Mercer[6], for example, has identified three kinds of talk in which school children regularly engage. The first is disputational talk, in which speakers are intent on winning the argument at all costs. This implies diversity but non connectedness. The second kind of talk is cumulative in which the talk is inter-active and cooperative but avoids conflict in case the (superficial) harmony of the group is threatened. Mercer calls the third and most complex kind of talk exploratory. This is characterised by the willingness of the participants to engage in the joint construction of meaning and to expose their own and others' reasoning to critical scrutiny. In this way, a new synthesis is achieved which would not have been otherwise possible. Exploratory talk implies a diversity which does not threaten the unity of the group but rather strengthens it. Teachers can begin to foster exploratory talk of this kind even with pupils in the early years but should recognise that it requires practice and reinforcement at all levels of education.

Talk is vital for the exploration of one's own and others' opinions. In a pluralist society young people cannot avoid moral conflict, a major source of which is what Heater has called multiple citizenship[7]. Individuals are members (citizens) of many different communities based on the family, ethnicity, religion, culture and nationality each demanding some measure of loyalty. Where these are in tension, serious conflicts can result, all too often accompanied by major human rights abuses. Education for human rights and European citizenship helps pupils come to terms with value pluralism such that they can feel themselves simultaneously members of a family and cultural group as well as citizens of the state and the international community. However, research suggests that teachers often find it difficult to promote the kinds of activity necessary for this level of reflective engagement. Woods[8], for example, found that teachers' questions are overwhelmingly directive and provide little opportunity for genuine reflection. He quotes one study in which the average pause after a question was found to be one second but when teachers lengthened the pause to three seconds (still a very short time), the amount of student response doubled. And when teachers shifted from a didactic mode of speech to a more reflective one, pupils' responses began to be correspondingly more thoughtful. Many other techniques can be used to improve the quality of discussion. Even the seating arrangements can impact on pupil interaction. Arranging chairs in a circle, for example, can make it easier to encourage all members of the group to contribute.

To sum up, we believe that human rights education should be offered to children at all levels of schooling but in a planned and systematic way, culminating in teaching about human rights as both universal moral norms and as international legal codes. Ideally, this requires a good level of coordination between teachers in primary and secondary schools to achieve an effective and systematic progression. Factual knowledge and conceptual understanding should be developed in tandem with skills of critical and moral reasoning. Moral conflict generated by the contested nature of human rights concepts, should be utilised to promote greater self-understanding and increase respect for the beliefs of others and the democratic processes. In the section that follows we describe some approaches we have developed to introduce human rights concepts into curriculum materials for both primary and secondary schools.

Some Examples of Approaches to Human Rights Issues in School

Human Rights Teaching in Primary Schools: In 1994, the Citizenship Foundation published a pack of teaching materials for primary schools (age 5-11) entitled 'You, Me, Us!, social and moral responsibility for primary schools'[9].

The pack mainly uses the medium of story to focus on a wide range of social and moral issues which the children are likely to encounter, including the right to be tree from violence, the right to be heard, the right to be free from arbitrary punishment and discrimination, the right to participate in community governance and the right to freedom of conscience. This material stresses the importance of discussion and reflective thinking, even for the youngest pupils. It emphasises the need for all students to develop confidence in expressing their viewpoint. The pedagogical model employed integrates the influential approach of the Philosophy for Children movement of Matthew Lipman[10] with Kohlbergian moral stage theory. Through the medium of story, it is possible to address both cognitive and affective aspects of human rights issues as they are embedded within situations familiar to the children. The teacher, acting as facilitator rather than the source of moral truth, uses a range of prompts designed principally to extend the children's individual and collective thinking. But the material is not only skills-based. In terms of knowledge and understanding there is a very clear framework provided by a number of key social, moral or political concepts, especially, rights, responsibilities, justice (fairness), rules, laws, equality, diversity, power, authority, democracy, and community. Material is provided to enable teachers to deal with these concepts in Key Stage 1 (age 5-7) and again, in greater complexity in key stage 2 (8-11 years) on a spiral curriculum basis[11].

One example of how the materials bring out human rights issues in Key Stage 1 is a story called 'A Friend for Farouk'. This is based on a true incident in which Farouk, aged six and newly arrived with his family from Africa, finds it impossible to make friends in his new school.

He is at last befriended by another new boy, Lenny, who comes from a family of gypsies. Lenny, too, is ostracised but is also subjected to racist taunts. For a while, the two boys are able to support each other but, unfortunately for Farouk, Lenny's family moves on, leaving Farouk alone again. Only then do the other children come to feel sorry for Farouk and realise that he needs friendship and respect, just as they do. The story offers the opportunity for the teacher to explore different kinds of prejudice and stereotyping and to challenge the children's thinking about common practices such as name-calling.

It is not essential to present young children only with situations relating to their immediate environment. For this pack, for example, we devised a light-hearted historical story about the captain and crew of a sailing ship who are wrecked on a desert island. The captain is incompetent but cruel, ruling the ship by fear. The shipwreck provides the opportunity for the crew to challenge his authority and a successful bloodless mutiny results. This presents the crew with a number of problems to consider, such as how to organise themselves, how to deal with the deposed captain and how to distribute the resources belonging to the group and some treasure which is discovered. Using this story, teachers can engage the children in discussing a range of very important rights issues, including the captain's wrongful treatment of the crew, the issue of what would be a just punishment for the captain, and whether the crew should be organised on a democratic basis now that the old authoritarian leadership has been deposed. Presented in this way, the issues are simple to understand but complex in nature and children will debate them vigorously and in surprising depth[12].

Teachers have found that regular use of this material, and the reinforcement of appropriate techniques, brings a rapid and noticeable improvement in the quality of the children's discussion as they grow in confidence that they can express themselves freely in a non-judgemental atmosphere.

Human Rights Issues in the Secondary Curriculum: At the secondary level (years 7 - 13), we have developed a series of books on the role and function of law in society. Human rights issues arise as an integral part of introducing students to their legal rights and duties and the working of the UK systems of justice and democracy[13]. The same key concepts provide a framework for the organisation of knowledge as were used in the primary materials, with particular emphasis in this series on justice, rights, responsibilities and law. Through discussion, group work, role play and other methods, the same kind of 'critical, democratic thinking' is encouraged. The materials raise issues such as children's (and parents') rights, the right to own property, to be free from discrimination, the right to the due process of law and so on. Whilst students gain knowledge of the law and their rights, they are encouraged, at the same time, to adopt a critical stance, constantly reviewing them in the light of the justice concept[14].

Education for democracy should constantly return to the idea that 'law' is not monolithic or immutable, that it is fallible, is often in need of change, that it can be unjust, and also, in an international context, that it may from time to time be in breach of the European Convention on Human Rights.

The law provides a very useful framework for the teaching of controversial human rights issues, such as abortion and discrimination. Teachers may well find themselves criticised from some quarters for promoting human rights but there are few grounds on which to object to teaching about the law. One sensitive area, for example, is the extent of parental control over their children. In a unit dealing with children's rights, two real cases are used as starting points, one concerning a baby abandoned at a railway station and the second involving a boy of eleven who was confined to his room by his mother and stepfather as a virtual prisoner, deprived of love and human comforts. Students are asked to discuss what they believe to be the reasonable limits of parental control in the context of the idea that children too have rights and become increasingly able to think and act for themselves. Specific reference is made at this point, to the development of the United Nations Convention on the Rights of the Child as an aspirational statement for all the world's children and students are asked to decide which of these they believe to be the most important. They are also asked to examine which of these rights were neglected in the cases mentioned and which might be being ignored in their own society. In this way, the unit clearly differentiates between rights embodied in operational legal codes and aspirational rights yet to be enforced.

The importance of context is again recognised in another exercise called 'The Islanders', a simulation based on the history of the early colonisation of Tasmania. Students are asked to take on the roles of the indigenous population and a group of European settlers who arrive on the island in search of a new life. The two groups have widely differing cultural values and, inevitably, many conflicts arise over rights issues such as the ownership of land, the treatment of the environment and property rights. The situation is complicated by the imbalance of power between the two groups. Students are provided with a series of hypothetical disputes which arise and to which there are two sides. After considering the issues amongst their own people, they role play a meeting with the 'enemy' to attempt to resolve the problems peacefully. This is far from easy, since the beliefs and values of the groups differ so markedly and there is a total lack of mutual understanding. Following this part of the exercise, students are asked to develop a set of rules which might help prevent the future outbreak of war. This demonstrates the need for a supra-national code of minimum rights as a bulwark against oppression and injustice. In the role play, students often find ways of coming to 'reasonable' agreements especially when they believe this is what the teacher expects. However, we felt it to be essential to refer back to the historical situation when the white settlers, in fact, had no intention of making concessions.

Students sensitised to the issues by the role play, are often appalled to learn of the genocide which took place when the Aboriginal population was systematically eliminated and few voices were raised against it. This is a successful example of human rights knowledge being integrated with moral reasoning and empathy work.

The above unit can demonstrate why the international human rights codes are necessary but at the other end of the spectrum it is important to show how apparently trivial issues can also throw up matters of fundamental importance. This idea is at the heart of a unit we developed focusing on life in school. As part of this work, we introduced the famous **Campbell and Cozans (1982)** case in which the British Government was challenged over its support for corporal punishment. A child's parents refused, on grounds of conscience, to allow their son to be beaten with a leather strap. The boy was suspended from school and, eventually, the European Court of Human Rights was asked to adjudicate. In this exercise, students are supplied with the facts of the case and the wording of the relevant texts (Article 3 against degrading treatment and Protocol 1.2 protecting parents' religious and moral beliefs). Their task is to judge for themselves what the Court should decide. Only after this, are they provided with the Court's ruling, which in fact went in favour of the parents and eventually led to the banning of corporal punishment in all UK state schools. This example demonstrates how useful real cases can be in teaching students in an understandable way, about the mechanisms of appeal to the European Court.

We were aware that this issues-based approach does not set out a coherent explanation of the origin of the human rights instruments themselves and we therefore developed a 'reference' unit, which attempts to define the meaning of the term human right and explains, briefly, the historical context out of which the European Convention arose. To do this, we first of all asked students to categorise a list of statements, such as 'killing is wrong' or 'people should be able to marry whom they choose', according to whether they should apply in all cases, most cases or some cases. This is a small group exercise and through a process of discussion and elimination, there emerges in each an agreed (or sometimes contested) set of fundamental values not unlike the ECHR. The difficulty of classification allows discussion of the fact that few of these rights apply universally with no exceptions whatever. This exercise is then followed with information about Hitler's regime in which the law itself was used progressively to limit the rights and freedoms of the Jews prior to the Holocaust itself. Students consider these restrictions in the light of their own list of basic human rights, after which they are presented with a simplified list of the main articles of the Universal Declaration and the ECHR which were developed partly to try to prevent such gross events from ever recurring.

We have made the claim in this chapter that human rights issues are best treated contextually for a number of important reasons. One objection to this may be that this approach results in piecemeal treatment of human rights and only partial coverage of some essential issues.

There is, of course, some weight in this argument particularly when more complex issues need to be addressed. This is why, for senior students, we are currently preparing materials which require a more in-depth study of some of the major human rights issues facing Europe as a democratic community. In this project, the main focus is on the key democratic rights enshrined in the European Convention

– freedom of conscience, belief, expression, the due process of law and protection of privacy. Using examples from all over Europe which have come before the European Court of Human Rights, the materials attempt to show how cases dealt with at national and international level arise from the experience of ordinary citizens. The right of an individual to petition the European Court was a profoundly important innovation for international law and has now been used by countless citizens of Europe. For example, we refer to the case of **Kokkinakis v Greece**, where the Court of Human Rights decided that Greek courts had violated the right of freedom of thought, conscience and religion by forbidding Kokkinakis, a Jehovah's Witness, to spread his beliefs. Other cases will be used to demonstrate the Court upholding citizens' rights to privacy against the British and French governments. In addition, using cases brought under Article 14, the whole area of discrimination will be examined. One exercise asks students to consider which groups in their own societies they think are included or excluded from a given list of freedoms. These range from freedoms which are determined to a large extent by the state, e.g. slavery and torture, to those which might be influenced by family and culture such as the freedom to marry whom you choose.

Teachers using this material will be encouraged to explore ways in which each of the rights dealt with by international law, also translates into more local, and possibly culturally specific, issues. For example, issues such as minority rights, must be applied to local contexts if they are to have any impact on students' attitudes or behaviour. At this level, students should also learn about governments' powers of derogation by which they can avoid bringing their domestic legislation in line with the ECHR. Students need to understand how and why this can happen and the means by which the Court has dealt with it. There is clearly a tension between the notion of inalienable human rights protected by supra-national law and the idea that the same law can support a country in opting out of certain obligations. It is important that older students understand the limits of the European Convention's powers and the political and economic realities which can stand in the way of the realisation of human rights in many societies.

In so many ways, the notion of European citizenship and a common European culture is a distant and difficult one for young people to grasp. We have argued that, taught sensitively, a human rights approach offers teachers an important yet manageable and interesting way forward. By showing how it has adopted a common standard of human rights, even as an 'ideal', Europe can more easily be shown as a developing entity. Defined in this way, education for European citizenship is inseparable from education for democracy and, indeed, from education for global citizenship.

Endnotes

1   Starkey, H. (1992): Back to Basic Values: education for justice and peace in the world *Journal of Moral Education*, vol. 21, no. 3, pp, 185-192.

2   Piaget, J. (1932): *The Moral Judgement of the Child* (London: Routledge & Kegan Paul)

3   Kohlberg, L. (1984): *The Psychology of Moral Development*, (New York, Harper and Row).

4   Gibbs, J. (1991): Toward an Integration of Kohlberg's and Hoffman's Moral Development. *Human Development*, vol. 34, pp. 88-104.

5   Hoffman, M.L. (1976): Empathy, role taking, guilt and development of altruistic motives, in Lickona, (ed.) *Moral Development: current theory and research* (New York: Holt, Rinehart and Winston Ed.)

6   G Mercer, N. (1995): *The Guided Construction of Knowledge: talk amongst teachers and learners.* (Clevedon: Multilingual Matters.)

7   Heater, D. (1990): *Citizenship: the civic ideal in world history, politics and education,* (Harlow: Longman.)

8 Woods, D. (1991): Aspects of Teaching and Learning, in Light, P./Sheldon, S./Woodhead, M., (eds.) *Learning to Think*. (London: Routledge).

9 Rowe, D. and Newton, J. (1994): *You, Me, Us!, Social and Moral Responsibility for Primary Schools*, (London: The Home Office).

10 Lipman, M./Sharp, A.M./Oscanyan, F.S. (1980): *Philosophy in the Classroom* (Philadelphia: Temple University Press).

11 Bruner, J. (1968): *Towards a Theory of Instruction*, (New York: Norton).

12 Costello, P., (1995) Education, Citizenship and Critical Thinking, *Early Child Development and Care*, vol. 107, pp. 105-114.

13 Rowe, D. and Thorpe, T. (Eds.) (1989): *Understand the Law*, (2nd ed.) Vols. 1-4 (London: Hodder and Stoughton); Rowe, D. and Thorpe, T. (Eds.) (1993): *Living with the Law*, Vols. 1-3 (London: Hodder and Stoughton).

14 Rowe, D. (1993): Law-related Education: an overview; in Lynch, J. and Modgil, C. and Modgil S., (Eds.) *Human Rights, Education and Global Responsibilities* (London: Falmer).

TOWARDS THE EUROPE SCHOOL: EDUCATING EUROPEAN CITIZENS THROUGH WHOLE SCHOOL DEVELOPMENT

CHAPTER 10

Gordon H. Bell

Background

Euro-citizenship, Euro-curriculum, Euro-schools - reality or illusion? The Europe Schools project in Hesse, Germany is well on the way to providing some clues.

The Land of Hesse centred in Frankfurt with an administrative core at Wiesbaden is a most prosperous area. Launched in September 1992, the project experience of the first five Europe Schools (EUROPE SCHOOLS) with an associated network of 14 EUROPE SCHOOLS including one primary, offers an insight into the prospects of a Euro-curriculum and the notion of European citizenship which would underpin it.

Unlike England and Wales which attempted educational reform by defining a structure of approved knowledge units backed by a system of surveillance and control through inspection, the EUROPE SCHOOLS project built on existing practice by highlighting five principles:

- *Intercultural and International education.* Staff exchange and pupil mobility schemes, foreign cultures integral to the curriculum

- *Extra curricular lessons* extending pastoral care, satisfying interests, and helping to find future jobs
- *Co-operation with the community* making them a centre of activity and the community supporting their aims
- *Reformpedagogik* featuring self determined methods of learning
- *Ecological education* as a subject facing the challenges of today's society

Commenting on the formation of this programme, Schwarz[1] identifies certain influences on German society: the Treaty of Maastricht including the removal of trade barriers, the effects of re-unification and breakdown of communist regimes in Eastern Europe, the migration of millions of workers into Germany over three decades resulting in a multi-cultural school population, the eruption of nationalist hatred focused upon 300,000 people migrating into Germany each year at a time of rising unemployment, and changes to child rearing practices modifying the traditional pattern of mother staying at home supported by a school system with lessons in the mornings only and with teachers trained principally for a didactic approach to teaching subjects in secondary schools. Finally, growing awareness of ecological damage to the environment caused teachers as well as parents and the Ministry of Education in Hesse to stress the importance of environmental education in the school curriculum.

The land government of 1991 (a coalition of Social Democrats and the Greens) was responsible for devising the EUROPE SCHOOLS programme and was re-elected in 1995 adding a further 3 EUROPE SCHOOLS and extending the associated EUROPE SCHOOLS network.

The first five EUROPE SCHOOLS were chosen from a list of 50 applicants. The selected schools ranged in size from 780 to 1,936 pupils. Three had advanced courses (sixth forms) ranging from 140 to 266 pupils. All were comprehensive schools able to convince

Ministry officials that they would achieve success after a developmental period of four years. The criteria applied in their selection related to each of the five principles and culminated in an agreement to fund facilities for lunch, afternoon courses, and to support exchange programmes.

The present account of their origins, development and effectiveness brings together a number of considerations relevant to being and becoming a European citizen. The EUROPE SCHOOLS represent one of the few examples of a whole school approach being taken to implementing the provisions of the EC Resolution of Ministers of Education of May 24 1988 on 'Giving Greater Emphasis to the European Dimension in Education' (Commission of the European Countries 1988). Whilst every member State was required to have such a policy prior to the Treaty of Maastricht, very few, if any, have identified this as a priority for school development subsequently. The gap between official satisfaction about what has been achieved and unofficial surveys[2] stands as a stark reminder of the gap between policy and practice.

The importance of the EC Resolution of 1988 in providing a definition of European citizenship is demonstrated both by the consensus of opinion amongst EU Ministers of Education it represents and through its provisions having been accepted by the wider Europe via member states of the Council of Europe. Moreover, in the case of Germany, an operational definition has been added which specifies the knowledge, skills and attitudes of the German pupil qua Euro-citizen and does so very explicitly in the following terms:

> The process of European integration challenges Europeans to see their national history and traditions in a new light, to appreciate other people's perspectives, to be tolerant, to express solidarity and to practice co-existence with people who speak different languages and have other customs. Europeans must recognise the responsibility for freedom,

peace, justice and social balance placed in their hands - above all with regard to the developing countries.

Turning to the application of these political principles in schools, the following policy guidelines are provided:

European Awareness as a Pedagogical Assignment of the School. The school has the task of making the European peoples and countries aware of the integration process and the realignment of their relations. It is intended to make a contribution towards developing awareness of European identity and fostering understanding of the fact that in many spheres of our lives European terms of reference apply and that European decisions are necessary.

In order to realise this European dimension in teaching and education, the school has to convey knowledge and views on:

- the geographical diversity of the European region as a result of its natural, social and economic structures
- the political and social structures of Europe
- the formative historical forces in Europe, above all the development of the European views on law, the state and freedom
- the patterns of development, features and evidence of what is despite its variety a common European culture
- the multi-lingual nature of Europe its inherent cultural wealth, the history of the European idea and the attempts at integration since 1945
- the harmonisation of interest and joint action in Europe towards solving economic, ecological, social and political problems
- the tasks and working methods of European institutions

The basic values of state, social and individual life on which the teaching and educational aims of the school orient themselves must be seen in their relationship to life in the European community of peoples and states. This involves:

- the willingness to reach understanding so as to overcome prejudice and to be able to recognise mutual interests whilst at the same time affirming European diversity
- an open-minded attitude to culture which transcends cultural borders yet preserves individual cultural identity
- respect for the values of European legal commitments and the administration of justice within the framework of human rights recognised in Europe
- the ability to coexist as neighbours and the willingness to make compromises regarding the realisation of the different interests in Europe, even when this involves sacrifice for the benefit of others
- support for freedom, democracy, human rights, justice and economic security
- the will to maintain peace in Europe and throughout the world[3]

I have attempted to express these matters in some detail to demonstrate that definitions of the European Dimension do exist and that these provide a grounded interpretation of European citizenship. Against critics who claim 'We don't know what we mean' we can show that we do indeed have definitions at a prescriptive level as expressed through official validation of central concepts; we do have operational evaluations of the European dimension in action particularly in the case studies reported in the 'Europe in the Primary School Project'(1982-88), amongst others; and we have a commitment to implementation of key concepts in the case of the EUROPE SCHOOLS[4].

The main aim of this contribution therefore is to present an interim account of the notion of becoming a European citizen by evaluating the experience of Europe Schools. The main hope is to stimulate critical scrutiny of some provisional outcomes in order to test the rhetoric and reality of European citizenship values in action.

Evaluating Europe Schools

The theoretical and practical background to the evaluation approach is rooted in collaborative action research. This approach has been tested through a network of projects over the past twenty years. These projects led to the development of teaching materials[5] which were based upon a conceptual model emerging from teacher based action research in eight member states of the EU (see Fig 1).

The role of evaluator evolved from an invited proposal following a conference on the European Dimension in Education jointly organised by the author with the Department of Elementary Education, University of Crete, Greece in 1992. During this conference, Hesse Ministry officials gave an account of the launch of the EUROPE SCHOOLS concept and heard at first hand how teachers in other member states had evaluated their teaching in developing a European Dimension in their schools.

The proposed evaluation model was grounded in concepts of process consultancy[6], action research[7] and collaborative action inquiry[8]. The notion of 'consultant evaluator' which formed the basis of the proposal (assessed jointly by the schools and Ministry officials) culminated in my appointment in August 1993. The evaluation contract essentially defined a relationship in which there was to be a joint intention to manage change with a view to improvement.

The central aim of bringing about worthwhile innovation through systematic collaboration meant:

- pursuing structural rather than marginal change
- encouraging resource use to sustain both immediate and self maintained growth
- using what is known to inform decision making

- maximising opportunities for the transfer of professional knowledge and experience
- making ethical and staff development issues explicit
- promoting objectivity through procedures for evaluating and validating outcomes
- seeking multiplier effects; clarifying role relations to minimise conflict

Such aspirations meant in turn that judgements would have to be made by those who took part, namely that change with a view to improvement was desired, that a critical level of dissatisfaction with the status quo had been reached, that efforts will or had been made to ensure quality and clarity of vision about some future state, that the possibility of proposed changes had been calculated, and that the costs both material and psychological would be less than the benefits[9].

The quality of these judgements made jointly by the evaluator and participants would be governed by an ethical code and be validated through criteria adapted from Lincoln and Guba's[10] account of naturalistic inquiry:

- credibility - judgements must be believable by those competent to assess the appropriateness of actions and the validity of claims
- transferability - judgements must make possible the exchange of evaluated experience and provide considered conclusions based upon the evidence presented
- dependability - judgements must be trustworthy through being grounded in evidence gathered by reliable procedures
- judgements must be capable of being scrutinised for absence of bias by making the evidence clear and methods of analysis explicit

The process of action, reflection and evaluation selected to systematically promote these types of judgements was collaborative action research following a long tradition developed from Kurt Lewin's pioneering efforts in the USA during the 1940's.

Collaborative Action Research

The concept of action research has been applied to a variety of settings including community relations, organisation development, and in recent years in the UK to teacher training. The main characteristics are that it:

- investigates everyday problems experienced by teachers
- deepens teachers' understanding (diagnosis) of their problems
- provides easily understood explanations
- generates evidence validated by dialogue between participants
- requires an ethical framework for the collection, use and release of data[11].

The action research model and the underlying processes that informed the approach to evaluation which EUROPE SCHOOLS project staff adopted are outlined in Figure 2. The proposed benefits of engaging with these processes can be summarised as ensuring that the evaluation strategy would be:

Formative: the knowledge gained through the investigation is fed back continuously to the project teams

Participatory: high priority is given to increasing the capacity of project participants (including teachers, pupils and parents) to evaluate and reflect upon their own practice

Consultative: the evaluator acts as a resource to project participants on problems and issues arising from the Europe Schools policy in practice

Practitioner Knowledge and Experience Based: the action of the project is progressively informed by knowledge and experience produced by participants' own enquiries, provided by evaluator feedback, and created through experience exchange with other participants

Supportive by giving access to the multi-lateral European Citizenship project (and similar projects running in parallel) with a view to enhancing the resources available to project schools

EUROPE SCHOOLS: An Interim Evaluation

This review reports on the first three years experience of the Europe school concept and focuses mainly on the five original EUROPE SCHOOLS (eight since September 1995). The account provided is based on six reports formally presented to the schools and to the client (Ministry of Education) between 1993 and 1996. Whilst the reported outcomes attempt to be an accurate portrayal of some main trends and issues, the selection of material is entirely my own.

At an official level, the evaluation outcomes up to 1995-96 have been acknowledged to have achieved the following aims:

- The eight EUROPE SCHOOLS co-operated together systematically

- Promoted dialogue with a variety of agencies including the 'outer network' schools

- Encouraged the structured transfer of evaluated experience amongst an 'inner network' of co-ordinators

- Installed a data capture system to secure the conditions for judgements to be grounded in evidence

- Provided training in the management of change and practitioner research

- Gained acceptance of the requirements for developing a 'site study' at each school to facilitate dissemination of evaluated experience

- Enabled the establishment of a European Network of schools in the EU countries and in countries of Middle and Eastern Europe

- Raised awareness amongst staff, pupils parents and the wider community of the concept of an ES

(Source: Hessisches Kultusministerium Evaluation 1996-98, 2 April 1996)

The history of these interim outcomes was predictably turbulent, especially bearing in mind the difficulties of language barriers to be overcome as a precondition of co-operation. (English was adopted as the main alternative vehicle of communication for project development purposes).

The initial 'unfreezing' stage in the move from the schools as they were to becoming Europe Schools was highlighted in the first of a series of evaluation reports in October 1993. Entitled 'Ten Critical Questions', it identified issues emerging from the first six months of the evaluation process in which the techniques and conditions for action research based teaching were being installed. The report was perceived as provocative and testing, but was nevertheless viewed in a positive spirit - 'Love with severity' as St. Augustine expresses the disciplines of fraternal relations!

The ten 'critical questions' posed can be summarised as follows:

1. Have pupils (and their teachers) had access to the Europe School concept? Central Problem: Mission Drift

2. Is there innovation without change? Central Problem: Paper Tigers

3. Can certain principles be afforded? Central Problem: Over ambitious planning

4. Is a Europe School two, three or more schools in one? Central Problem: 'Soft money' failing to transform the curriculum

5. Who controls the success of a Europe School? Central Problem: Radical content: Conservative structures

6. What is the European Dimension of a Europe Schools? Central Problem: What is this thing called 'Europe' amongst the five principles that don't specify it?

7. How are the focal points of innovation in Europe Schools to be integrated? Central Problem: Developing the weakest whilst maintaining the best

8. In order that genuine alternatives are developed, have needs been identified in relation to evidence and to what extent have wants been neglected? Central Problem: Defining alternative curricular needs and cross checking against pupil/parent wants

9. What steps need to be taken in primary schools? Central Problem: Restricting innovation to one level

10. How might internal and external project coherence be achieved? Central Problem: Implementing whole school development policies and networking outcomes

In my judgement, it was this last issue that was the most immediate concern. Accordingly, a project management structure was defined in which school based planning groups were formed to include the head teacher and key staff and a nominated co-ordinator who would act as liaison link between the planning group and myself and the Ministry-based project director.

These then were some of the initial barriers to be overcome in developing European citizens. The parallel focus of training key staff and supporting them in becoming change agents was begun through the five EUROPE SCHOOLS' co-ordinators taking part in the EC workshop on 'Citizenship Values and the European Dimension'[12].

One year later in September 1994, the Final Evaluation Report (validated by both schools and Ministry participants) recorded some summary recommendations arising from the three questions: Where are we now? Where do we want to be? How do we get there?

The evaluation style was not without its critics at this stage. For example, certain head teachers would have welcomed more statements about their individual schools. This was resisted on the grounds that allotted evaluation resources prevented this approach and in any event would have created tendencies towards a divisive climate both between schools who would seek to compete, and between researchers, schools and the Ministry who would have required wholly independent access to school activities and produced reports without reference to staff or parents.

This challenge and its response helped to underline the collective possibilities arising from innovation at multiple sites and gave rise one year later to the concept of an 'Ideal Type Europe School' (described later). Notwithstanding these reservations, it was becoming clear that the objective of becoming a self evaluating institution in which values were not only transmitted but systematically appraised was becoming a reality - at least amongst the planning group of key staff.

The central intention was, and still remains, to create the conditions under which evidence would be provided to support claims each EUROPE SCHOOL would itself make about its capacity to fulfil the objectives of the five principles and through them to effectively develop European citizens.

Even at a relatively early stage, the quality of dialogue between the five EUROPE SCHOOLS was such that they were able to identify the main outcomes of their change efforts and express them in a structured form through adoption of a group evaluation technique[13]. Repeated use of the same technique has yielded comparative data sufficient to track progress over the period of innovation and has provided a systematic account of the consensus of evaluated experience.

One should perhaps pause for reflection here and ask whether *any* five schools in any region of the E.U. would be able to satisfy the rigours of such a challenge, to appraise their strengths and weaknesses - not simply in the 'protected' categories of the conventional curriculum; eg language, science, mathematics, - but on the kinds of ethos indicators that produce educated persons (as evidenced in the five EUROPE SCHOOLS' principles) and moreover do so publicly! In short, in developing European citizens, should we not be concerned to produce performance league tables on the basis of a school's attested contribution to peace and security, tolerance and international understanding, ecological awareness and intercultural knowledge, skills and attitudes to note but some of the key categories implied by the ES concept?

This digression is meant to illustrate the radical dynamics of the process engaged in by the Europe schools in Hesse. It should not be taken for granted that such commitments were easily achieved, and there is a continuing effort particularly towards increasing the participation levels achieved amongst staff, pupils, and parents both in the process and the outcomes.

By September 1995, the evaluation evidence provided a set of issues from which hypotheses about the process of developing European citizens could be derived and this data led to certain summary recommendations:

To Ministry -

- Give greater emphasis to consultancy and training role
- Focus on strengthening European Dimension
- Facilitate development planning on whole school basis
- Establish an EUROPE SCHOOLS schools network

To Schools -

- Consolidate and maintain those activities that meet agreed objectives for 1994-95
- Re-examine allocation of resources to do fewer things with increased rigour

- Release more time for in-house training particularly for co-ordinators/planning groups
- Review resources for supporting the European dimension on a whole school basis
- Review information/communications technology strategy
- Use the evaluation data to inform decision making and policy development

Six months later in March 1995, an Interim Evaluation Report was produced in the form of a checklist to planning groups on the progress made on the five key principles. Responses were used to construct an Action Plan to guide the collective development of the EUROPE SCHOOLS in the years ahead.

The Final Evaluation Report for 1994/95 processed the resulting data together with other sources of evidence arising from the pattern of visits and group evaluation meetings over the year as a whole. The results of this analysis is described in what follows.

Developing European Citizens Through Europe Schools

Implementing the five EUROPE SCHOOLS principles had presented a formidable challenge in their management. By September 1995 four out of five schools had established between three and five task groups each to take special responsibility for implementing the necessary changes.

The agreement to conduct in house, teacher based evaluation studies resulted in two schools conducting them in five key areas, two schools in one to three areas, and one school had carried out studies in five to ten key areas. All five schools had conducted them in at least two areas. The uses to which evaluation studies were to be put both within and across EUROPE SCHOOLS was acknowledged to be an important factor in the process of curriculum reform.

All five schools developed a mission statement reflecting the five EUROPE SCHOOLS principles. Their relation to development plans and the Governing Body still require further clarification. The process of developing policy statements and action plans by task groups had however been successfully completed in two schools. In three schools, this was ongoing with a target completion date of January 1996.

All five schools confirmed their intention to have a medium term development plan for the European Dimension formally adopted by the end of 1995. In order to install a development planning process in the school to manage change effectively, it was accepted as desirable to have a medium term, whole school development plan (1994/97) in place for all key areas and an action plan managed by a task group relating to the year ahead (1995/96) in each one.

Four out of five schools claimed that they had identified performance indicators in order to determine how distinctive their own success had been. They were at this stage too general. However, the process of developing more specific, measurable (or verifiable), achievable, relevant and time related success criteria was accepted as necessary and the results of the schools' subsequent deliberations are presented below:

EUROPE SCHOOLS Performance Indicators

School A (875 pupils)

Performance Indicator Data

1. Number of afternoon activities: 34
2. Number of pupils attending afternoon activities: 529/week
3. Number of Partner Schools: 9
4. Number of Exchange Programmes: 5
5. Number of link activities: 6
6. Number of community based activities:
   - community activities: 6
   - community workshops: 9
   - co-operation with different partners: 53
   - regular co-operative projects: 12
7. Number of work placements: 125
8. Parental survey data: outcomes of questionnaire
9. Local community partners: 20
10. Sponsorship and external funding:
    mainly by Förderverein and parents' fees
11. Public relations:
    a) press articles: 16
    b) commemorative publications (96 p.): 1
    c) school documentation (400 p.): 1
    d) TV production (Open Channel Kassel):
    our school video: 1
12. Number of dissemination activities:
    a) Conferences: 8
    b) Meetings of Planning Group: 20
    c) ES information evenings: 3
    d) Network conferences: 1
    e) Visitors/visitor groups to school: 12
13. Applications for entry 1996/97: about 150 pupils
14. First destination:
    a) GO/BG(Forms 11-13): 26
    b) FOS: 40

	c) BFS	21
	d) Vocational Training	68
	e) Others	12
15.	Level of qualification awarded:	
	a) G10	28
	b) R10	70
	c) H10	12
	d) H 10/R-level	5
	e) H9	54
16.	Number of Staff Development Events and Activities	4
17.	Number of volunteer helpers	about 90
18.	Number of assistant teachers	1 (Finland)
19.	Number of university trainees (initial teacher tr.)	22
20.	Number of academic researchers	2

School B (2090 pupils)
Performance Indicator Data

1. Number of afternoon activities — 66 projects
2. Number of pupils attending afternoon courses — 978
3. Comparative examination results (over past 3 years): no data; statistic inquiries could not be made with 2.090 (!) pupils for lack of personal resources
4. Number of partner schools — 18
5. Number of link activities — 32
6. Number of exchange programmes — 10
7. Number of community based activities — 17
8. Number of work placements
   forms 9/10 (France, England) — 2
   sixth form (England) — 1
9. Parental survey data: feed-back at parent days, Schulkonferenz, parent council meetings and other bodies which cannot be recorded for lack of resources
10. Pupil satisfaction data: Largely positive feed-back from pupils' representation and teachers' reports; no specific data. Again we point out the short resources for such inquiries at our extremely big school

11. Local community partner data: see school development plan
12. Amount of sponsorship and external funding achieved: The parents as well as the 'Friends and Supporters of the School' have their own funds; they make contributions towards school events, anniversaries and project weeks. Amounts vary, and the money is always given for specific purposes so that data here are not representative
13. Public relations: At regular intervals the school publishes project results and topical information on school life in eight regional newspapers
14. Number of:
    - dissemination activities   8
    - publications   12
    - conferences and meetings   5
15. Applications for entry data:
    - Hauptschule   31
    - Realschule   108
    - Gymnasium   161
16. First destination data:
    - Hauptschule: 45 leavers, 21 of which attend training colleges, 24 start a job
    - Realschule: 121 leavers, 54 of which attend further schools, 67 start a job
    - Gymnasium: 87 leavers, 25 of which go into job training, about 62 to university
17. Resources data: Resources allocated in 1995/96 by the state of Hesse and the Main Kinzig-county follow an established distribution system; they can therefore not be used as performance indicators.
18. Completion/non completion of programmes: With a few exceptions in the afternoon options, homework supervision and support courses in particular, the activities described in chapters 1.1 and 1.3, are firmly incorporated in the school programme and are continued every year

19. Level of qualifications: Pupils' reports testify to their participation in ES projects. In some courses project leaders write 'documents' and similar evidence
20. Number of staff development events and activities   42
21. Number of volunteer helpers   32
22. Amount spent on infrastructure improvement: Partial amounts, the size of which we ignore, are included in the total costs of renovation paid by the county; data can therefore not be given
23. Equipment inventory data: Inventory lists have been made individually for all areas of the ES programme by the subject groups who use the specific equipment. Based on these individual lists an overall review is set up for each area at the end of the school year e.g. computer science, audio-visual media. These lists can be made available on request

Modifications in the light of the European Dimension to teaching and learning activities were reported to have been achieved in five schools with an average range of three to six subject activities having been modified. The development of European Dimension action plans at subject leader level with relevant success criteria identified were in the process of being formulated.

Innovation had proved to be resource intensive, especially when related to reforming teaching activities (Intercultural and Reformpedagogik) and in reconstructing teaching materials (Ecological Education and European Dimension). Three out of five schools reported that an audit of teaching resources including information technology had been carried out. It was recommended that this exercise be re-examined and independent advice sought on policy and practice for 1995/96. The issue of effective curriculum change through strategic management of the transition years and curriculum continuity policies is now on the agenda of the Europe schools. three to five schools reported they had begun to address this issue and the remainder reported an intention to do so within the timetable of their development plans.

In relation to student centred, topic based, autonomous learning (Reformpädagogik), all five schools reported that their respective Planning Groups had achieved their own level of satisfaction in pursuing an explicit policy. The Europe schools made a significant step forward in defining what they considered to be success criteria in achieving such policies and outlined 19 indicators to guide good practice in implementing key principles. The detail here offers an interesting insight into the management of the European pupil qua citizen.

What Does the School Define as Success Criteria in Achieving Reformpädagogik Policies?

- A policy statement being formulated
- Project days plus evaluation
- Project weeks
- Project activities as an accepted and welcomed form of preparing and evaluating class/group activities e.g. class trips, exchange programmes
- Teams of teachers being formed
- 3 days preparatory meeting of all new form teachers to organise and co-ordinate curriculum activities.
- A planned programme of topic work
- Explicit linkage with citizenship education
- Formation of task group
- Extension to all classes including 6th form
- Day conferences on policy with all staff involved
- Cross curricular co-operation planned in examination classes and all three branches (Hauptschule, Realschule, Gymnasium)

- Linkage with social care and social welfare - the development of 'pupil profiling' and the management of behavioural disturbances
- Approval at Schulkonferenz and Gesamtkonferenz of policy and procedures
- Group evaluation sessions conducted by teaching teams
- Buoyant pupil recruitment
- Outcomes of learning reported in records of achievement
- Linkage between format of examination and style of teaching and learning e.g. submission of project work for determining grade levels
- Fully minuted and monitored meetings of teams of teachers pursuing cross curricular work.

The EUROPE SCHOOLS are now considering the possibility of collectively developing 'best practice' statements in other areas of their activities.

Having an explicit and effective staff development policy was reported in three schools. It was recommended that this aspect be reviewed and guidelines produced during 1995/96 to secure a balance between internal and external providers and to include mobility of project staff as 'key trainers'. The notion of 'staff appraisal' was suggested as a developmental support strategy but so far has been rejected.

The development of networking based on encouraging the transfer of experience across the partner schools proved to be highly successful. All schools reported they were clear about the objectives of networking and their role in the inaugural Europe Schools Network Conference which was successfully launched in May 1995 through the organisational skills of one of the EUROPE SCHOOLS

The initiative taken by each school to hold a pre network conference meeting was an important factor in contributing to the acknowledged success of the main conference itself which was attended by 150 delegates from 14 countries.

Two out of five schools reported that they had established a clear role for parents in the development of such a network. It was recommended that the European Parents' Association be contacted to become involved and that the experience of surveying parental opinion be more widely shared as a means of keeping the EUROPE SCHOOLS on track.

All EUROPE SCHOOLS had prepared an outline action plan for the year ahead including an evaluation element for negotiation with prospective partner schools and colleagues were consulted about its content. The management of this action plan in the context of multi-lateral school partnerships will require detailed monitoring. The designation of a partnership co-ordinator in addition to the project co-ordinator was recommended and adopted. But the role of the associated network of Europe schools in Hesse requires further clarification in terms of purpose and effectiveness.

The development of the EUROPE SCHOOLS over the two years of evaluated activity were judged by co-ordinators and staff to have certain strengths and weaknesses. Their main strengths were considered to be growing understanding of the importance of action planning, increased identification with the EUROPE SCHOOLS concept by teachers, new structures taking shape, and the sharpened profile of the EUROPE SCHOOLS including the implementation of the European Dimension in subject curricula.

The main weaknesses were perceived to be continued overload amongst innovative and competent colleagues, in house teacher training being insufficient, Reformpädagogik considered to be an outsider activity, and not everyone yet being convinced of the programme.

It may be recalled that structural change in educational institutions is considered to occur in the 15-20 year range. Against this perspective, the progress made by the EUROPE SCHOOLS schools is highly satisfactory. Whilst a number of shortfalls have been identified against aspirations, the schools have strategies in place to address them and are energetic and effective in pursuing identified objectives.

Evaluating the EUROPE SCHOOLS networking strategy overall suggests that a very promising start has been made. The programme is an inspiring and ambitious one that appears to have developed a successful approach to managing the early stages of multilateral co-operation. This development is, of course, highly relevant to the aims of the recently approved EU funded Socrates programme which promotes multi-lateral partnerships as a foundation for active intercultural citizenship.

It was recommended that the future development of the EUROPE SCHOOLS network be considered in relation to eight key features;

- An EUROPE SCHOOLS Network comprised of those schools who have negotiated an action plan, exchanged a memorandum of agreement and are working within the framework of a multilateral school partnership

- A pre network conference held in May annually which brings together the co-ordinators and/or head teachers of each school in partnership

- An Associated Europe Schools Network which has a formally defined membership of schools expressing an interest in the five EUROPE SCHOOLS principles and willing to fund a delegate to attend a conference held in October each year to share experience and report progress

- A Networking Manual updated annually which sets out the criteria for EUROPE SCHOOL membership and contains documents for networking management including protocols for

action research, action planning and in house evaluation reporting
- A suite of databases established for network maintenance which is regularly updated by EUROPE SCHOOLS co-ordinators and correspondents in Associated EUROPE SCHOOLS
- A dissemination policy that meets local, national, European and international interests in the process and content of developing EUROPE SCHOOLS
- The use of a common European Awareness Audit to map pre and post network achievements amongst pupils
- An evaluation programme in support of the development of EUROPE SCHOOLS and future networking policies

In summary, the Europe Schools during 1994/95 maintained the advances made in the previous year and developed innovative and enterprising strategies to enable the changes introduced to become structurally embedded within the educational policy framework in Hesse.

Data on the current strengths and weaknesses of the EUROPE SCHOOLS (June 1996) can be gathered from a reading of the co-ordinators group evaluation which, for the first time, included the three new EUROPE SCHOOLS (established in September 1995).

Ranked Priorities:

First Round of Voting

Perceived Strengths	*Votes*	*Total*
Networking	3+5+2+1	= 11
Extension of Budget	5+5+1	= 11
Getting More Members of Staff Involved	3+1+5+2	= 11

Positive Acknowledgement by Other Länder and EU Countries	4+2+3	= 9
Planning Group Established and Working with Large Number of Staff	5+4	= 9
Implementing European Dimension	2+3+4	= 9
Improving Effectiveness of Planning Group: Intensity, Efficiency, Co-operation	4+4	= 8
Planning Group Eases Changes	4+4	= 8

Second Round of Voting

Getting More Members of Staff Involved	3+4+3+5+4+3+2+3+5	= 32
Implementing European Dimension	2+5+2+3+1+4+3+1+4	= 25
Improving Effectiveness of Planning Group: Intensity, Efficiency, Co-operation	4+5+5+1+4+3	= 22
Networking	3+2+3+2+2+5+4+1	= 22
Positive Acknowledgement by Other Länder and E.U. Countries	2+1+1+4+2+1+2+2	= 15
Extension of Budget	1+1+4+3+5	= 14
Planning Group Established and Working with Large Number of Staff	5+5	= 10
Planning Group Eases Changes	5+4+1	= 10

N=10

Ranked Priorities

Perceived Weaknesses	Votes	Total
EUROPE SCHOOLS Activities Vs. Regular Teaching	2+3+5+4+3+5	= 22
Too Many Things At One Time	4+4+1+3+4+4	= 20

Outcomes of the Financial Audit	3+2+5+5+3	= 18
Insufficient Monitoring	1+5	= 6

N=10

It will be clear from this evidence that developing European citizens is not a dilettante business. It may also be clear from a U.K. perspective just how insular schools (at least in England and Wales) are. For example how many secondary schools have any partner schools, let alone an average (across the EUROPE SCHOOLS) of 10!

And this point is crucial from the standpoint of citizenship values, for if one accepts Heater's[14] analysis that citizenship is the notion of belonging to community then the ability to identify with and sustain a community of interests and ways of life on a multilateral basis is the acid test of tolerance and of inter cultural understanding in action.

Conclusion

The EUROPE SCHOOL concept is a pioneer development and its lessons merit close scrutiny. It demonstrates what can be achieved in both mainstream and extra curricular activities from a base of professionals and volunteers who adopt a whole school approach to managing change and who are willing to engage in research based teaching and learning.

From the evaluated experience of the Europe School to date, an 'Ideal Type EUROPE SCHOOL' has emerged which claims to represent an archetypal organisation within which we might expect the development of European citizens to arise.

Whether such a specification is either necessary of sufficient is an open question. On the evidence of the Europe schools in Hesse, the criteria outlined below are acknowledged by their members to be necessary.

An *'Ideal Type EUROPE SCHOOL'* has: *A Mission Statement* reflecting the five ES principles i.e.,

Intercultural and International education activities, staff exchange and pupil mobility schemes, foreign cultures integral to the curriculum with special reference to the European Dimension of the curriculum

Extra Curricular lessons extending pastoral care, satisfying interests, and trying to find future jobs

Co-operation with the community making them a centre of activity for the community supporting their aims

Reformpedagogik featuring self determined methods of learning

Ecological education as a subject facing the challenges of today's society

A Whole School Development Plan implementing the above principles over a medium term, three year programme, endorsed by the relevant authorities and school community

A Planning Group comprised of head teacher, staff, pupils and parents who provide impetus and direction to the strategic aims of the development plan and monitors agreed performance indicators

One or more *Task Groups* comprised of staff with curricular responsibilities who devise an annual action plan to implement the five principles in key areas of delivery within the school and monitor success criteria

A commitment to and capacity for contributing to the development of *multilateral school partnerships* in order to develop joint teaching and learning activities, facilitate staff and pupil mobility programmes, and maximise the involvement of parents. A *dissemination* policy designed to facilitate the transfer of evaluated experience.

A systematic *evaluation* programme structured to promote collaborative action research within the framework of an ethical code

A capacity to provide an *Annual Review Report* to an agreed format which describes strategic aims, provides a self assessment report on activities, responds to the detail of external evaluation reports, includes an executive summary of a whole school development plan, provides a summary of the European Dimension Development Plan within it, defines an Action Plan for a Planning Group, identifies key priorities for the year ahead together with success criteria, and records performance indicator data agreed with the Governing Body relating to five central principles.

Whether such criteria for a Europe school are considered sufficient is yet to emerge. Whatever the detailed criteria may be, the notion of developing European citizens in the Europe schools of Hesse is firmly set within a rationale of knowledge-power in which the aim of enlightenment is attained through supporting both staff and pupils to change and develop through the use of reason and evaluated action. The opposite path of coercing and prematurely shaping future citizens through a regime of power-knowledge represents a contrasting model that awaits the verdict of history to supply its own evaluation.

Endnotes

1. Schwarz, W. (1995): Europe Schools, in Bell, G.H. (ed.) *Educating European Citizens: Citizenship Values and the European Dimension* (London: David Fulton Publishers).Ch. 10.

2. Ryba, R. (1995): Developing a European Dimension in the Curriculum, in Bell, G.H. (ed.), Ch. 12.

3. Standing Conference of the Ministers of Education and Cultural Affairs of the Lander of the Federal Republic of Germany (1990): *Europe in the Classroom.* (Bonn: Germany).

4. Bell, G.H. (1991): *Developing a European Dimension in Primary Schools* (London: David Fulton Publishers); Bell 1995.

5. Bell, G.H. and Dransfield, R. (1993): *Europe in the School: The School in Europe* (London: Shell Education Service).

6 Schein, E.H. (1969): *Process Consultation: Its Role in Organisation Development.* (Cambridge: Mass., Addison Wesley).

7 Elliott, J. (1991): *Action Research for Educational Change* (Milton Keynes: Open University).

8 Bell, G.H. (1990): Collaborative Consultancy through Action Inquiry in Aubrey, C. (ed.) *Consultancy in the United Kingdom, Its Role and Contribution to Educational Change* (London, The Falmer Press).

9 Bell, G.H. and Pennington, R.C. (1988): Action Learning and School Focused Study. Collected Original Resources in *Education,* vol.12, no. 3.

10 Lincoln, Y. S. and Guba, E. G. (1985): *Naturalistic Inquiry* (London: Sage Publications).

11 Elliott.

12 Bell, G.H. (ed.) (1995).

13 O'Neil, M.J. (1981): Nominal Group Technique: An Evaluation Data Collection Process. *Society for Research into Higher Education, Evaluation Newsletter,* vol. 5, pp. 44-60.

14 Starkey, H. (1995): From Rhetoric to Reality: Starting to Implement Education for European Values, in Bell, G.H. (ed.) (1995). Ch. 2.

THE EUROPEAN MONETARY UNION: A CROSS-CURRICULAR TEACHING PROJECT

CHAPTER 11

Peter Krapf

Introduction

European citizenship has at least two dimensions. First, there is the formal, legally defined citizenship of a member state of the European Union. The Maastricht Treaty envisages a political union as a longterm objective, but in the minds of most citizens in the EU - and apparently some of their political leaders - this goal is very far away, and perhaps not even desirable. This points to a second dimension of European citizenship: the formal status of belonging to a political entity, be it a nation state or confederation of several states, must be complemented and supported by a political culture, i.e. a set of shared basic values, attitudes, cultural traditions etc. without which no political system can survive[1].

European citizenship has, therefore, a 'hard', namely a legally and formally defined dimension, and a 'soft', i.e. an informal and more diffuse, cultural dimension, which may be more difficult to describe, but is nonetheless real. We may be on the way to becoming citizens of Europe, but most of us feel more strongly tied to our nationstates or regions. There is not yet any such thing as a political culture underlying the European Union - or the continent of Europe. The 'hard core' of European citizenship, however incomplete, is still more developed than its 'soft' complement on a cultural level. This development lag may become clearer if viewed in a historical perspective. The stages of development leading to the Treaty of Maastricht from the European Economic Community (1957) up to the Single European Market (1993) - reflect the problems and rapid changes in economy to which the leaders of the member states felt compelled to respond.

The development of multinational corporations and a world market left economic policy at a national level increasingly powerless, and European companies had to deal with competitors who served a bigger home market (USA). Challenges such as these, inducing a structure of interdependence - of 'problem sharing' within Europe - led to the creation of European institutions long before the citizens of the European nation states could develop any feeling of belonging towards the emerging 'mega-state'.

Citizenship education must respond to this feeling of not-belonging, by attempting to help political attitudes and behaviour to catch up, as it were, with the economic and political developments creating a new, bigger political entity within Europe which needs to be understood and accepted by its citizens if it is to be democratic - and stable. As I understand it, this is where the discussion of methodical approaches, curricular development and projects in the classroom sets in.

In this chapter I would like to present a report on how we have attempted to respond to the task outlined above in political education at the *Gymnasium* type schools in Baden-Württemberg. After having outlined the federal, i.e. decentralised, structure of the German education system and the curricular development in the regional state of Baden-Württemberg, I will attempt to sketch the treatment of European integration in a cross-curricular approach. The project brings together three school subjects: political education and two foreign languages, French and English. While a basic element of the political culture of a nation state is often a single language community - all citizens are native speakers of English, German, Italian etc. - the political culture of Europe will be multilingual. A cross-curricular teaching project including foreign languages may therefore help pupils to appreciate the importance of learning other European languages.

Cross-Curricular Teaching in Baden-Württemberg

General School Education in the Federal Republic of Germany

Before we look at the curriculum for the *Gymnasium* in Baden-Württemberg, it might be helpful to clarify for which type of school, and which region within Germany, the curriculum applies.

Germany is a federal republic, which means that legislation, decision-making and jurisdiction are not only distributed among three separate powers, but also among respective institutions at a national and regional level. Thus there is not only a horizontal, but also a vertical dimension to the division of powers. The Federal Republic of Germany has sixteen regional states *(Bundesländer,)* one of which is Baden-Württemberg, situated in the south-west. Each of these *Bundesländer* has its own constitution, government, parliament and jurisdiction. In national legislation, the chamber of representatives from the regional states, the *Bundesrat*, forms the second chamber next to Parliament, the *Bundestag*. The regional states are solely responsible for state school education, which caters to the vast majority of pupils; private schools are of much less importance than in the US or the UK. Depending on which major party is in power (and very often has been for decades) in a regional state, the school system and the curriculum will be found to differ considerably.

In the regional states governed by one of the Christian Democratic parties, a tripartite system of secondary education has prevailed. The Social Democrats, on the other hand, have introduced comprehensive schools in secondary education.

In Baden-Württemberg, which has been governed by the Christian Democratic Union for several decades, we have a tripartite school system. Pupils enter school at the age of six and receive four years of elementary school education at the *Grundschule*, which is comprehensive, as it caters to all ability groups. In secondary education, the pupils are split between three types of school: the *Hauptschule*, the *Realschule*, or the *Gymnasium* (see Figure 1).

Figure 1
The Tripartite School System in Baden-Württemberg

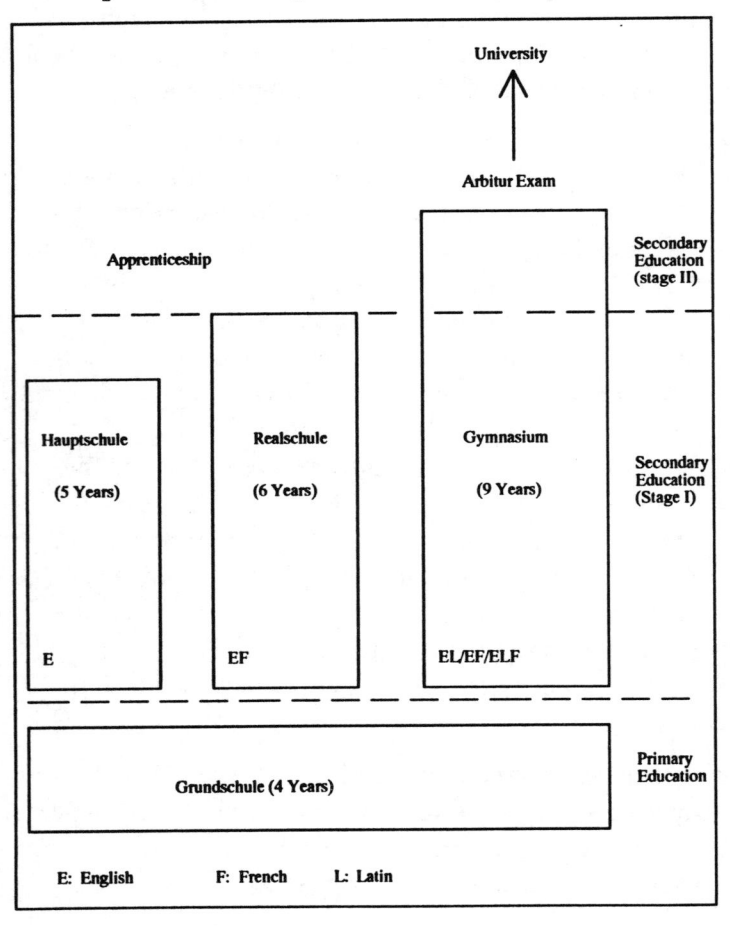

```
                              University
                                 ↑
                            Arbitur Exam
                                                    Secondary
        Apprenticeship                              Education
                                                    (stage II)
    - - - - - - - - - - - - - - - -        - - - -

     Hauptschule    Realschule     Gymnasium
                                                    Secondary
      (5 Years)     (6 Years)      (9 Years)        Education
                                                    (Stage I)

         E            EF           EL/EF/ELF
    - - - - - - - - - - - - - - - - - - - - - - - -

              Grundschule (4 Years)                 Primary
                                                    Education

      E: English    F: French    L: Latin
```

The duration of schooling and the range of foreign languages, which are shown in Figure 1, may suffice to indicate for which ability groups the different types of school are intended: the *Hauptschule* and *Realschule* lead to non-academic careers, which usually require an apprenticeship of three years. The final *Abitur* exam at the *Gymnasium*, which caters to approximately 35% of all pupils, has the status of a general university entrance exam.

This brief summary might give readers who are not familiar with the federal, i.e. decentralised, structure of the German public school system an impression of the great variety of school types and curricula within the Federal Republic of Germany. The curriculum which I shall refer to in the following applies solely to the regular *Gymnasium* in the regional state of *Baden-Württemberg*.

Political education and cross-curricular teaching in Baden-Württemberg

Political education is included in every school curriculum in the Federal Republic, but there are considerable differences within the regional states, e.g. in the age groups which receive political education, the number of lessons per week assigned to the subject, or the topics included in the curriculum[2]. In *Baden-Württemberg*, pupils are taught *Gemeinschaftskunde* (community affairs) twice a week in forms 10 and 11. In the final two years leading up to the Abitur exam, pupils must either take politics as one of their two major subjects (five lessons per week) or as a minor subject (one lesson per week).

In 1994, a new curriculum was introduced for all academic subjects at the *Gymnasium* in Baden-Württemberg. A major innovation is cross-curricular teaching *(facherübergreifender Unterricht)*. A wide variety of topics require cross-curricular teaching, the foreword of the curriculum stated[3], including topics such as the European unification process, peace, intercultural understanding, or the gender issue. Still more important than the *content* is the *method*, which prepares pupils for complex studies at university. While the *method* of cross-curricular teaching has been made compulsory, the teachers have been given great flexibility as far as the *content* is concerned. The curriculum merely requires the new method to be employed once per school year in each age group. It is left to the teachers to decide, however, which academic subjects to include, and which topics to treat. A substantial proportion of the annual time budget (approx. 20%) has been set aside to allow for the timetable to be suspended for several days and even weeks to facilitate project teaching.

The curriculum includes five optional cross-curricular teaching-units for each form (5 - 11). These units are based on compulsory topics of each individual academic subject. The teachers are free to choose and modify one of the five teaching units suggested for a particular age group. They may also replace the units suggested by the curriculum by developing their own model of cross-curricular teaching.

'Developments and Changes in Europe' *as a topic of* Cross-Curricular Teaching

After having outlined the federal structure of school education in Germany and some general aspects of curricular development in Baden-Württemberg, we can now focus on the treatment of Europe in cross-curricular teaching.

The curriculum for the regular *Gymnasium* suggests *'Development and Changes in Europe'* as a topic for cross-curricular teaching in form 11. The 11th form introduces the pupils to more advanced methods of study on the upper level of secondary education. In the 12th and 13th form, the class splits up into courses (general and advanced level) leading to the *Abitur* exam.

A translated version of the teaching-unit on Europe for the 11th form is given in *Appendix* 1. The 'T' form of presentation is used to distinguish between different levels of teaching-objectives and suggestions.

The *General Objectives*, which are presented in the top horizontal section, outline insights which should be arrived at (i.e. understanding the importance of different sets of cultural and historic experiences and viewpoints, the common historic and cultural heritage based on Christianity and the traditions of ancient Greece and Rome). While these objectives are basically cognitive, the curriculum also includes 'soft' teaching-objectives, e.g. tolerance towards other nations and their specific ways of life and mentality, and the willingness to engage in intercultural communication.

In the two columns which follow this first section, the left-hand column contains a list of teaching objectives on a more elementary level - i.e. knowledge. Obviously, each of the keywords given in this column could easily provide material for fifteen or twenty lessons; take, for example, *'Civilisation in the Ancient World'*, *'Renaissance and the Age of Enlightenment'*, or *'Common Challenges in Europe'*. Further details on the topics have been deliberately omitted to leave the decision of what to treat in detail in an exemplary approach to the teachers. This principle of a 'medium level of abstraction' is also employed throughout large parts of the whole curriculum for political education. The column on the right contains suggestions on how certain topics could be treated. The concluding section, *References to the curriculum*, lists the academic subjects which could contribute to the treatment of Europe in a broader perspective. The list of contents in the right-hand column refers to the compulsory topics which must be treated within each of these subjects, regardless of whether they participate in cross-curricular teaching or not. Thus the time budgets of the teachers participating are not drawn on too heavily. All teaching-units in the curriculum for the Gymnasium in Baden-Württemberg are presented in this T-structure. The content presented in the left-hand column is, however, compulsory in regular teaching-units, whereas it is optional in units for cross-curricular teaching to ensure the greatest possible flexibility in planning and classroom work for teachers.

The Topic of the European Monetary Union in Cross-Curricular Teaching

One major obstacle to cross-curricular teaching has been a lack of adequate materials, as the majority of textbooks for pupils do not include references to other subjects. The ministry for education in Baden-Württemberg therefore assigned the task of preparing special teaching materials[4] to the teams who had prepared the draft for the new curriculum.

Exemplary Approach

Two colleagues, Giselher Birk and Otto Gauss, and I formed a team which has produced materials to support cross-curricular teaching on Europe. We reduced the scope of academic subjects which are included by the curriculum to those which we teach ourselves: English, French and Politics. We also felt an exemplary approach was appropriate in dealing with the vast topic of 'Developments and Changes in Europe', and we focused on one aspect in the curriculum, *'Europe Today - The European Union'*. We finally narrowed this down to the issue of the European Monetary Union (EMU). Our reasons for this decision were the following: one of the major issues at the top level of the EU today is the question if EMU, which the EU member states agreed on in 1991 in the Treaty of Maastricht, should ever go into effect, and if so, which schedule should be applied. Across the EU, however, the citizens seem to be most deeply concerned about unemployment and the problems related to it - poverty, violence, and the collapse of our social security systems. We therefore considered it worthwhile to ask what EMU could contribute to creating new jobs throughout the EU.

In an introduction for the teachers, we briefly outlined the possible contribution of EMU to more employment: EMU is a policy guided by the theory of supply-side economics. It is intended to encourage investment and production by reducing costs and improving business prospects in the Single European Market. Provided that the new European currency is stable and is introduced in a substantial number of EU member states, EMU is a necessary, but not a sufficient measure to create new jobs.

Didactical and Methodical Approach

By focusing on EMU, we would cover substantial parts of the regular curriculum in Politics, which contains units on economics (unemployment) and the European Union. We also hoped the pupils would take a new interest in foreign language learning if they could experience multilingual communication within Europe (see Figure 2).

Figure 2

Teaching Objectives related to European Citizenship in Cross-Curricular Teaching

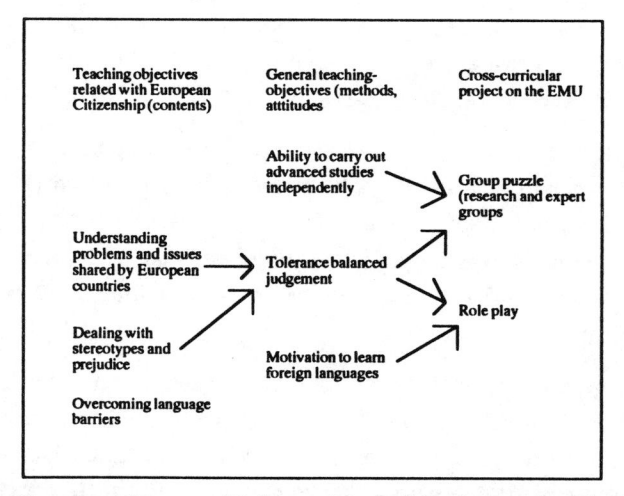

```
Teaching objectives        General teaching-         Cross-curricular
related with European      objectives (methods,      project on the EMU
Citizenship (contents)     attitudes)

                           Ability to carry out
                           advanced studies          Group puzzle
                           independently             (research and expert
                                                     groups)
Understanding
problems and issues        Tolerance balanced
shared by European         judgement
countries
                                                     Role play
Dealing with
stereotypes and            Motivation to learn
prejudice                  foreign languages

Overcoming language
barriers
```

The diagram shows which teaching-objectives related to European citizenship education may be dealt with by the cross-curricular model presented in this paper. These are primarily elements of content. In addition, some important skills (independent work) and attitudes may be developed. The column on the right suggests student-centred methods when using the model in the classroom.

To support cross-curricular teaching, our materials must meet certain requirements both in terms of content and methods. As far as *content* is concerned, our materials must ensure that:

- The topics which we deal with in detail cannot be fully evaluated within the limits of one academic subject alone, but rather call for *complementing studies* for the viewpoint of other subjects. Foreign language teaching should not only be involved as a means of overcoming language barriers; rather, foreign languages should become *a means of communication*. Therefore, topics of political education should be presented and discussed not only in German, but also in English and French. Thus the order of presenting our materials follows topics, not academic subjects, leading to a mix of all three languages in most chapters.

We included some brief suggestions on the *methods* and organisation of cross-curricular teaching, which is a new experience for most teachers and pupils.

- The simplest form of cross-curricular teaching consists of *co-ordinating teaching schedules*. Each teacher continues to work alone in class, but the timing of schedules allows for links to be made between academic subjects. If one teacher is responsible alone for several subjects, this method may be applied 'quietly' and flexibly

- A more sophisticated set-up is the *group puzzle*, details of which are given in *Figure 3*. The teachers taking part pool their lessons, which allows group sessions and project work to take place in the time slots available *within the regular timetable*. In this way, the group puzzle puts little stress on school organisation, but offers flexibility to account for student centred teaching. We therefore recommended this method to the readers of our materials and developed it in somewhat greater detail

- An even more advanced form of cross-curricular teaching is *a project* which the pupils work on for several days or even weeks. This, however, requires the *regular* school timetable to be suspended for a certain time

Figure 3
The Group Puzzle in Cross-Curricular Teaching

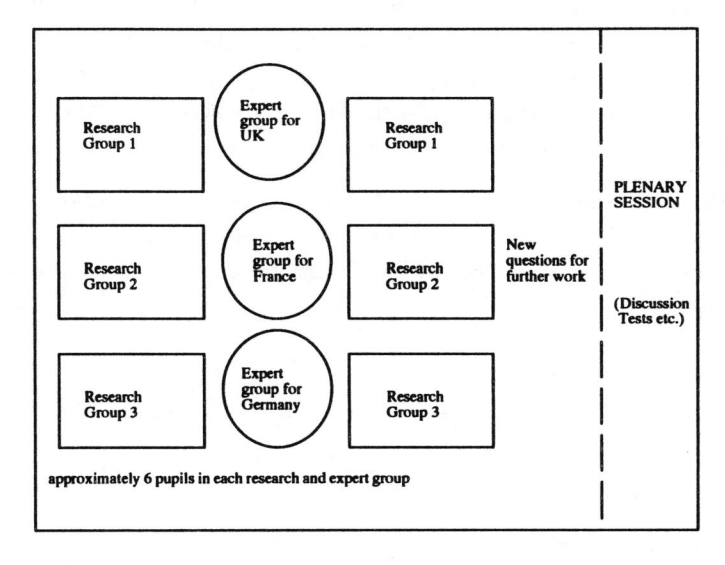

```
┌─────────────────────────────────────────────────┬──────────────┐
│  ┌──────────┐    ╭─────╮    ┌──────────┐        │              │
│  │ Research │   ╱ Expert╲   │ Research │        │              │
│  │ Group 1  │  │ group for│ │ Group 1  │        │              │
│  └──────────┘   ╲  UK   ╱   └──────────┘        │              │
│                  ╰─────╯                         │  PLENARY     │
│                                                  │  SESSION     │
│  ┌──────────┐    ╭─────╮    ┌──────────┐   New  │              │
│  │ Research │   ╱ Expert╲   │ Research │ questions for          │
│  │ Group 2  │  │ group for│ │ Group 2  │ further work           │
│  └──────────┘   ╲France ╱   └──────────┘        │              │
│                  ╰─────╯                         │ (Discussion  │
│                                                  │  Tests etc.) │
│  ┌──────────┐    ╭─────╮    ┌──────────┐        │              │
│  │ Research │   ╱ Expert╲   │ Research │        │              │
│  │ Group 3  │  │ group for│ │ Group 3  │        │              │
│  └──────────┘   ╲Germany╱   └──────────┘        │              │
│                  ╰─────╯                         │              │
│  approximately 6 pupils in each research and expert group       │
└─────────────────────────────────────────────────┴──────────────┘
```

Suggestions for procedure

1. The teacher(s) explains the method of work alternating between 'research groups' and 'expert groups' to the class

2. The pupils form research groups with approximately six members in each group. They may like to give their group a name to increase integration

3. Each group sends two members to one of three expert groups. In the model suggested here, the expert groups specialise on the UK, France and Germany, communicating in the respective languages of their countries under study. The groups working

on France and the UK are provided with information and texts in the teaching materials. Vocabulary annotations and comprehension questions have been supplied with each text to assist the pupils in overcoming the language barrier. The pupils working in their native language on Germany are expected to obtain their information on their own initiative

4. The research groups reassemble and listen to the reports from the three expert teams. This amounts to the pupils teaching each other in turn, communicating in English, French and German. New questions may arise, leading to further study in the former expert groups or new ones, with different tasks

5. The plenary session may serve to discuss issues of general interest (e.g. a debate on the monetary union, either solely in German or including the foreign languages) or to carry out a final written test

Outline of Content

Our attempts to support cross-curricular teaching may become clearer by summarising the structure of content and presenting excerpts from the materials.

Our materials comprise two parts. Part I deals with unemployment in the EU in general, and how it has affected France and the UK in particular (see *Appendix* 2). Part II offers an outline of how EMU will work, and a debate on EMU. This chapter includes authors from France, the UK and Germany who represent both EMU-supporters and Euro-sceptics (see *Appendix* 3). Throughout the book, materials in French and English are supplied with annotations on vocabulary and comprehension questions to facilitate independent work by pupils.

Appendix 2 presents excerpts on the malnutrition problem and sweatshop labour in the UK. The context of the chapter on unemployment and poverty in the UK, from which these texts have been taken, may be summarised as follows: Poverty in the UK has caused widespread malnutrition and compels people to accept housing considered unfit for habitation. Poverty is not only caused by unemployment, but by third-world-style employment, e.g. in sweatshops which pay wages as low as one pound an hour. The government has shown great reluctance to admit that poverty exists in the UK, let alone link poverty to its rigid application of supply-side economics.

A further chapter in Part I, excerpts of which could not be included for reasons of space, deals with 'chomage', i.e. unemployment in France. Here, unemployment is shown to have aggravated the problems of youth violence and illegal immigration and to have laid the ground for mafiose drug trafficking in the 'cites interdites', the parts of the big cities which the police do not dare enter without special precaution. The government has promised to create new jobs, but the shortage of cash limits its scope of action.

We did not add a chapter on the effects of unemployment in Germany, as ample material from other sources is easily available to our pupils. However, Part I does include statistics on poverty and unemployment in the EU to enable the pupils to compare the situation across the EU. After studying the reports on poverty and unemployment, the pupils will come away with the impression that millions of people in all three countries suffer under these problems. This result could lead the pupils to the question why unemployment has been so hard to overcome, and which policy might be successful. We have omitted the discussion on the reasons for unemployment, as this is part of the regular curriculum in politics, but offer materials for the following step - the issue of EMU, more investment, and the creation of new jobs.

Appendix 3 presents excerpts from the debate on EMU in Part II. The German texts have been translated for the readers of this paper, but the French text is given in the original to preserve some of the flavour of the multilingual debate which the pupils are encouraged to engage in. The pupils will find that scepticism about EMU is strongest in the UK, but is also voiced in Germany. Both the British and French contributors express their uneasiness about Germany and its dominant position in Europe. The materials convey a surprising richness in shades of opinion and styles of argument, thus reflecting the cultural and political diversity in Europe which makes communication both fascinating and difficult.

The notes on the group puzzle in *Figure* 3 give an idea of how the materials could be applied in a student-centred approach to cross-curricular teaching.

The treatment of Europe in cross-curricular teaching is a pioneer project in our *Gymnasium* type schools; not only is the teaching method new for teachers and pupils, but so is the experience of acting as *European citizens*. As far as our teaching materials are concerned, 'the proof of the cake is the eating', which has yet to take place; at present I therefore cannot report on our teaching experience in the classroom.

Appendix 1

The Cross-curricular Teaching-Unit on Europe in the Curriculum for the Gymnasium in Baden-Württemberg

Gymnasium	Cross-curricular topics
Form 11	

Topic No 1:	Developments and Changes in Europe

General Objectives

The process of integration in Europe affects our daily lives in numerous ways and may be experienced in individual, regional and national contexts. The pupils are to be introduced to the background of political developments, both past and present, in Europe, including changes in Middle and Eastern Europe. The pupils should understand how differing national attitudes to Europe have been influenced by a people's respective historic experiences and their particular cultural and regional identities. This insight may help pupils to become aware of their ties to their own culture and to develop a deeper understanding of the ways of life and mentalities in other nations. In this way, cross-cultural co-operation and tolerance is encouraged. Moreover, the pupils should understand the common origins of our European cultural heritage and appreciate the richness of cultural diversity in Europe today, which will help them to understand the necessity of intercultural communication.

Contents	Teaching Suggestions
Our common European heritage	
Links between languages	Relationships between lanugages
Civilization in the ancient world	Influence of foreign languages on the development of the German language; loan words, foreign words
	Influence and spreading of mythological topics in works of art and literature
	Tradition of literary genres and motifs
	Democracy in ancient Athens
Ancient ethics	Socrates: a pioneer of western ethics
Christianity in the western world	Universal significance of the Christian conept of man
Medieval Civilization	Monasteries: their contribution to preserve and spread the cultural heritage of Europe
	Themes of literature in Middle High German; subjects in works of art; sacred buildings
Renaissance and the Age of Enlightenment as European movements	Emergence of a secular culture and the revisiting of antiquity Descartes, Hobbes, Locke, Kant
The making of civil society	Movements for emancipatiion and ccivil rights
	Literature and publicity
	Development of democratic institutions (constitutional state)
Europe Today	
The European Union	Development and institutions of the EU
	The four fundamental freedoms in the European Single Market
	Chances and problems from the viewpoints of different countries

Contd/.....

Contd/.... .

National and regional particularities:	
France - our western neighbour	The Franco-German relationship and the unification of Europe
Great Britain - the isles in front of the European continent	How the British see themselves ('*island mentality*')
Russia - a country in the midst of radical change	Russo-German relations in past and presen
The Europe of the regions	Regions in partnership with Baden-Wurttemberg: Alsace; Cataluna; Emilia Romagna; Lombardia; Rhone-alpes; the middle Ural; Wales
Common challenges in Europe	Migrants from the Third World; migration within Europe
	Environment problems
	Combating crime
	The development of a binding system of social security
	Ambivalent implications of ethnic; cultural and linguistic diversity
	Nationalism and the bid for political unity
	The search for a set of shared basic values

References to the regular curriculum of the academic subjects included in the teaching-unit

Protestant religious education	The changing Europe - economic ethics
Roman Catholic religious education	The changing Europe - a challenge for Christians
German	The ancient drama Medieval literature Literature in the Age of Enlightenment Linguistics, Grammar and Style
History	The early modern age: the emergence of the modern world
Politics	The process of European unification and the Federal Republic of Germany
Modern foreign languages	Political and cultural studies (Landeskunde)
Latin	Influence of literature and art
Greek	Literature, Socrates' ethics
Ethics	Concepts of ethics in philosophy: Socrates, Hobbes

Translated by Peter Krapf

Appendix 2

Excerpts on Poverty in the United Kingdom

1. *Judy Jones, The Bad Food Trap*

Malnutrition, literally, means a lack of the nutrients vital for good health and long life. In the last century, the big killers from inadequate nutrients were scurvy (Vitamin C deficiency) and rickets (Vitamin D deficiency). Now their modern equivalents are cancers and heart disease - Britons suffer some of the West's highest rates of these often preventable diseases - which are in large part the result of high-fat, low-fibre diets.

Britain's hidden malnutrition problem worsened as the gap widened between rich and poor through the Eighties and the numbers living in poverty grew. The income of the poorest 10 per cent fell from 73 pounds a week to 61 pounds in real terms (after housing costs) between 1979 and 1991, according to an Institute for Fiscal Studies report in 1994. Put another way, the number living on less than half average earnings - the EU definition of poverty - was five million in 1979, compared with 13 million in 1990. The Government has never accepted that UK poverty exists, preferring instead to refer coyly to 'health inequalities' and 'low-income families'.

In Britain, the average household spends about 17 per cent of its income on food. Surveys suggest that the poorest need to spend between a quarter and a half. In September 1994, Sainsburys compiled a low-income shopping basket for a family of four costing 11.66 pounds a week per person. In the same year, the average two-child family was living on benefits of 1 £13.05 a week, so the Sainsbury's basket would take a 40 per cent chunk of income.

The parent's anguish

'I normally buy four packets of bread, but if I', running out of money we just buy two. So those who have six slices, I'll tell them to take four... those taking four, I tell them to take three - and I don't eat. Sometimes I lie to them... they say *"Mummy don't, we know you're trying to keep us alive, but don't starve yourself, let's share it"*... they're very good children, they understand.'

Parent on income support. Two dependent children

'I buy apples and bananas every fortnight... It's horrible when she has a banana and then says *"Can I have an apple?"* and you've got to stop because it's got to last.'

Parent on income support. One daughter.

'I've walked about with holes in my shoes, no winter coat and haven't eaten for three days to look after them... I won't let my kids go without. I won't have anyone look at them and think *"Oh, isn't it a shame".*'

Parent on income support. Three children.

2) *Neasa MacErlean: No Place Like Home Sweated Home*

Shirley - who sews skirts as she looks after her two young children - is relatively well paid for a homeworker. She earns more than 3 pounds an hour, usually bringing in between 60 and 80 pounds a week. But her daily routine is a scramble to combine childcare and sewing. 'I get up with the baby. I get her ready and give her her breakfast and then get my son ready. He goes to nursery three mornings a week. Then I do a few jobs. The baby usually has a sleep and I try to do three hours work in the afternoon - with interruptions. I make the tea, then my husband comes home. I get the children ready for bed and usually do a couple of hours or more at night,' says Shirley. Like most homeworkers, she does not get a pension, holiday pay, sick pay or any other basic benefits from her employer. No safety equipment has been provided by the company. She has been given no guidance on health and safety - on the dangers to her eyesight and back, for example.

The Observer, Business section, 2 June 1996, p.8

Appendix 3

Excerpts from the Debate on EMU ('Die Wähungsunion im Meinungsstreit - La deuxieme bataille de Maastricht - Should we stay out or should we go in?')

1) *Wilhelm Hankel: New Single European Currency will split Europe*

What is more... it is precisely in periods of waning economic growth and massive increases of unemployment - in the EU there are now 20 million people out of work, almost a third of which are, in effect, in Germany - that the state cannot remain inactive. The government must tackle the problem comprehensively, i.e. not merely by spending reductions, downsizing and cutting social security benefits. Rather, what is required are incentives for more production, financing aids and job subsidies, in short, measures which will cost money. A government which refuses aid and subsidies to its jobholders will have to pay a double and treble bill in supporting its unemployed. Therefore, with steeply rising unemployment looming ahead, it is contrary to any economic and political reason to pin oneself to rigid, and utterly arbitrary, rules and criteria of budget discipline...

Südwestpresse, 19 March 1996, p. 3; translated by Peter Krapf.

2) *Will Frankfurt be the New London?*

To accept monetary union means accepting that Britain stands in relation to the rest of Europe as Wales stands to Britain and that Frankfurt is the new London. Most British people are not ready to accept that; not yet, perhaps not ever.

The Daily Telegraph, 17 January 1996.

3) *Timothy Garton Ash: Damned if We're out and Damned if We're in*

If it comes to the crunch, going in would seem for me the lesser evil. But the least bad option for Britain would be for the project of EMU to be quietly dropped. I would argue that this would in fact be the best thing for the whole of Europe, too. If monetary union failed, much else would fall with it. The Europe which emerged would be closer to the Europe of nation states which Eurosceptics want. Yet Britain might actually find itself doing worse in a Europe in which Germany and France start behaving like Britain than in a Europe in which Britain and France have to behave a little more like Germany. If this suspicion is right, then our position is difficult indeed. We reach the conclusion not only that we are damned if we do (join in) and damned if we don't, but also we are damned if they (go ahead) and damned if they don't. Alas, poor Albion.

The Observer Review, June 2 1996, p.3

4) *Pour une Europe à deux*

L'Europe se meurt. Depuis l'adoption du traité de Maastricht, elle n'a pas arrêté de prendre de l'embonpoint et de perdre des forces.

C'est le triomphe posthume (au sens politique) de Margaret Thatcher et la défaite de tous ceux qui, sous des formes diverses, de Jean Monnet à de Gaulle à Mitterrand, de Konrad Adenauer á Helmut Kohl, ont placé leurs espoirs dans l'Union européenne. Nous sommes à la veille d'un immense gâchis. Parce que les egoismes nationaux étaient trop forts dans le domaine politique, on avait décidé de donner la priorité a l'économie. Pourquoi pas? Mais on ne doit pas s'y tromper: L'Europe était, dans l'esprit de ses pères, un moyen d'assurer la paix entre ses membres et de se protéger contre la menace extérieure. Aujourd'hui l'Europe est menacée de toutes parts. Elle doit relever le défi. Sans une initiative franco-allemande, la conférence de Milan risque d'accoucher d'un monstre ingouvernable. Or depuis Maastricht, la France se tait. Elle n'a même pas répondu au document allemand Lamers qui proposait la création d'un noyau dur franco-allemand pour relancer la construction européenne. Pourtant, a côté de l'Europe thatchérienne à trente qui se profile à l'horizon, il est temps de faire une Europe politique vraiment opérationnelle. Et vite. A combien? Ma foi à deux, pour le moment.

D'après: Jacques Juillard, 'Le Nouvel Observateur', 19 January 1996

5) *Helmut Schmidt: Our Second Attempt, Our Last Chance*

Moreover, many opponents against monetary union are also opportunists, who would like to surf on a wave of what they believe to be the public's opinion which they themselves have created. Some of the opponents among economists who have so often erred in their experts' reports in recent years are no better; so just for once, by a self-fulfiling prophecy, they would like to be right. The monetary union must not come, for it would mean unbearable sacrifices.

But once it has been prevented, nobody will be able to prove that the 'sacrifice theory' - sacrificing the Deutschmark for the Euro - was utter nonsense. All economic arguments against the single currency in the European Union may be dismissed as unfounded.

On the other hand, the economic advantages of the monetary union will be obvious if we consider what will happen if EMU is put off or completely cancelled, and postponing the union would most probably mean abandoning it.

Die Zeit, 5 April 1996, p.4; translated by Peter Krapf -

NB: *Helmut Schmidt (SPD) was Federal Chancellor of Germany from 1974 to 1982*

Endnotes

1. Derek Heater has analysed European Citizenship along similar lines. See chapter 1 of this book.

2. For more detailed information, see Weidinger, D. (1995): Politische Bildung an den Schulen in Deutschland: Stand nach Ausweis der Stundentafeln und Lehrpläne, in *Gegenwartskunde* vol. 3, pp. 327 - 341.

3. See Ministerium für Kultur und Sport Baden-Wurttemberg (ed.), Bil dungsplan fur das Gymnasium, in Kultur und Unterricht, *Lehrplanheft* vol. 4, p. 10.

4. Landesinstitut für Erziehung und Unterricht Stuttgart (ed.). Die Europäische Währungsunion. Fächerverbindendes Thema Klasse 11. Handreichungen zum Bildungsplan Gymnasium. Forthcoming.

5. This Diagram is based on Dietrich Steinbach, Thomas Kopfermann, Helmuth Kern: 'Herbst 1989 - Ein historischer Wendepunkt für Europa: Innere Auflösung and Zusammenbruch der DDR', in: Lothar Schaechterle (ed.), Deutschland und Europa (Hannover, Metzler Schulbuchverlag 1992), pp. 5 - 39.

PHILOMEL: A PROJECT FOR EUROPEAN UNITY

CHAPTER 12

Ernesto Macaro

Beyond the extensive writings on European Awareness, the European Dimension and European Citizenship lie the practicalities of getting a school based activities off the ground. Where does one start?

Information sources such as the Central Bureau for Educational Visits and Exchanges (CBEVE)[1] and the European Parliament office in London clearly have a part to play in providing teachers and curriculum planners with packs of information on the EU, access to European Commission funding and lists of interested partner schools. However, it has been argued[2] that European Citizenship is not going to be simply handed down from knowledgeable teacher to uninformed pupil. European Citizenship is unlikely to take the form of a neat package or educational manual which will do the job of creating European citizens during Personal and Social Education lessons. Still less is it the case that many teachers will feel confident and competent to engage their pupils in the process of understanding and experiencing citizenship without themselves having undergone a process of self-questioning, self definition and reappraisal of the meaning of citizenship in a supranational context. School staff are composed of individuals who do not necessarily act with homogeneity and coherence faced with socio-political change. It is much more likely, therefore, that the European dimension and

European Citizenship education will be delivered through process rather than content. That process will involve the school's gradual examination of its own policy towards citizenship against, on the one hand, a background of the aspirations of the local community and the current political climate at the national level, and on the other, against a background of universal principles and values. Moreover, this examination will necessarily be on-going and dynamic rather than an immutable document residing in the filing cabinet marked 'school policies'.

It will involve the pupils themselves, as future citizens of Europe, discovering alongside their teachers the meaning of the process of Europeanization as the Union tries to move from adolescence to maturity.

Any citizenship project, therefore, undertaken by teachers and pupils, will itself be a voyage of discovery. It will answer questions such as: what do we mean by building bridges across nations? How can we appreciate a common cultural heritage? How can we tap into the cultural dynamism of Europe? In what way is the image of Europe multi-faceted? What constitutes respect for one another's languages?

The Philomel project has as its overarching aim to provide young people with a tool which will assist in answering some of these baffling but urgent questions.

Philomel is the brainchild of Sophia Kakkavas. The project, launched by her in 1992, is based on a modern Greek fable, that of the forest nightingale (Philomel), written but unpublished by Ange S. Vlachos[3] in 1943 and rediscovered by her many years later. In order to understand the many schools' already considerable involvement in this unusual and fascinating project as well as its future potential we will need to summarise the story here.

Chea is a beautiful princess who, unknown to her husband, is lured to the Marshes by an Ogre with offers of riches and jewels. Her husband discovers her there, covered in mud and with the Ogre beside her. The Ogre laughs at him. In his fury the husband asks his mother, a witch, to turn Chea into a snake who will 'crawl on her belly' for the rest of her life. The only way Chea can be released from her curse is if she kills a bird while it is singing. Chea spends her days and nights attacking the animals of the forest in the vain attempt to regain her true identity and form. Fear and evil thus permeate the forest. Only the song of the nightingale, in the early evening, is able to lift the hearts of those who live there.

Philomel is the youngest of the nightingales in the nest and, at first, merely seems foolhardy. He ignores his mother's cautious advice as well as that of the wise owl, Vigo.

Philomel gradually draws away from the safe world of the tree tops to frequent the dangerous world of the forest floor. When the time comes for his family to migrate he announces that he wants to save the world by confronting Chea and singing to her. He flies off and spots Chea about to bite Vigo and draws her away from him. Chea kills Philomel and in so doing not only casts off her evil spell but also brings peace and security to the forest.

Many of the themes which this fable encompasses are timeless and universal: good and evil; conflict and peace; segregation and co-existence; innocence and experience, the quasi-religious individual self-sacrifice. Written, as it was, at the height of the Second World War it draws its inspiration from a European continent torn apart by political and ethnic divergence and now speaks to a new generation by holding out the hope of European unity.

The Philomel project's aims are to encourage communication between pupils in as many European countries as possible through the medium of the fable and to draw upon the resources offered to education by the European Commission in order to facilitate eventual exchanges. In so doing it hopes to contribute to the creation of European citizens through a process of greater understanding of people's different languages, cultures and traditions. Through the understanding of meanings in the story and through its variety of representations by children in schools, the project tries to plant the seed of the idea that whilst opinions, reactions and interpretations may differ, all our existences are necessarily entwined. At a curriculum level the project seeks to reinforce the prospect of European unity through the study of a common subject.

The fable has been translated into 23 languages. The story can thus be studied and interpreted either in the children's first language (L1) or their second or foreign language (L2). Each participating school receives at least one hardback copy of the book which is beautifully illustrated by Christos Georgiou, a Greek artist of some renown.

Following are some of the ways in which schools have taken part in the project. If any school has been omitted from this description it in no way reflects the quality of their endeavours but rather lack of space afforded by this chapter. Many of the comments below pertaining to evaluation of the project were made by the teachers or the pupils themselves.

Purcell School - London

The school, in association with member of the London Symphony Orchestra, produced a semi-improvised musical composition entitled 'Philomel' and drew its inspiration by exploring selected ideas and images in the fable. The piece was performed in July 1996 at the Guildhall School of Music.

Holy Child Girls School and Scoil Nairhi, Dublin

Classes of 12 year olds studied the fable in Irish (their L2). They did this by first carrying out an in-depth reading of the story, analysing the characters and reflecting on the reasons for their actions. This study not only stimulated the youngsters' thinking about universal values, but was also influential in helping the pupils to acquire a greater belief in and love of the Irish language that they were studying. The latter school is a minority language school and the idea of so many children in different countries working together on the same story in different languages reinforced the ethos of the school. The class made a collage of the story and then went on to write a sequel. For personal reasons the schools were not immediately able to set up links with other schools in Europe. Nevertheless this became an aspiration for the teachers and the pupils. As one teacher said: 'With enough links, the chain of fear and hatred can be broken and replaced with a chain of friendship and understanding of others'. The symbolism of working on such a project on the island of Ireland will certainly not go unnoticed.

Robert Piggott CE Infant School, Wargrave (near Reading), Berkshire.

In this school the project was undertaken by 102 children aged between 4 and 7 in early 1996. The school's curriculum is designed around topics. Teachers decided to use the story to develop the theme of colour and light, a decision encouraged by the illustrations in the book.

Thus a variety of disciplines came into play including art and design, technology, media, literature and language. In addition, the 'selflessness and sacrifice' theme in the story was used as a comparison in Religious Education with the Easter story. The final product of the project was a narrative of the fable involving dance, movement, speaking parts and mime performed to an audience of parents. The school extended this experience by setting up a link with schools in Germany and Greece. Teachers hoped that the communication and collaboration which would ensue would enable children at the school to acquire a closer understanding of their European neighbours. The school, a rural one, also hoped to use Philomel to forge links with a school in the UK with a much greater multicultural ethos and having a number of minority languages.

The Forest School, Winnersh (near Reading), Berkshire

Year 9 (13 year olds) pupils involved themselves in Philomel by incorporating it into their art/photography project. They made background, masks and costumes related to the Philomel plot. They then used Information Technology (Revelation software) to enhance the photos they had taken of their art work. Art teachers hope to set up links with continental schools also working with Philomel in order to compare art-centred outcomes. In addition, this school used the Greek version of the story to enhance the teaching of Modern Greek at the school (L2).

Lycee Franco-Hellenique, Athens

10 year old pupils at this school studied the beginning of the story in French (L1) then were asked to imagine and invent the rest for themselves by producing cartoons and drawings. One drawing, showing the nightingale Philomel sacrificing himself to the snake Chea has the caption:

'Once upon a time a little bird did a tour of Europe. He went past Athens, Paris, London, Madrid, Rome, Brussels, Luxembourg, Budapest, Monaco and lots of other capitals. When he came back to his own country, Greece, he looked in Chea's eyes and he lost his mind. Chea bit him and became a beautiful girl again'. In the speech bubble issuing from Philomel's beak are the words: 'For Europe, which I love'.

College Valeri, Nice, France.

The high involvement of this school in the project was almost entirely due to the efforts and enthusiasm of a student teacher working at the school. She took on the project as material for an assignment for her CAPES (teaching qualification) in English as a foreign language. The school drew from a multicultural and fairly deprived part of the Nice suburbs and she involved a group of mixed-ability year 9 pupils (13 year olds) in their English lessons

(L2). Key words in her aims for the project were: oral and written communication; universal values; Europe. In her assignment she points to the disappearance of the oral tradition in families as a vehicle for transmitting culture and its replacement with television's mass and stereotyped cultural images. The primary school is virtually the only place where children come into contact with fables. Yet oral narration, myth and fable are the vehicles which gradually awaken in children the awareness of feelings and how to react to them: justice, generosity, love, loyalty, etc. This awakening gives the child the instruments with which to elaborate its thoughts and its judgements. This was her rationale for adopting the project. She also hoped that working with Philomel would provide a counterbalance to the daily diet of Anglo-American culture.

After reading the story and working on exercises to help comprehension, the pupils began corresponding with a school in Italy and telling their partners about Philomel in addition to information about themselves and their regional and national culture. For this they used English (their common L2). Dialogues based on characters in the story were also sent to their exchange partners. The student teacher summarises the positive outcomes of the work as being: something concrete for the pupils to produce; progress with second language acquisition; an increased sense of solidarity and belonging. The difficulties and negative aspects were entirely linked to practical difficulties she encountered with the corresponding schools and with the amount of time required.

The class also made a collage of the Nice Carnival and sent it to a link school in Belfast (Meanscoil Feirste). Pupils from Meanscoil Feirste replied with descriptions of St. Patrick's day. Correspondence here was carried out in respective L2s. One particularly pleasing outcome of this aspect of the project was the effort and enthusiasm that one boy at the College Valeri (often in trouble with the police and absent from school) put into writing a letter to the Belfast school. The student teacher 'couldn't believe her eyes!' watching him write the letter.

It is hoped that the children will continue to correspond until the year 2000 when some sort of meeting between them all is envisaged.

Institut Universitaire de Formation des Maitres (IUFM), Nice

This teacher training department decided to use the idea of Philomel with its student teachers of German (L2) in conjunction with primary school children. The story was first translated into French (L1) by the student teachers purely to enhance their own language learning and to really get to know the text. It was then adapted into play form. The fable is seen as having enormous potential for teacher training in general and for cross-curricular teacher education in particular. Staff at the IUFM envisage using it with Mother Tongue teaching - poetry involving nightingales; with Civics - the resolution of conflict and the European dimension; with Science - astronomy[4] and the animal food chain; with art and music.

Ladispoli Primary School, Ladispoli (Rome), Italy

This school's involvement in Philomel resulted in pupils producing drawings inspired by the fable and by the style of artwork already in the book. From these they then produced 50 slides and added a commentary and music.

This work was then taken further by the **Istituto di Stato per la Cinematografia e la Televisione**, (a specialist upper secondary school in Rome) which planned the production of a cartoon sequence in film form of about 30 minutes, drawing on the semiotic approach already inherent in the original story. The film is given a dual audio narrative: the voices of the actual characters in the story as established by the original text; the 'inner voices' of the characters, the imagined feelings, sensations and memories of the characters are added.

One teacher from the primary school comments that 'the project is unique in that for the first time it involves the co-operation of different levels of schools and puts together the different skills and abilities of young children and teenagers'.

Teachers from the upper secondary specialist school were particularly optimistic about the process outcomes of the project - the actual investigation, the understanding and skills that it engendered. They hoped students would have a clearer understanding of the way 'nations have used film to spread their cultural roots towards the attainment of a common cultural European heritage'.

Odelcalchi Scuola Media, Ladispoli (Rome), Italy

This lower secondary school planned an operetta adaptation of the story involving two of its classes and drawing on both L1 and L2 versions of the book. Its educational objectives were to help:

- overcome selfishness
- accept diversity and remove prejudice
- encourage in pupils inter-personal communication and socialisation
- develop the pupils creativity and emotional involvement

Kopanaki Primary/Secondary School, Messinias, Greece

This school produced, in 1994, an outdoor performance of the fable of Philomel on a set constructed in the courtyard of the primary school. Narrators were positioned behind the scenery but were visible to the audience. Adults paid 1000 Greek Drachmas per ticket. Proceedings went to the Community Centre of Kopanaki.

Clearly not all of the activities related to the project have resulted in direct work on European citizenship. However they have laid the foundations both in terms of attitudes and in terms of organisation for further development work on European citizenship to occur. Future developments of the project must and do contain applications to Socrates for funding for educational visits. At time of writing funding for joint educational projects has been obtained from Socrates in at least three of the above schools.

There are plans for collaboration between University Teacher Training departments and preliminary meetings were held in September 1996. The University of Reading's Centre for Languages, English and Media in Education aims to use the project as a cross-curricular tool in order to involve its student teachers in bringing a European dimension to their work in specific subjects such as MFL, English and Drama.

A partnership bid (with the IUFM in Nice and the III University of Rome) is currently being submitted under Comenius Action 3. Although the main thrust of Philomel is that schools should have free rein to bring to the story a multiplicity of meaning and interpretations, there are, nevertheless, plans to produce materials and teachers' guidelines on how the Philomel fable might be used.

Conclusion

A number of issues are raised by the project which need to be addressed within the conceptual framework of Socrates funding. The first issue is how is it possible to evaluate, objectively, a diffuse project such as this? Is there a need for a centralised and co-ordinated evaluation of educational outcomes? It must be borne in mind, on the other hand, that the very fact that it is diffuse means that it is the participants themselves who are generating paths to citizenship at grassroots level. As one teacher commented: 'it was a case of feeling our way as we went along'. The project's strength lies in its organic nature. Its weakness, if it has one, might be seen by some to lie in the very eclectic nature of its interpretation. That it builds bridges and affords cultural insights is unquestionable. To what extent it helps young people understand the meaning of European citizenship and act as citizens of Europe, remains to be seen. We shall only have a clearer understanding of this as a result of a detailed evaluation of the project.

The second issue concerns Sophia Kakkavas herself. Until now she has given generously of her time and personal finances to attend, personally, the launch of every project in every school. It has been this personal touch, her infectious enthusiasm and the very fact that, in most cases, she is from another European country that has so obviously motivated pupils to produce such high quality work on the project by making them feel that they are special.

If the project is to grow, clearly she cannot bring to it the personal contact nor the financial resources. The book alone costs about £18 and the Commission will not at present fund it directly, although it is prepared to have it included as part of costs incurred for the future production of materials. Clearly, without the illustrated version of the book there is no starting point for a project.

The third issue concerns the attitude of the European Commission towards the project. Regulations regarding Socrates bids actually prevent the project from mushrooming, funding being made available for a limited number of schools and institutions under one project title. This unfortunately runs counter to one of the important ideals behind the Philomel project, namely that no one should be excluded. This is clearly a case of a European ideal running up against the harsh reality of the limited funding available.

Nevertheless Philomel continues to attract interest. Its flexibility and adaptability to cross-curricular approaches, its opportunity to discuss abstract values, its many levels of understanding from the simple to the complex, all contribute to an extraordinary potential for exploration of the self and for collaboration with others.

Endnotes

1. Central Bureau for Educational Visits and Exchanges.
2. Convery, A./Evans, A./Green, S./Macaro, E./Mellor, J. (1996): *Pupils Perceptions of Europe*. (London:Cassell).
3. Vlachos, A. S. (1993): *Philomel: A Modern Greek Fable*. (Dublin: Philomel Euromyths).
4. Chea, on shaking off the curse of the witch rises, to the sky and turns into a constellation.

BOOTHVILLE MIDDLE SCHOOL: EUROPEAN CITIZENSHIP INITIATIVES

CHAPTER 13

Mary Clark

The School

Boothville is a 9 - 13 years Middle School in Northampton. It was established in 1972 and has approximately 500 pupils on roll and 27 staff. The projects described initially began with pupils from the top two years of the school but ultimately involved pupils and staff throughout the school. We have good links with the local community and frequently draw upon their assistance and support.

Introduction

At Boothville Middle School we have always been aware of the need to provide a broad spectrum of experience which provides exposure to a wide variety of adults other than teachers, thus presenting more than the teacher as a role model. We also recognise the importance that one of the purposes of education is to prepare the child for the world outside of their school experience.

Increasingly this has come to mean a wider arena, where the children learn to perceive themselves not just as citizens in a small society, but as citizens of the EU.

It has been with this aim in mind that we have embarked upon a number of initiatives which have presented opportunities for pupils to work within the world of industry and thus develop not just their citizenship skills, but their awareness of being European Citizens.

Traditionally these initiatives have developed from existing and ongoing curriculum work and have developed as a result of either teacher or pupil interest.

Aims and Objectives

The Curriculum for Citizenship Education should help pupils to know and understand their own developing characteristics, skills and abilities. In particular it should help them to develop the following attitudes, values and skills:

- respect for different ways of life, beliefs, opinions and the legitimate interest of others
- valuing oneself and others
- constructive interest in community affairs
- independence of thought
- open-mindedness
- consideration for others
- flexibility
- enterprising approach to tasks and challenges
- self-respect, self-confidence, self-discipline and recognition of their own worth
- self-appraisal, especially the ability to recognise their own aptitudes.

Citizenship Education should also help them to:

- recognise different adult roles within the home and community, how labour is divided and tasks are shared
- understand the nature of work and occupations and how these

affect peoples' lives and attitudes
- understand the ways in which people contribute to, are dependent upon and are affected by industry, commerce and technology
- recognise ways in which social and economic circumstances, locally, nationally and internationally, affect peoples' lives

PROJECTS UNDERTAKEN

Case Study One: Leisure and Tourism in Northampton

Over the past few years we have undertaken a number of projects where we have attempted to fulfil some of our targeted aims and objectives and enhance our pupils' awareness of their role as European Citizens.

Our first venture developed from a well-established module of work in Humanities on the subject of Settlement. In this module pupil studied the growth and development of their town. I took this theme and developed a sub-project which was entitled 'Leisure and Tourism in Northamptonshire'. It was this that was to be the launching pad for our first foray into Citizenship Education.

The pupils, a class of 12 -13 year olds, initially spent a period of time in preparation learning about their town. They participated in a town trail, surveyed places of leisure and tourism and visited leisure and recreation centres. In turn they received visits from local industrialists, including the town's Leisure and Tourism Manager.

The next stage was for the pupils to each spend a day in a local hotel working alongside members of staff from each of the departments in the hotel. The pupils became chefs, cleaners, receptionists, chambermaids, waiters, maintenance staff, porters and so forth. At the same time pupils were also spending time in the Training Restaurant at the Northampton College of Further Education working alongside staff and BTEC students learning restaurant skills.

Bursting with new-found skills the pupils then began preparations for their own catering enterprise. This was to run a cafe of their own, to take place in school over a period of two days. The cafe was to have a French theme, tying in with a visit being made to the school by the pupils of Henri Quatre School, Poitiers, France.

Day one was a fast-food snack bar where children, parents and other visitors sampled the delights of French food. All customers had to pass through a 'Bureau de Change' and change their money into francs before venturing into the cafe. In order to assist with the running of their 'Bureau de Change', pupils had visited the Foreign Till at their local branch of Barclays Bank where they received a taste of foreign finance.

Day two of the cafe gave the pupils a chance to display other newly acquired skills. This day involved them in running a formal restaurant, serving a three-course meal to various invited guests, including the Mayor and Mayoress. French still prevailed and another dimension was added by the provision of a cabaret including music and dance, all with a French flavour.

Throughout both days pupils were aided by a range of adults other than teachers. College staff helped by providing cutlery, crockery and table linen and rehearsing the waiters in the necessary skills. One of the pupils' fathers was a chef and he helped in the preparation of the meal.

It was a hectic few weeks. Pupils declared that they had never worked so hard. Many new skills were gained and pupils voted it the best experience they had been involved in during their time in the school. Later we learnt that, of the class involved, seven went into the leisure industry, one of them became assistant manager at the London Hilton and later, at the age of 21, started her own restaurant.

Having seen what the experience had done for the pupils involved we then developed the project further the following year. This time an entire year group, 120 pupils, participated. They followed the same course as our trial group, working in local hotels and with the college but also spent time at other leisure outlets. The culmination of their work was when they took over a local restaurant and ran it for the day, cooking, serving, managing all aspects of providing a restaurant service for the general public.

Case Study Two: Boothville's Berlin Wall

This project was designed to heighten the pupils' awareness that they were members of Europe during a European Awareness week.

The idea grew out of some work we were doing in Personal and Social Education (PSE) lessons. The idea followed a discussion on the concept of freedom. The issues raised included:

- freedom for the individual - what should each individual be allowed to do?
- freedom for the individual within a group
- freedom for the individual as a citizen

Apart from our overall aims and objectives for Citizenship Education, as previously outlined, there were some specific aims for this particular topic:

These aims and objectives were:

- to increase children's awareness of the concept of personal freedom
- to develop attitudes, skills and knowledge necessary for making informed decisions and exercising responsibilities and rights in a democratic society
- to develop knowledge and understanding of how communities are organised and the importance of rules and laws

- to see how communities reconcile the needs of individuals with those of society, and how society, and how societies react with each other
- to encourage planning, organisation and reviewing

The project intended to consider the following ideas:

- The Declaration of Human Rights
- Patterns of distribution of wealth in the E.U.
- Industrial organisation
- People as resources
- The rise and fall of the Berlin Wall.

The project began with a PSE lesson about individual rights and how these need to be accompanied by individual responsibilities. This progressed to a case study of a group of people whose freedom had been denied them.

We discussed in class discussion groups the issue of human rights and the pupils drew up their own charter of children's rights. This they then compared with the United Nations' Charter and found many similarities.

We then embarked upon our chosen case study which took the project in to many different curriculum areas.

The class learned something about the country of Germany through a variety of methods, including the involvement of a German student who was on work experience at a local firm. He visited the class and spoke about his knowledge of the Wall and his feelings about its coming down.

He opened our eyes to the economic implications of the event. He also spoke about his country and taught us a little of his language; we even learnt to sing in German, which proved very useful later in the project.

A soldier, who had served in Berlin whilst the wall was up, came to speak of his experiences and the children were fascinated by his tales. Other aspects included use of video and photographic material, and personal research work.

One of the key parts of our project was a link made with local industry. This took off when we decided to build our own Wall.

We had the opportunity to work with apprentices from a local building firm, under the supervision of Building Studies' staff at one of our local colleges where we actually did some bricklaying! During the course of this activity, and in conjunction with work being carried out in science lessons testing strengths of various building materials, we came to understand why the Berlin Wall had been built the way it was - truly active learning.

We then took our new-found knowledge back into the classroom and set about constructing our own wall. This was achieved by using 1200 cardboard boxes donated by another local firm and by working under the direction of the apprentices lent to us by our building firm. Once our Wall was complete we then moved into the realm of graphic design and set about decorating our Wall with graffiti, as the Berlin Wall had been. The art work was an expression of the personal feelings of the children.

We were fortunate to have the help of 6th form graphic design students from a nearby Upper School to help us with this.

We next decided to use the wall in a dramatic presentation and so evolved the idea of Boothville's Berlin Wall Day. The decision was made to divide the school into two sections - East and West. Exterior division proved quite a problem but yet another local firm came to our aid by providing metres of crash barrier fencing which we erected across the playground. A parent, who restores old army vehicles, lent us a military vehicle which we parked at the main entrance - a most impressive touch.

Both inside and outside the school checkpoints were set up and manned by 'soldiers'. The class worked on the checkpoints throughout the day taking shifts, one shift inside and one outside.

The outside 'soldiers' had the experience of stopping visitors to the school and challenging them. They also had the disadvantage of torrential rain nearly all day. The 'soldiers' were supplemented by a group of army cadets, 15-18 year olds, from a local school, who arrived complete with guns. Another touch of realism.

The drama of the event for most pupils throughout the school was that they were not aware of the building of the Wall until after their arrival at school. Much like it had appeared in Berlin - suddenly and with little warning - so it appeared in Boothville, or 'Boothlin' as it was now referred to. Some pupils were deprived of material 'wealth' in the form of computers, science lab, PE facilities etc., thus heightening feelings of privilege or deprivation.

Each child was issued with a personal Identity Document, which clearly identified them as citizens of either East or West 'Boothlin'. These had to be carried at all times and produced on demand.

The day culminated with a presentation of dance/drama which encapsulated the whole story of the rise and fall of the Berlin Wall and included the singing of the German folk song we had been taught by our German student. Local dignitaries, industrialists, parents and friends were all invited to share the children's interpretation of events.

The whole event grew with the enthusiasm of the staff and pupils but we never lost sight of our original aim, namely to encourage active citizenship and participation within a European context.

Ultimately the project involved work in a number of curriculum areas and developed and enhanced many skills, notably those of co-operation, team-work and commitment. The industrialists involved all commented on the enthusiasm, commitment and hard work of the pupils involved and expressed a willingness to work with us again should the occasion arise.

Perhaps the final word should come from the pupils involved. I shall conclude the account of this initiative with two pieces of work produced by pupils who participated in the project. The first is an account written by a lower school pupil of his experience of the day. The second, a poem written by one of the class primarily involved, expressing his feelings about the real event.

BERLIN WALL DAY - A PUPIL'S ACCOUNT

On Berlin Wall Day the school was split into two sides, East and West. We all got identity cards with our name on and an ID number, mine was 6GG23, our address and our occupation. Everybody had to carry their card because if they didn't they could be arrested and go to jail, also if there was anything wrong with their card they could go to jail. In some of the lessons soldiers came round and checked the cards and some people got taken out of lessons.......... The East side did not have as many rooms as the West so this made a few difficulties for the teachers and people in the East trying to get lessons...........I would have hated to live in Berlin because the soldiers were real and jail is not a school hall and I would feel frightened to go out on the streets.

From the Berlin Wall Day I learnt what it would be like to be separated from people you know and I found out how many privileges one side had.

THE BERLIN WALL

It happened overnight
We were trapped as prisoners,
We were separated from our friends
And relations,
As the wall and armies
Swept through the country.
People trying to get into the West,
No matter what,
People getting shot

In the process.
Concrete slabs being lifted
About by people of the East,
The wall was gradually built,
And stood for twenty years or more!

Case Study Three: Northampton to Paris via Waterloo Experience

This project was also designed as a European awareness raising exercise. It was extremely successful, leading to awards for the school. In our usual tradition, it came out of an on-going module of work on Settlement, part of the National Curriculum Key Stage 3 Geography syllabus. The class involved, a year seven group of 11-12 year olds, had been looking at the growth and development of their home town. They had learnt that from earliest times Northampton had been a routeway town. It was just a small step from this point to begin to consider Northampton as part of a routeway to Europe, especially considering the amount of interest being generated in the completion of the Channel Tunnel, a major step towards drawing Britain even closer to Europe. Many of the children had spent more than four or five hours travelling to holiday spots in England; now it would be possible to travel to Europe in the same way and in about the same time. So the decision was taken to begin work on a project that would highlight the ease of this routeway to Europe with Northampton being the start of their journey.

Planning

The first planning meeting included a consultation with someone who had been of invaluable help in our earlier projects, namely, our local SCIP (School Curriculum Industry Partnership) Co-ordinator, as this seemed an ideal project to also involve an element of industrial and economic awareness. In consultation with her we learnt of a schools' competition being run by European Passenger Services (Eurostar) to raise European awareness and we felt that our project might well fit into this area. Entry into the competition would give us an added interest. It was during these discussions that the project plan was decided.

We decided that we would explore in detail the routeway from Northampton to Paris, via Waterloo Station and the Eurostar Express. The work with the children would culminate in the creation of this routeway through the school using a variety of media, such as artwork, written work, design and craftwork, computer simulations, language work, home economics, dance and drama, communication skills, research skills etc.

Paris was chosen rather than Brussels as we have a very strong link with France through a long standing exchange link with a school in Poitiers. We felt this would heighten the pupils' awareness that we are all citizens of Europe. There is also quite a lot of curriculum Humanities' work, which focuses on France, taking place throughout the school, so we felt that interest levels would be high and staff would be reassured that this was relevant to National Curriculum targets. The project was to be very cross-curricular.

The second stage of planning was then to consult with the other members of staff who would be most likely to be involved in this exercise. This was initially done at a full staff meeting and then continued in smaller departmental meetings. There was a tremendous amount of interest and support from all the staff approached and new ideas were quickly generated.

The idea was to begin the journey at one end of the school and to finish it at the other, a task easy to achieve as the school is built with four year groups forming the corners of a square with other teaching areas being the heart.

The Project

The point of 'departure' was to be in year five; this was to be Northampton station. The staff in this year group became interested and decided to develop a unit of work into a local study which would produce a display all about Northampton and enhance this aspect of the route. So year five became Northampton.

The 'journey' continued through the school with displays of work on the subject of the stopping points on the train journey from Northampton to Euston Station, London. The children had each chosen one of these towns and done some individual research work about their choice. This had involved them in visiting the places, writing to local tourist offices, chatting to friends and relatives, or library research skills. This part of the journey culminated in a display of work about London, in particular London of the tourist, which had involved more research work. At this point a computer simulation was set up called 'Let's Explore London'.

This involved an exercise in using the Underground Train system, a necessary part of the journey. The pupils instructed the 'travellers' in the operation of this simulation.

From here the 'traveller' entered the main hall where we had attempted to create an impression of Waterloo Station, both old and new. In order to fulfil this part of our task we had taken the children on a visit to the station where they had made notes, produced sketches and taken photographs from which we worked back at school. It was at this point that we had one of our major inputs from industrialists. We had managed to acquire the services of an 'artist-in-residence', Mrs. Jenny Bicat, who spent three days working with various groups of children on some major artwork.

The work consisted of a huge mural depicting a perspective view down the track at Waterloo International. This was based on a photograph taken by one of the children on their visit to the station. It was memories and impressions from the children , as well as the photographs that inspired the work produced with the 'artist-in-residence'.

In addition to this mural, the children also produced a another depicting shop-fronts in the old part of the station, an arch, a clock, chicken-wire models of a guard and an abseiling window cleaner. In their science lessons they had been carrying out work on circuits and using this they designed and made a ticket machine that would take your ticket and return it, an attempt to imitate the very hi-tech system they had seen at the new terminal. This also involved a group in simple programming on the computer in order to produce a system of changing lights.

With great difficulty a large pillar was also constructed and other items of interest that had captured the children's imagination during their visit. As part of their circuitry work, and with the help of a local firm, ADT Alarms, they also constructed a security system for screening people as they went through 'Customs'.

On leaving the station the 'traveller' then reached the Channel Tunnel. The work for this part of the journey was based on a trip made to the Channel Tunnel Exhibition at Folkestone, Kent. In order to facilitate this visit, which would have been exhausting if attempted in one day, we arranged with a school on the Isle of Sheppey to 'host' our children overnight. This experience involved the children in letter-writing activities and a host of new experiences, for some of them the first residential visit of their school lives.

The 'traveller' then continued his journey into the Tunnel. At this point one of the major design elements came into play. The children were involved in constructing both the facade of the Tunnel and a structure simulating the Eurostar Express which seated ten people and which involved the 'passengers' in a sound and light experience which attempted to simulate the train journey. This also involved the use of poetry written by the children using the rhythm of the train, a commentary on the countryside through which they would pass.

The production of this poem on tape involved a visit to a recording studio, owned by one of the parents, where the children recorded their poem to an accompanying sound track.

The next piece of design work occurred at this stage as the children were also involved in screen-printing the Eurostar logo to make cushions and curtains for their train.

Journey's End

At the end of this part of the journey the 'traveller' was in France and a whole range of experiences awaited him! His journey first took him into a French cafe where the children had devised and prepared a menu with a French flavour, served by French-speaking waiters and waitresses. These were identifiable by the T-shirts that they had designed and we had printed.

This had not been the first use of a Modern Foreign Language experienced by our 'travellers', as at Waterloo Station the children had been broadcasting station announcements in French, German, Italian and English. We had capitalised on the language talents of some of our members of staff.

After leaving the cafe, which the children had called 'L'Escargot', because all travellers to France expect snails, our 'traveller' now continued his journey through France.

He now entered another hall where he was able to view paintings and sculptures that the children had produced in the style of French artists as part of their curriculum art lessons. This had also involved them in research work into the lives and times of their chosen artists.

The experience continued with a slide show and commentary, in French and English, about Paris. The children had researched the information for their commentary and had worked with the French assistante to perfect their French for this, for the cafe and for their announcements at Waterloo Station. The slide show was interspersed with pieces of entertainment, a performance from the recorder group, a dance, a song, a playlet, a piece of mime in the style of Marcel Marceau, and all with a French flavour.

Our 'traveller's' journey ended with a trip through year six, who had also been infected by project fever, and this was France. The children had worked on various regions and symbols of France to create France in their year area. This was in conjunction with their first steps in language work where they begin by studying the country and its culture before embarking on learning the language. There were skiers in the Alps, bathers in St Tropez and champagne, bread and wine all over the place!

This was the culmination of our 'traveller's' journey, the end of our experience. An experience that had served to further the knowledge and awareness, not only of the class who had been at the core of the project, but of every class in the school who had become involved in some way, not to mention the many guests who had been invited to participate in our experience. Many of these guests had been people who had helped and worked with us during the course of the project. Apart from our artist, we had received support from local builders' merchants, who donated materials, the TSB and National Westminster banks who sponsored various activities, Yorks' Travel who supplied posters and sponsored travel on various trips, ADT Alarms who helped with the circuitry work and many parents who had been dragged by their offspring to various places in their quest for information for their research work. Another element we tackled was a foray into the world of advertising. The children wrote to various local firms and sold them advertising space at their 'Waterloo Station'.

They then produced advertising hoardings and the money raised helped fund the cost of the project, as well as further enrich the pupils' experience.

What began as a small European-awareness exercise turned into a fascinating and extremely valuable cross-curricular experience which achieved many of our targeted aims and objectives for European Citizenship education, not just for one class but, in some way, for every pupil in the school.

An unexpected event that occurred was being invited by the School Curriculum Industry Partnership to make a presentation of our project at their International Conference which was to be held in Paris. The invitation was initially made to me, as teacher in charge of the project, but I felt very strongly that this was the children's project and that they should be the ones to present it. Naturally this had financial implications, to the tune of over £2000. So we set about raising the money and, by dint of many varied fund-raising events and tremendous support from local firms, we achieved our aim and took thirty pupils to Paris to make their presentation This was to an audience of over three hundred people, a daunting experience for 11 year old children, not to mention their teacher! We presented in French and English and the pupils rose magnificently to the occasion. I am including a copy of a letter they received after the event which pays testimony to the fact that they had displayed many of the citizenship skills which had been at the heart of our project.

Dear Pupils,

Many congratulations on an outstanding contribution to the International Partnership Conference in Paris. As we expressed by the standing ovation that you all received at the end of your presentation, the delegates felt that the presentation was the real high point in the conference. The work displayed in the exhibition, as well as in the accomplishments of the musicians, speakers and performers was of the highest quality and you must be very proud of your performance.

You worked very hard and showed the very best qualities of team-work in preparing and presenting your project. You impressed a large international audience who had a memorable experience when they watched 'The Northampton to Paris via Waterloo Experience.' We have received many positive comments about you all!

Congratulations and very well done again.
Chris Lea.
Conference Manager.

Conclusion

It is very difficult in a few words to sum up what the children gained through these projects. Almost all areas of the curriculum were involved in one, or all, of the projects and learning was clearly enhanced by adding new dimensions to the syllabi. Teachers these days are concerned that all work fulfils National Curriculum criteria and, therefore, tend to stay safely within prescribed bodies of content as laid out in the Programmes of Study. All of the projects described will have fulfilled many National Curriculum requirements in many curriculum areas. They can easily be justified, if justification was needed, in the percentage of time recently allocated by Dearing for other aspects of the curriculum other than that which has been prescribed. Cross-curricular work and development of Citizenship skills are also a necessary part of the National Curriculum. Good teachers will, however, perceive their role as that of being an educator, their job to produce well-rounded, confident citizens.

One of the most valuable outcomes of such projects is the opportunity it presents for pupils to develop their skills of citizenship. It gives them the opportunity to meet and work with other, and different, adults thus developing their awareness of a wider community and of a world that extends beyond the world of education, beyond the confines of their own town and country into a community where they will be the citizens of the future, the Community of Europe. It fosters a team spirit where they have the opportunity to recognise skills within each other that may not always be apparent in the normal classroom situation. It gives them ownership of their learning situation, developing their self-confidence and preparing them for their place in the adult world.

CONCLUSION:
SOME FINAL THOUGHTS
Andreas Sobisch & Ian Davies

In this book we have attempted to provide an integrated approach to the issue of education for European citizenship. We proceeded from the assumption that any discussion of educational initiatives concerning European citizenship could not be divorced from their specific 'European' political context. We felt this to be the case not just because the concept of citizenship is an inherently political one (since citizens are, ultimately, political actors). More important for the purpose of education for European citizenship is the fact that there is no consensus across the EU over how the European 'polity' should evolve and what its final form should be (and consequently there is no consensus over what European citizenship really means). Yet, as we argued in chapter 3, true citizenship can only be realised in a polity. Education for European citizenship is thus hopelessly entangled in the web of controversy of EU politics. All this is reflected in the so far rather meagre advances made at the member state level toward establishing any kind of European citizenship education (see chapter 4). However, we do not wish to argue that there can be only one 'vision' of what the future Europe should look like and, therefore, only one form of citizenship and citizenship education (namely an overtly 'political' one with citizenship defined as nationality).

In fact, as is clear from almost every one of the chapters in this book, there are a number of different aspects to 'citizenship', and not all of them involve political matters to an equal degree. There is a world of difference between, for example, teaching basic awareness of the European Union (its history, institutions, purpose, etc.) on one hand, and the development of a European consciousness or identity, on the other. The former would, presumably, be more factual, whereas the latter may involve attempts at promoting certain specific 'European' values. Thus, whether or not we can all agree on a common definition of European citizenship, in practice we may come to emphasise different aspects of such citizenship in the classroom. This is not to say that a common definition across the EU would not be desirable. But, notwithstanding the legal codification of 'European Citizenship' in the Maastricht Treaty, at present such agreement seems hardly feasible.

What we are interested in more than anything else at this time is a higher level of commitment to European citizenship education, a commitment that might eventually be equally high across the EU. Currently such a commitment is clearly lacking, at least at the national level. Therefore, what we have documented in this book are a number of specific individual educational initiatives (see chapters 8-13). These initiatives have been developed almost exclusively by individual educators or school districts rather than by national or supra-national agencies.

However, there are other barriers to the objective of a European citizenship education than the reluctance or ignorance of individual member states' policy makers. Some of these barriers are legal or structural in nature. For example, given the Maastricht Treaty's mandate of subsidiarity, there are limits to the types of initiatives that can be undertaken at the level of the EU itself, although EU institutions can certainly play a supporting role - as exemplified by programs such as ERASMUS or Youth for Europe. Member states also vary greatly in the degree to which their educational systems are centralised. Some, such as France, are highly centralised, while others, such as Germany, are more decentralised. In the latter, a coherent approach to European citizenship education would have to be undertaken by sixteen separate educational authorities with relatively little coordination at national level (see chapters 10 and 11). Moreover, it should not be overlooked in this context that education is a policy area where the public's enthusiasm for intergovernmental (much less supra-national) cooperation is at best guarded (see chapter 6). Thus, if major progress in European citizenship education is desired, it would have to be initiated at national levels or below, at least for the foreseeable future.

How might progress towards the goal of education for European citizenship be realised then? Perhaps this book is unlikely to be a vehicle for mobilising local and national educational authorities to be more daring and take greater strides toward developing at least the semblance of European citizenship education for their jurisdictions. But if we have accomplished anything at all in the preceding chapters it is this: citizenship and citizenship education should not be so narrowly defined as to be perceived as a threat by anyone, least of all by member state governments (it is they, after all, who gave their consent to forming the EU along with formally codifying EU citizenship). European citizens are not just, and perhaps not even primarily, political actors, especially at a time when the EU as a real polity is still in its infancy. Rather, at present they are much more likely to be tourists, consumers, workers, students, scholars, entrepreneurs - or simply private persons. In that capacity they are in need of certain skills to take advantage of the opportunities before them. These would include a basic awareness of, and knowledge about, Europe, its institutions and purposes, as well as their role within it; foreign language aptitude; as well as a rudimentary understanding of European (and member state) history and culture. It is difficult to see how anyone could object to that. In fact, chapter 5 documented very well the deficits that exist in the area of knowledge and interest - although these deficits are not necessarily greater than they are with respect to the domestic context.

And even in the attitudinal domain, which is more subjective and thus potentially more controversial, the development of a European identity need not be considered a threat to national identity. Instead the two should be viewed as complementary - corresponding to the idea of multiple citizenship outlined by Heater in chapter 1. In fact, as chapter 5 had also shown, this is precisely how they are viewed by the majority of the European public right now. But the pleading by academics is unlikely to be heeded by anyone, certainly not by those in charge of educational policy in local and national governments. What we need are more practical ideas to show the way forward - ideas which can be communicated effectively to those responsible for educational policy. It is in this context that we hope that our six substantive chapters have provided some examples of strategies that could be emulated, discussed, developed, or - if found unsuitable - rejected.

But this is not to say that anything goes. On the contrary, whatever strategy is being implemented, it should always be tied to a specific purpose that can be identified, defined, achieved, and, importantly, evaluated. The reader is invited to judge for him/herself whether or not that is the case with our six case studies. It might therefore be useful to adopt our conceptual framework, which we developed in chapter 3 and which consists of the three dimensions - political-legal; normative; and psychological - to the three key learning objectives identified by Derek Heater and others: knowledge, skills, and attitudes. Such a framework, however, should not be seen as a straightjacket into which everything has to fit. Rather it is an attempt to provide some order and coherence to the confusing muddle that is citizenship education.

1. Political-legal: Clearly, European citizens should be aware of the existence of the EU, their place within it, as well as their rights under the Rome and Maastricht Treaties (see chapter 9). But knowledge goes further: it includes the history, purpose, and opportunities of the EU; beyond that, European citizens should be aware of the political context: the challenges, controversies, and

debates surrounding the EU (see chapter by Peter Krapf, for example). They should possess the requisite skills to act as European citizens. This would include not only such obvious items as language competency, but also the ability to search for information in the European context, critically evaluate it, and act upon it (e.g., contacting one's MEP or Ombudsman). On the attitudinal level, European citizens should be able see themselves as such - without in any way compromising their national identity. This may sound ambitious and even controversial, but given the current level of development of the EU (i.e., its lack of being a truly federal system), the potential level of tension and conflict between national and European citizenship (i.e., competing loyalties) is small indeed.

2. Normative: As discussed in chapter 3, this is probably the least developed aspect of European citizenship. It is unclear what it means to be a 'good European citizen'. Partly this is because the EU is still relatively new, unfamiliar, and remote. But it is also related to the lack of European institutions and organisations to which individuals can attach themselves and to which they can donate their time and efforts. Nevertheless, a good citizen in this context would be one who is willing, motivated, and able to exercise his/her rights and obligations as a European citizen. This would not only entail such things as voting, but also keeping informed about current EU affairs and being able to engage his/her political leaders and fellow citizens in a dialogue about European affairs. This area would appear to be a very fruitful one for further research into the meaning of European citizenship.

3. Psychological: At the psychological level, European citizenship probably begins with feelings of empathy and mutual understanding among fellow Europeans (see chapters 12 and 13). This would not at all be unlike cultural education. But, as Hugh Starkey has pointed out, empathy also means coming to see fellow Europeans as people who are very similar to oneself. This could

contribute to lowering the anxiety and fear that still exists between certain countries and peoples. The psychological dimension would further include an appreciation for the common European historical and cultural heritage and culminate in the knowledge of being bound together in a 'Schicksalsgemeinschaft' (common fate). The latter is particularly important if the EU member states come to see the EU more and more as a way to compete in the global economy - and thus as a defence of its unique European identity and standard of living (see chapters 6 and 11).

This brief outline is not meant as an exclusive or exhaustive catalogue. Rather, it is an attempt to begin a more systematic way of thinking about education for European citizenship. Not everything that has been advertised as such in recent years necessarily qualifies. Equally important, we realise that the 'ideal' citizen described above - that is the well-informed, public-spirited and loyal individual who is willing and ready to take on his or her citizenly responsibilities - rarely exists in actual practice, even in the domestic context. In fact, democracy has so far been able to survive without many such individuals. Why should this be any different for the European Union? In fact, one school of thought in political science argues that too many active and informed citizens may be a bad thing - leading to government overload, paralysis, and perhaps even eventual breakdown. Whatever the merits of this line of argument, it would certainly be foolhardy to use the 'model citizen' as a practical goal for European citizenship education. Instead it should serve as no more than a theoretical construct - a heuristic device, as it were - around which educational policies might be designed.

But there is one crucial difference between the EU and the domestic context that must not be overlooked: the national polity already exists and its legitimacy is not in question. Moreover, it has a proven track record. This is not the case with the European Union. It is still in its infancy and a true European polity is not yet in sight (and may - for better of worse - never exist). To come about, if that is desired, it must make its case before the people of Europe. In this context a practical and appropriate education for European citizenship is all the more relevant.

Index

Adenauer, Konrad 162

Adonnio Commission 102

Amsterdam Treaty 57, 61, 66, 71, 84

Aron, Raymond 81, 86

Brittan, Sir Leon 63

civil rights 37, 41, 75, 79, 81-2

civil society 116, 144

Committee of the Regions 68

Common Agricultural Policy 56

Common Foreign and Security Policy 57, 136

COREPER (see Council of Permanent Representatives)

Council of Europe 41, 53, 97, 114, 187ff, 209

Council of Ministers 59ff

Council of Permanent Representatives 67-8

Court of Justice (see European Court of Justice)

De Gasperi, Alcide 162

De Gaulle, Charles 55-6, 166

Delors, Jacques 56, 64, 189-90

Delors Commission 64

Deutsch, Karl W. ii, 142, 144, 160

Economic and Social Committee 68

ECOSOC (see Economic and Social Committee)

ECSC (see European Coal and Steel Community)

EMS (see European Monetary System)

EMU (see European Monetary Union)

ERASMUS 103-4, 308

EURATOM 55, 63

EU educational initiatives 103-5, 308

Eurobarometer 124ff, 321ff

European Citizenship 41, 73, 81ff, 123, 133ff, 190, 206, 223, 277

European Coal and Steel Community 53-4, 59, 63, 65

European Commission 63ff, 131

European Community 136, 141

European Convention on Human Rights 40, 76, 81, 187, 209ff, 219

European Council 59ff

European Court of Human Rights 41, 66, 76, 218, 220

European Court of Justice 41, 65, 66ff, 84, 133

European Defence Community 54-5

European Economic Community 55ff, 63

European identity 86, 133ff, 167

European Monetary System 151

European Monetary Union 151, 260ff

European Parliament 57, 65ff, 82ff

European Union 57ff, 73, 100ff, 131
EUROPE SCHOOLS 223ff
EURYDICE 99-100
human rights 42, 209ff
identity 79
ICJ (see International Court of Justice)
International Court of Justice 88
Janne Report 102
Justice and Home Affairs 57, 136
Kinnock, Neil 63
Kohl, Helmut 56, 62, 166
language learning 187ff, 281, 286
Maastricht Treaty (see Treaty on European Union)
Major, John 62
Marshall Plan 37, 89
Marshall, T. H. 35
Mitterrand, Francois 56, 62
Monnet, Jean 7, 63, 162
multiculturalism 39-40, 47
National Curriculum 298
Nationality 74ff
NATO 55
Nordic Council 109
Open University 197ff

permissive consensus 141

Pleven, Rene 54

Pleven Plan 54

political rights 37, 75

Qualified Majority Voting 60, 64

Rifkind, Malcom 166

Santer, Jacques 66

Schengen Agreement 141

Schmidt, Helmut 275

Schuman, Robert 54, 162

SEA (see Single European Act)

Single Currency (see European Monetary Union)

Single European Act 56ff, 129, 141, 164

Single Market (see Single European Act)

Social Chapter of the Maastricht Treaty 70ff

Social Charter (1989) 82

Social Europe 143

social integration 143ff

social rights 37, 75-6, 81

SOCRATES 103-4, 245

Subsidiarity 11, 83

Thatcher, Margaret 18

Treaty of Rome vi, 55, 102, 147

Treaty on European Union v, 12, 21, 41, 51, 57ff, 62, 66, 68, 73, 81ff, 102-3, 132, 141, 145, 187, 253

unemployment 261
UNESCO 188, 192
world citizenship 34ff, 42
You, me, us! 214ff

APPENDIX

The survey data upon which the analyses of chapters 5 and 6 are based are from the Eurobarometer Public Opinion Surveys, which have been conducted on behalf of the Directorate-General for Information, Communication, Culture, Audiovisual (DG X) of the European Commission each Spring and Autumn since Autumn 1973. These data are available for purchase in Britain from the ESRC Data Archive at the University of Essex (dawww.essex.ac.uk). Aggregate summaries of each Eurobarometer are available directly from the Unit 'Surveys, Research, Analyses' of DG X (Rue de la Loi, B-1049, Brussels).

Sampling

Identical sets of questions are asked of representative samples of the population aged fifteen and above in each member state. The standard sample size is 1,000 for all countries, except Germany (1,000 West, 1,000 East), Luxembourg (500) and Northern Ireland (300). To be representative of Germany/United Kingdom as a whole, the eastern German and the Northern Ireland samples are adjusted when combined with the western German/British samples, respectively. The basic sampling design for each country is a multi-stage, random (probability) sample. In each country a random selection of 'sampling points' is made in such a way that all types of area (regions, urban, rural, etc.) are represented in proportion to their populations. For each survey different individuals are interviewed in the master sample of sampling points. Within sampling points addresses are drawn at random. All interviews are face-to-face in people's homes and in the appropriate national language.

Sampling errors, that is the margin of error of sample estimates at the 95% confidence level, are +/- 3.1% or less at a sample size of 1,000 (larger for smaller samples or subsamples). So, for example, if we find that 50% of respondents in the UK sample favour their country's membership in the EU, we are 95% confident that the 'true' percentage in the UK favouring membership is no smaller than 46.9% and no larger than 53.1%. Expressed more technically, if we drew 20 independent samples of the same size, 19 of them would fall within the 46.9 - 53.1 percent range.

Questions

Following is a catalogue of all questions used in chapters 5 and 6. The catalogue is organised in the order in which the respective questions appear in the chapters, i.e, beginning with Figure 1 in chapter 5. The readers should be aware of the fact that most, though not all, questions appearing in this catalogue are asked in every, or almost every, Eurobarometer. For 'unusual' questions, variable (V) and question (Q) numbers in the original codebook and questionnaire (EB) are noted. For any further detail, please consult the Eurobarometers directly or contact the author/s. Please note that all questions allow respondents to indicate that they 'don't know', are 'unsure' or have 'no opinion'. However, for reasons of economy these options have been omitted from this appendix in most cases.

Chapter 5

Figure 1

'In general, are you for or against efforts being made to unify Western Europe?' (very much for; to some extent for; to some extent against; very much against; don't know/not sure)

Figures 2-3

'Generally speaking, do you think that our country's membership of the European Community is a good thing, a bad thing, or neither good nor bad?'

Figure 4

(see also Figures 1 and 2 above)

'Taking everything into consideration, would you say that on balance our country has benefited or not from being a member of the European Community?' If you were told tomorrow that the European Community had been scrapped, would you be very sorry about it, indifferent, or very relieved?'

Figure 5

'Compared to 12 months ago, do you think that the general economic situation in this country now is a lot better, a little better, stayed the same, a little worse, a lot worse?'

'Compared to 12 months ago, do you think that the financial situation of your household now is a lot better, a little better, stayed the same, a little worse, a lot worse?'

Table 1

'To what extent would you say you are interested in European politics, that is to say matters related to the European Union?' (a great deal, to some extent, not much, or not at all)

'All things considered, how well informed do you feel you are about the European Union, its policies, its institutions?' (Very well, quite well, not very well, not at all well)

'How much do you feel you know about the Maastricht Treaty?' (a great deal, a fair amount, know just a little, heard of it but know nothing else, never heard of it before today) (EB 39, Q.30, V.120)

'Here is a list of countries of Europe as a whole. Please give me the numbers or the names of all countries which are members of the European Union' (EB 43)

'Do you happen to remember the date on which the latest European election has taken place in our country or not? If yes, on which date?' (year/month) (EB 42, Q. 45, V. 183)

'What is the capital where the European Commission and several other European Community institutions are located?' (EB 39, Q.43, V.293)

Table 2

'There is talk of establishing a European citizenship, that is to say defining rights, freedoms, and obligations common to all citizens of member countries of the European Community. In your opinion, would such a European citizenship be a good thing or a bad thing or neither good nor bad?' (EB 35, Q.14, V.18)

'Do you ever think of yourself as not only (nationality), but also European? Does this happen often, sometimes or never?'(EB 37, V.178/9, Q.32A/B)

'People may feel different degrees of attachment to their own town or village, to their region, to their country, to the EC or to Europe as a whole. Please tell me how attached you feel?' (EB 36, Q.64, V.171-175)

'This symbol is the European flag. I have a list of statements concerning it. I would like to have your opinion on each of these: I am proud/not proud of this flag'. (EB 37, Q.39, V.200)

'Do you see a European Union rather as a threat or as a protection for your national identity or culture?' (EB38)

'Do you consider a sense of European identity as being compatible with a sense of national identity or do you see your country's identity disappearing over time if a European Union came about?' (EB38, Q.26, V.234)

'In the near future do you see yourself as (nationality) only, (nationality) and European, European and (nationality), European only or don't you know'? (EB 37, Q.33, V.180)

Chapter 6

Table 1

'Irrespective of the other details of the Maastricht Treaty, what is your opinion on each of the following proposals? Please tell me for each proposal, whether you are for it or against it. e) The EC member states should have some basic common principles on social policies, but the details should be left to national governments.'(EB 39, Q. 31e, V.125)

'The Council of Heads of states and governments of the European Community has adopted a declaration which constitutes a 'Community Charter of Fundamental Social rights', i.e., a set of common principles in all member-countries concerning the rights and responsibilities of workers and employers. Do you think such declaration is a good thing or a bad thing or neither good not bad'? (EB 33 Q.31, V.78)

'The European Community is committed to complementing the Single European Market with a social dimension. This consists of a basic set of rules concerning the rights and duties of workers and employers in all members countries. In your opinion, is such a European social dimension a good thing or a bad thing or neither good nor bad'? (EB 35, Q.44, V.81)

'After the declaration which constitutes a 'Community Charter of Fundamental Social Rights', the European Commission prepared a programme of community legislation. For each of the following areas, would you be in favour or not of the basic regulation being applied to all the countries of the European Community'? (Social protection/setting minimum income; job related training for all citizens of the EC throughout their working lives; information, consultation and participation for workers in matters concerning the company where they work; health and safety protection in relation to work; protection of young workers; protection of the social rights of the elderly; protection of the disabled, e.g., their integration into working life; hours of work, rest periods, holidays, night work, and weekend work; social rights in the EC for people from non-member countries, protection of women in relation to work, part-time and temporary work) (EB 33, Q.32, V.80-90)

'Many people are concerned about protecting the environment and fighting pollution. In your opinion, is this an immediate and urgent problem, more a problem for the future, or not really a problem?' (EB 37, Q.74, V.304)

'Which of these two statements comes closest to your own opinion? (1) I find that both freedom and equality are important. But if I were to make up my mind for one or the other, I would consider personal freedom more important, that is everyone can live in freedom and develop without hindrance. (2) Certainly both freedom and equality are important. But if I were to make up my mind for one or the other, I would consider equality more important, that is that nobody is underprivileged and that social class differences are not so strong'. (EB 30, Q.164, V.121)

'I am going to read you three opinions which you sometimes hear about environmental problems. Which one comes closest to your own? Economic development should get a higher priority than concerns about the environment; economic development must be ensured but the environment must be protected at the same time; concerns about the environment should get a higher priority than economic development'. (EB 37, Q.76, V.311)

Table 2

'If you were asked to choose one of these five names for your social class, which would you say you belong to'? (Middle class, lower middle class, working class, upper class, upper middle class)

'I am going to say some things that some people say they sometimes feel. Do you yourself ever happen to think that the rich get richer and the poor get poorer?' (EB 30, Q.125, V.61)

Table 3

'Do you strongly agree, agree, neither agree nor disagree, disagree, or strongly disagree that a man's job is to earn money and a woman's job is to look after the home and family?' (EB 42, Q.40d, V.148)

'Do you strongly agree, agree, neither agree nor disagree, disagree, or strongly disagree that it is not good if the man stays at home and looks after the children and the woman goes out to work?' (EB 42, Q.40e. V.149)

'Do you think that homosexual couples should, or should not, have the right to marry each other?' (EB 39, Q.91, V.636)

Table 4

'Whether you do, or do not, follow religious practices, would you say that you are religious, not religious, an agnostic, an atheist'?

Table 5

'Do you attend religious services several times a week, once a week, a few times a year, once a year or less, or never?'

Table 6

'To what extent would you say that you are interested in politics?' (a great deal, to some extent, not much, not at all)

'When you hold a strong opinion, do you ever find yourself persuading your friends, relatives or fellow workers to share your views?' (often, from time to time, rarely, never)

'Here are ten cards. On each, you will find a description of a particular action that people sometimes take to protest about something or to draw other people's attention to their objectives. Are there any you have never heard about or do not understand?' [remove card]. Please, place the remaining cards as follows: place the card on this space, if you have personally done what is on this card during the past ten years. If you have not done it up till now but would do it if it were bout something very important to you, place the card on space 2. If you would only do kind of action under very exceptional circumstances, place card on space 3. And if you would never, under any circumstances, do this kind of thing, place card on space 4.'

(1) Taking part in citizen's action groups

(2) Signing a petition

(3) Taking part in a boycott

(4) Taking part in a lawful political demonstration

(5) Refusing to pay rents, taxes, or installments

(6) Taking part in unofficial or wildcat strikes

(7) Occupying factories, offices, or other buildings

(8) Blocking traffic

(9) Damaging property, for instance breaking windows or removing roadsigns

(10) Using violence against others, for instance fighting with the police or with opposing demonstrators (EB 31, Q.462-471, V.460-469)

'I would like you now to consider some other kinds of action. For each one, I would like you to tell me whether you approve strongly, approve, disapprove, or disapprove strongly'.

(1) The police batton-charging demonstrators

(2) The courts giving severe sentences to protestors who refuse to follow police instructions

(3) The adoption of laws to forbid all public protest demonstrations, in the interest of public safety

(4) The government using troops to break strikes (EB 31, Q.472-475, V.470-473)

Table 7/8

'I would like to ask you about how much trust you have in people from various countries. For each, please tell me whether you have a lot of trust, some trust, not very much trust, or no trust at all' (EB39, Q.10, V.73)

Table 9

'There is a certain way of life, or standard of behaviour and values, that may be considered more specifically European than others. To which of the following aspects of Europe are you personally most attached'? (Culture, Peace, Democracy, Way of Life, Standard of Living, Quality of life, I don't think specifically European Values exist) (EB 33, Q.19, V.33-40)

Table 10

'Some people believe that certain areas of policy should be decided by the (national) government, while another areas of policy should be decided jointly within the European Union. Which of the following areas of policy do you think should be decided by the (national) government, and which should be decided jointly within the European Union?' (Defence; protection of the environment;

currency; cooperation with developing countries/Third World; health and welfare; education; basic rules for broadcasting and the press; scientific and technological research; rates of VAT; foreign policy towards countries outside the European Union; participation in workers' representatives on company boards of directors; industrial policy; cultural policy; immigration policy; rules for political asylum; health ad safety of workers; the fight against unemployment; the fight against drugs) (EB 42, Q.30, V.69-86)

Table 11

'On this list are four descriptions on how Europe might be organised in the future. Please tell me which one you would prefer: (1) each country keeps its sovereignty and cares only about its own affairs; (2) the countries work together sometimes, but do not give up their sovereignty and never have to submit to decisions taken by a majority of countries; (3) the countries regularly work together on certain matters within common organisations, to which they transfer a part of their sovereignty, that is, they have to submit to majority decisions of these common organisations on these matters; (4) the countries transfer all their sovereignty to a single common European state (EB 42, Q.83, V.367)

Table 12

'Generally speaking, how do you feel about foreigners living in (our country): are there too many, a lot but not too many, or not many?'

'Some people are disturbed by the opinions, customs, and way of life of people different from themselves. Do you personally find the presence of people of another nationality (race) disturbing in your private life?'

'If people from different countries of the EC (South of the Mediterranean; who are seeking political asylum) wish to work here in the European Community, do you think they should (1) be accepted, without restrictions; (2) be accepted, but with restrictions, (3) not be accepted?'

'Do you think immigrants and/or political asylum seekers are a big problem for our country, or are they not a big problem?' (EB 39, Q.37, V.164)

'Thinking of people living in our country who are not EC nationals, do you think that their rights should be extended, restricted, or left as they are?' (EB 37, Q.72, V.300)